The
of Be

The Late Years
of Benedict Arnold

Fugitive, Smuggler,
Mercenary, 1780–1801

Jane Merrill
with John Endicott

McFarland & Company, Inc., Publishers
Jefferson, North Carolina

Library of Congress Cataloguing-in-Publication Data

Names: Merrill, Jane, author. | Endicott, John, 1946– author.
Title: The late years of Benedict Arnold : fugitive, smuggler,
mercenary, 1780-1801 / Jane Merrill ; with John Endicott.
Description: Jefferson, North Carolina : McFarland & Company, Inc., Publishers, 2022
Includes bibliographical references and index.
Identifiers: LCCN 2022021516 | ISBN 9781476676531 (paperback : acid free paper) ∞
ISBN 9781476638645 (ebook)
Subjects: LCSH: Arnold, Benedict, 1741-1801. | American loyalists—
Canada—Biography. | Smugglers—New Brunswick—Campobello Island—
Biography. | Arnold, Benedict, 1741-1801—Last years. | BISAC: BIOGRAPHY
& AUTOBIOGRAPHY / Historical | HISTORY / Military / United States
Classification: LCC E278.A7 M47 2022 | DDC 973.382092 [B]—dc23/eng/20220503
LC record available at https://lccn.loc.gov/2022021516

British Library cataloguing data are available

ISBN (print) 978-1-4766-7653-1
ISBN (ebook) 978-1-4766-3864-5

Front cover image: the red jacket of Arnold's uniform
as a British general in beautiful condition. He first wore it in a parade
to congratulate him at Fort George, New York. It has been passed down
along the John Sage line for many generations and now belongs to Jayson
Arnold of White City, Saskatchewan, who states, "It was given to the eldest
son of the eldest son; stored in closets and trunks, it rarely came to light.
In the early 1980s a gentleman from the Smithsonian authenticated it.
When I was seven or eight, my dad and grandfather sat me at the kitchen
table and said, 'You're the eldest. You are given the responsibility to pass
this to the eldest in turn. My grandmother was in the room but had no idea.
It was an aunt who educated me about it after my father died.' The chest
measurement of the jacket is 48 inches" (courtesy Sasha Dale Photography);
inset "Benedict Arnold" The New York Public Library Digital Collections

Printed in the United States of America

*McFarland & Company, Inc., Publishers
Box 611, Jefferson, North Carolina 28640
www.mcfarlandpub.com*

Acknowledgments

In writing this book I have had the generous help of the following people:

David Arnheim, Jayson Arnold, Bill Batty, Jr., Gail G. Campbell, Joselyn Calder, Sasha Dale, Stephen Davidson, Captain Ralph Dennison, John Endicott, Burton Filstrup, Chris Filstrup, David Goss, Bonnie Huskins, Stephen Kimber, Joseph B. Gough, Joselyn Calder, Hugh French, Will Kernohan, Jessica Cline, Koral Lavorgna, Christine Lovelace, Barry Murray, Eric Pena, Ronald Rees, Charles Ripley III, Ian Robertson, Benedict Sayers, Martina Scholtens, Ed Surato, Deirdre Whitehead, Barry K. Wilson, Kenny Wing, and Colin J.C. Windhorst.

My sincere thanks to each of them and especially to the Leffingwell Museum, Norwich, Connecticut, who gave Jason Arnold and me a bandbox welcome.

Table of Contents

Preface

Judas hanged himself. Benedict Arnold, after he betrayed the American patriots, lived on a busy twenty years. This book tells the story of his life as a general-turned-traitor–turned international trader–turned smuggler–turned mercenary, an ostracized lion condemned as a conspirator in the U.S. and subject to suspicions in England. He became, by the end of this period, during the French Directory and Consulate, a virtual soldier of fortune and privateer to support his family and declare to the world his worth.

General James Robertson wrote in the 1780s to London of Arnold that "He never does anything by halves."[1] No person became a cliché so fast and he remains an object of fascination as the toppled hero.

There are more than 200 books about Arnold in the Harvard libraries. A reader perceives many of their authors repeating a point to draw a negative portrait. Their calumnies echo one another. One amusing instance (not amusing for him as a story going around when he was alive) was comparing his cruelty in battle to his having pulled wings off birds as a boy in Norwich and put glass on the street while an apprentice to injure black children passing by. A key anecdote that may be partly, conveniently, made up, relates to the aftermath of the 1788 court case in Saint John, New Brunswick, where he had been accused of burning his

Lithograph by an anonymous American artist accents a fierce, determined character (courtesy Peter Newark Historical Pictures/Bridgeman Images).

1

warehouse for the insurance money (his son Henry was sleeping in the office when the building caught fire), and Benedict sued for slander. The case was resolved in his favor. Some accounts say that the following day a mob looted his premises and left an effigy bearing the sign "Traitor." Even though a mob gathered, the details are suspiciously like an incident at the beginning of the decade in Philadelphia—fact woven with fiction, a collective memory of a villain.

This book combines original research and fact-based speculation on the question of what the notorious do after great failure. For Arnold, there is no journal as Aaron Burr left for his sojourn in Europe, but there is documentation regarding each of the various points on the map where the restless Arnold operated and lived, pursuing wealth, status, and pure and simply being right.

The structure of the book takes its form from where he was based from time to time. It chronicles the period from his defection to the British after plotting to surrender West Point in 1780 to his death in London in 1801.

Chapter 1. Growing Up Benedict. This encapsulates his background. It looks at qualities that helped and hindered his after-life: overconfidence, fearlessness, energy, and strategizing.

Chapter 2. How the General Viewed His Treason. A novel approach is to take him at his word.

Chapter 3. John Champe's Ride. After the defection, Arnold lived first in Bowling Green in a townhouse overlooking the Hudson River. As a Loyalist British officer, he hobnobbed, and was nearly abducted through his back garden door. The failed attempt made Sergeant John Champe of Virginia a quasi-hero by being a pretend traitor.

Chapter 4. Peggy's Nerves. This chapter revisits the attempted "sale" of West Point and how Peggy, the wife of the disgraced man, is caricatured.

Chapter 5. Maneuvers in the James River Valley and New London, Connecticut. This chapter takes Arnold, newly turned out as a British officer, to more military action in the James River Expedition fleeing which Thomas Jefferson moved up river with his family (and suffered humiliation for not calling up the militia in a timely fashion); and New London, Connecticut, which earned Arnold perhaps his greatest infamy.

Chapter 6. Ups and Downs in London. The Arnolds sailed to Britain and a period ensued when Benedict made transatlantic voyages and resided in London five years. He was welcomed by King George and Queen Charlotte, met Lord Germain, sometime Secretary of State, continued with self-justification, helped Loyalist friends with their claims, and was overlooked for military appointments.

Chapter 7. Sanctuary Province. This sets the scene of Benedict's residency in Canada in the context of the Loyalist emigration from New York City in 1783.

Chapter 8. Arrival in Saint John. Arnold's landing in Saint John, New Brunswick, in December 1785 was fraught with difficulty which he faced with a tourbillon of activity.

Chapter 9. Benedict Advances on the New Province. After the government moved to Fredericton as the seat of power, Saint John continued to be the commercial center. Benedict was aggressive getting into business in the fast-growing city.

Chapter 10. A Smuggling Culture. During the period Arnold was in New Brunswick, trading contraband goods "on the lines" was virtually unopposed.

Chapter 11. Elyseum: A Potential for the Gentry. Biographer Willard Randall aptly calls Arnold's time in Canada "seven tempestuous years." Keeping up appearances and out of debt was a challenge for everybody. His dicey personal experience paralleled what was going on in the newly formed province. This chapter parallels him with individuals whom he knew.

Chapter 12. The Benefit of Friendship. A look at the interactions of genteel Loyalist refugees in the Arnolds' social circle.

Chapter 13. On the Island of Welsh Squires. His proper business was conducted at Saint John and he had a store up the river at Fredericton but his wharves and warehouse on Campobello Island were the hub of Arnold's enterprises.

Chapter 14. Benedict's Depot. Campobello appears to have been the hub of Arnold's smuggling enterprises.

Chapter 15. Breaking Point and Departure. A fire and accusations of insurance fraud. Soon after the fire, Benedict and Peggy must have concurred that New Brunswick was no longer for them and departed.

Chapter 16. Challenging a Duke. During his life it is said he engaged in numerous duels; the duel with Lord Lauderdale in England is well documented and revealing.

Chapter 17. Guadeloupe. During the peculiar period of personal triumph in the West Indies, Arnold was trying to crush a slave uprising but may have been sickening of the brutality of warfare.

Chapter 18. Correspondents. Benedict shared his activities and unburdened his feelings in letters to Jonathan Bliss, a Loyalist attorney and friend from their days as refugees in London.

Chapter 19. Last Years in London. Benedict and Peggy lived in London from their departure from Canada to their deaths. The focus is on the Loyalist circle which provided the couple's fulcrum while their sons were gearing up for army careers. This was a time of involvement in privateering and general financial overreach for Benedict; Peggy is heralded rightfully for paying his debts as a widow.

Appendix. The Children and Hannah. For the Arnolds, their children were their achievement. The appendix summarizes what is known of them. It also delves into the substantial legacy in Benedict's will to an apparent love child, John Sage.

1

Growing Up Benedict

By heaven, methinks it were an easy leap,
To pluck bright honor from the pale-faced moon.
—Shakespeare, *Hamlet*

Sea commerce was the life Arnold grew up with. At this point we will call him "Benedict V." The male line was dynamic and high-achieving and had great expectations. The gentlefolk of Norwich, Connecticut, followed the tradition of giving first sons of each generation the same forename. He never called himself with a Roman numeral, of course, but biographers use the conceit for clarity. It is recounted that he sailed a ship himself from Nova Scotia to Jamaica at eighteen.

The treason for a moment aside, he was all ambition, little ruth or soft edges. His father, Benedict IV, collapsed from the inside while his son was a boy. Benedict V formed his character into a man that people thought his father was before he sank into depression and drink. Benedict V was a quixotic redeemer of his family. Intensifying Benedict V's drive was that he had a brother born before him who died in infancy.

The younger surviving child has much to prove against a standard that is not even present. My older brother was a shining star. When he died at 24 there was a question of foul play. At the funeral, the college president where my brother taught took me aside and said, "Now you have to live for two." A trite, well-meant remark like this is what the next child in birth order hears when predeceased by the firstborn. Thus, the family members including proud but eventually derelict Benedict IV and his godly wife imbued the stand-out Benedict who is the subject of this book with fiery zeal.

The paternal great-grandfather, Benedict II, was the governor of Rhode Island. The paternal grandfather (III) was a leader in Rhode Island who served in the Assembly but had financial problems. He apprenticed his son as a cooper, but the son was restless and left for Norwich, Connecticut, where he continued working as a cooper but married up. The sea captain who had given him passage died of smallpox, leaving a young widow, Hannah King, whom Benedict IV married. He purchased sloops and schooners and traded in the Long Island Sound, and down to the West Indies, with pork and lumber, returning with rum and sugar. The cooper became a prominent citizen who lived in a fine house on Norwich's Washington Street. The townspeople of Norwich elected him to offices from surveyor to tax assessor and constable. Then yellow fever took the lives of four of his children, and it is supposed that Benedict IV drank his grief. The son had to drag the father home from the taverns in town, what is now the Leffingwell Museum being one. (When the father died it is said in Norwich that several taverns failed.) His dereliction caused his wife and the two remaining children, Benjamin and Hannah, duress. All the same, Benedict Arnold was a proud name and Benedict V was Captain Arnold's son.

What did Arnold look like? His penetrating dark eyes are mentioned as are his muscularity and broad shoulders and that he was of medium height. He was agile and sportive. He rode a mill's water wheel and once jumped over a cart without touching it. An apt impression of him would be skating on a pond in Norwich, speeding across with his strapped-on skates, and pausing to impress the other skaters with his figures. A townsperson recalled him as "the most accomplished and graceful skater" he had ever seen. Benedict captained ships and rode horses, even after his war injuries, but it must have been a great hardship for someone who was a magnificent skater to lose that power to fly across the ice.

Selective hindsight has it that Arnold was a bad child, egotistical and sneaky, from childhood to that act of treason. Once he was demonized, his boyhood was cast as a series of nasty acts. Primers and abecedarians of the times usually had a picture of a boy stealing from pure meanness from a bird's nest. And so, the aforementioned story that Benedict was the prototype of the bad boy in the old nursery books who not only robbed baby birds but maimed their wings.[1] But we can get a general picture of his appearance and his nature.

To visualize Benedict, I consider my Uncle Jerome a model in face, bearing and temperament (not disloyal actions). Jerome was of medium height, with a muscular physique, prominent cheekbones, aquiline nose, piercing black eyes, and, sensual mouth, and even a beautiful French wife named Peggy. Jerome was a forward-thinking minister, fired three times, and, on a small scale, a driven entrepreneur. When stationed in North Africa in 1944, he asked the Ladies Aid Society to send him bedsheets. The church women did their best, hemming for the soldiers, while the scamp (of 21 or younger) was selling the sheets. Jerome had a brisk business making lamps of decoys and repairing a fleet of VWs in the big back yard of one parsonage in New England. He parted from a big Midwestern church after a disagreement over his charging a fee for Sunday school (parents were using it as a drop-off). He sold language laboratories to private schools and sets of photographs door to door in Harlem; and when used decoys became dear he carved his own. Meanwhile his sermons were brilliant.

Jerome with his blue-black hair, strong features and sparkling eyes looked more like a buccaneer than a pastor. People said he looked like Richard Burton in the movie version of *The Night of the Iguana.* They noted my uncle was Irish on his father's side and had the same kind of charisma as the great actor. Sparks seemed to fly off this uncle when he gave his sermon, like from flint.

When Benedict's mother couldn't pay the fees of his Canterbury prep school, he had to be pulled out. As a lad in Norwich he gained a reputation for being athletic and competitive. This must have caused dismay to his mother, who had him on her mind all the time, and lectured him to be upright and god-fearing, and had sent him chocolate when he was at boarding school. But she had connections and came up with a gold-chip apprenticeship for him with two of her cousins, Daniel and Joshua Lathrop, apothecaries. They were Yale-educated, and Daniel had learned his

Benedict boarded at 380 Washington Street with Mr. and Mrs. Daniel Lathrop in Norwich, Connecticut, during his apprenticeship (courtesy Charles C. Ripley III).

trade in London and operated in Norwich the only drug store between Boston and New York. During the Seven Years' War he supplied the army fighting up in Lake George, New York, with surgical instruments and young Arnold delivered them. Daniel and his wife Jerusha lost all three boys in infancy and treated Benedict as a son. His little room was in the house where he lived from about 13 to 20. Soon Benjamin was sailing in ships for the apothecary. It was natural that when Benedict was taken out of school and apprenticed, his trade related to shipping. Benedict moved to over a dozen addresses in his life but this two-chimney center hall gambrel roof house, now a bed-and-breakfast called Lathrop Manor, is his only dwelling-place in America which still exists. The gardener and his wife had a daughter, Lydia Huntley, born 1791, who was, like Benedict, treated as family by Mr. and Mrs. Lathrop and thereby improved her station in life. Lydia became a teacher, mother, an editor of *Godey's Lady's Book* and popular author of verse, often as "Mrs. Sigourney." Her poetry ranged from public issues of the day to personal grief to proper conversation for women. Daniel bequeathed the town a grammar school, built in 1782, a brick building on the green, today a visitors' center for the Norwich Historical Society.

While performing well as an apprentice, Benedict was keen to become a soldier, and ran away to enlist in Westchester County. His mother and Daniel Lathrop interceded, and he was brought home. The next spring, he answered the call for volunteers in the campaign against the French. This time he did a very telling thing. His provincial company moved north on an expedition to Montreal and word came to the camp that his mother was gravely ill. He departed without permission and walked for days to home, feigning that he was on leave to go see his mother. The *New York Gazette* of May 21, 1759, carried a notice of a reward of 40 shillings for a deserter "18 years old, dark complexion, light eyes and dark hair." That summer his mother hid him in her house and the houses of neighbors. She died, and with his employer's permission, Benedict V rejoined the army just as the war ended.

At 21, Arnold had a ship that he sailed between ports of Nova Scotia and the West Indies. In context, New England boys became sea captains in the era often at age 21. He was even sent on a business trip to London. Then the Lathrops generously helped him set up his own shop in New Haven. This exceptional store was stocked with elixirs, cosmetics, necklaces and earrings, stationery supplies, pictures and maps. The inventory of books at his store brings one close to the young businessman's relations with the Yale community: Latin, Greek and French grammars, and the Old Testament in Hebrew. He carried how-to's—e.g., *Every Man His Own Lawyer*; and contemporary novels such as *Tristam Shandy, Joseph Andrews*,

Clarissa, and one called *Romance of a Night-Vision's Fancy.* His first shop was successful, so he bought a larger shop by the harbor. His broadside advertised 150 items "imported via New York" as well as recipes for fancy body wash, pumice tooth powder, red sealing wax, and hog's fat soap; it is at the New Haven Museum.

Benedict valued the intelligence of women: his sister Hannah often managed the shop while he was away trading, the same as she would while he was fighting for American independence. He had pried her away from Norwich where a Frenchman, rumored to have been a dancing master, was courting her. Arnold, in line with his inveterate dislike for the French, scared the gentleman off by firing a pistol toward him.

As an enterprising merchant he invested in enterprises beyond his shop. He made several trips to Quebec where he gained a reputation as a "horse jockey."[2] He bought a sloop, sailed to the West Indies for sugar or rum, and kept warehouses and vessels in New Haven. An aperçu has come down to us of Arnold's style as a young seafarer merchant. There was a custom that when vessels of one nationality gathered in a port, the captain of the largest vessel, or the oldest captain, invited the other skippers for a party at his ship. Arnold was in Honduras and received an invitation from Captain Croskie, an Englishman, to come over for the evening. Arnold, who was finishing up loading to depart, decided he had no sailor to spare to go and explain his absence. The next day, Arnold went over to offer his apology, but Croskie replied with a snarl: "You damned Yankee! Have you no manners?"

Arnold challenged this sea captain to a duel which was set for the next morning at a small island. Croskie arrived late with a backup party of local people, as well as his second and a surgeon. Arnold let the members of the dueling party come ashore and told the others to row away. Croskie as the challenged party fired first and the bullet went wide. Arnold's shot wounded Croskie along an arm. This was bandaged, the pistols were reloaded. Then Arnold cried out, "I give you notice. If you miss this time, I shall kill you." It is said that Captain Croskie apologized, which ended the duel. This seems consonant with Nathaniel Philbrick's characterization that Arnold's approach was to put out a fire before it turned into an inferno.

British mercantilism had taken shape in the second half of the seventeenth century. Just as the design of ships stayed much the same from the Renaissance through the modern period, so British trade was regulated like a dancing school. British colonies in North America were permitted to trade certain commodities like tobacco and sugar with each other or England. Vessels engaged in trade with an imperial territory had to be British and manned by British crews, as well as subject to import and export duties. But Peter Andreas states that "Informal practice was another matter entirely. Mercantilism leaked like a sieve!"[3] He states that some New England merchants were such old hands at smuggling that insurance policies were available to cover them if their vessels were seized, while New York's privateer fleet was employed before the American Revolution to escort ships doing trade with enemies of the British.[4]

Cathy Matson describes "a well-trodden course" among New York smugglers after 1760:

> They gave the illusion of trading within their own region, then their ships proceeded to the West Indies, and then they brought back "French sugars" to the middle colonies and New England. A network of city merchants kept one another informed about the fictitious clearances. Many clearing vessels took goods to New London, North Carolina, Pennsylvania, and Jamaica that could never be sold there, but probably went on to Hispaniola instead.[5]

Complicitous customs agents falsified documents to help along the sugar trade. Matson quotes one who had a wry sense of humor about the illegal trading:

> Inclosed is a list of Vessels Cleared out of this Port with Provisions which are suspected to be on illicit trade. Among them it is observable that the sending of Onions, Boards, Hoop-poles Apples and Oyl to New London, the sending of Tar to South Carolina, Beef and Butter and the sending of Provisions, Bricks and hoops to Pennsylvania are all of them like sending Coals to New Castle.[6]

Because Arnold rode the crest of the great wave of coastal smuggling from the middle to the end of the eighteenth century, by understanding the contemporary colonial view of smuggling we understand his attitude. There are identifiable keys. First, smuggling was an old practice dating back to the early years when "the Dutch set the standard for free-flowing transnational trade."[7] Secondly, smuggling was ubiquitous and not seen as a crime by those who indulged in it. Thirdly, the mix of contraband with lawful trade that kept up the North American economy was inextricably linked with the plantation economy and its huge force of enslaved people. Lastly, mid-century, more vigilant customs house officials were appointed but ways of avoiding duties were ingrained. Truxes gives the example of bringing in sugar, rum and coffee from the French West Indies to a Connecticut port or to Perth Amboy, New Jersey, as if the cargo consisted of prize goods taken by one of the privateers of that port—though everybody knew no privateer ever claimed those ports as home or sailed from them.[8]

When the Stamp Act was repealed in 1766, the colonies celebrated, but the Parliament asserted that it had the power to tax them as it wished. The Townshend Acts (1767), named after the person who introduced them to Parliament, imposed duties on glass, lead, paints, paper and tea, all of

Fireplace mantle from Arnold's house in New Haven, now at the New Haven Museum (courtesy New Haven Museum).

which colonists could only buy from Britain. Merchants such as Arnold were keenly aware that greater freedom from restraint was a condition for the economy to thrive. The more taxes were levied, the more the colonists turned to smuggling, and local government deliberately took no notice. Economic concerns and the thrilling ideology of freedom both played roles in the revolutionary consciousness of the young Arnold. When he was accused of smuggling by a sailor he had previously employed, Arnold resorted to violent aggression, knowing that the illicit trading network was approved by the community.

Peter Boles was the sailor on Arnold's vessel the *Fortune* who in 1767 demanded wages that Arnold was unwilling to pay. Boles went to the customs house to inform about Arnold. The customs officer was not there but an assistant named Sanford was. Boles asked Sanford what his share of a seized cargo would be as an informer. The assistant didn't know so Boles said he would return to talk with his boss after the Sabbath. Arnold, hearing of this, pursued Boles and, by his own account, "gave him a little chastisement."[9]

Boles left town but soon was back. Now Arnold got tough. He had Boles write a confession that the devil had instigated him to turn on his employer, that he would never in his life inform on anyone in Connecticut again, and that he would leave New Haven at once and never return.

Boles hung on though. That a written document didn't get the result Arnold wished is a harbinger of his legal issues with business associates after the Revolution, as a trader in New Brunswick, and more briefly privateer in England. In defiance of Arnold, the sailor Boles was in the house of a tavern keeper named John Beecher, outside which a gang of sailors had gathered. Arnold took charge of the gang and broke into Beecher's house and dragged Boles out to the green. Boles was tied to a whipping post and given 40 lashes; afterwards he was run out of town.

A court action against Arnold ensued wherein he was fined 50 shillings. Ironically, the stamp collector Jared Ingersoll, whose job was to enforce the law, was his defense counsel. After the incident, Arnold wrote an open letter to the *Connecticut Gazette* that expressed the opinion of self-interest as the righteous path. Considering how the trade regulations "suppress our trade ... that one would imagine every sensible man would strive to encourage trade and discountenance such useless, infamous informers."[10]

Smuggler Nation has a salient example of the discrepancy between official imports and the amount of molasses needed to keep colonial distilleries running: "a mere 384 hogsheads of molasses per year officially arrived in Boston in 1754–1755, but 40,000 hogsheads per year were required to run the regions' 63 distilleries."[11] John W. Tyler describes, in his *Smugglers and Patriots: Boston Merchants and the Advent of the American Revolution,* how the activity of merchants at the fringes of the mercantile system led them to realize that their interests lay beyond the empire. Thus, Arnold had a concerted background of illegal trade, shrugging off imposed duties and taxes, from his earliest days in Connecticut. The ethos when he lived in Canada after the American Revolution was also favorable to smuggling, but there, smugglers like Arnold were taking advantage of vague borders. During the pre–Revolutionary period the smugglers were angry, not acquiescent, to be pushed by imposed taxes into disobeying the law.

Arnold had great material success ten years after coming to New Haven, emblematic of which was his marrying the county sheriff's seventeen-year-old daughter, Margaret Mansfield, and joining the Freemasons. Besides the store he owned three small ships. He advertised in the *Connecticut Gazette* of January 24, 1766, for "large genteel, fat horses, pork and oats and hay," and stated his wish to sell "choice cotton and salt, by quantity or retail: and other goods as usual." He had a sloop that sailed to Quebec and traded to Barbados for molasses and rum. By the time Arnold left off being a merchant and went to fight at Bunker Hill he was imbued with a tradition of coastal smuggling and thumbing a nose at governments hampering the making of profit, that he picked up again after the American Revolution.

He is often described as lavish and living beyond his means but there was one way for a gentleman, in particular a merchant gentleman, to live, without a lot of variation. Sometimes only a man's connections kept him from being a pauper when his house burned down, or his vessels sank at sea. Arnold wanted to be in the thick of commercial action. The sign now in the collection of the Museum of New Haven, which first hung over the store on George Street, and then just west of his house on Water Street, closer to the docks, is telling. The sign reads, "B. Arnold Druggistt/Bookseller etc. / From London" with the confident motto in Latin "For himself and for all."

He had already made a voyage to London for supplies for the Lathrop brothers' pharmacy. The distance between Water Street and the harbor has been filled in over the years. In 1775 he was near Long Wharf, which had been important for trade since 1736. His home too was directly off the harbor. Not only the premium location but the high style was the pattern of the homes Arnold would have all his life. When the Arnolds fled to London and Benedict's funds were short, the family would downsize several times, but when his prospects were up he would move to a finer house in a tonier neighborhood. The house into which he brought Peggy in Saint John, New Brunswick, was called "pretentious" by a contemporary, and that was the idea.

Today all that is left of the Water Street dwelling is a wooden painted mantle, which was a gift to the Museum of New Haven, dated 1777, described only as "Chimney Piece and Window from the Benedict Arnold home." The fireplace was the centerpiece of the main gathering room; and this mantle which surrounded it has Georgian moldings—decorative pilasters of matching design at either side of the opening and projecting slightly from the wall, inset panels, and a handsome cornice. It is very elegant. There are no dentils, which are more Greek Revival architectural features. It is easy to imagine it a prime thing to be rescued if the house was burning down.

Having a commodious house may have had clandestine purpose as well. According to an account written when the Arnold house in New Haven was still standing, the attic had a hiding place, and the cellar had "the ruins of what was once a tunnel that connected the house with the wharf, through which smuggled goods were carried."

In New Haven in 1764 he and another merchant formed a partnership and had three trading ships, the *Fortune, Charming Nancy* and the *Three Brothers*. Their trade connections were with the West Indies and Arnold often sailed his own ships. The greater profit came from smuggling molasses for rum. He brought in quantities in kegs marked "red claret." He was able with the profits of his business to buy back the Norwich house where he and Hannah had grown up, which had been sold to pay for his father's debts. He resold it at a profit and was already on his way to affluence when he married Sheriff Mansfield's daughter Margaret.

Mr. Edward Surato of the New Haven Museum encapsulates Arnold as he was before the Revolution as

> an important businessman in town, whose success as a pharmacist and bookseller allowed him to form a partnership in 1764 with merchant Adam Babcock. The pair bought three trading ships and established trade connections with the West Indies. Hence the move to Water Street where he could be close to the docks.

But taxes and restrictions on trade made a dent in his prosperity by the time he joined the local chapter of the Sons of Liberty. While in the West Indies he heard news of the Boston Massacre and wrote home, "Good God, are the Americans all asleep and tamely yielding up their liberties, or are they all turned philosophers that they do not take immediate vengeance on such miscreants?"[12]

In New Haven on April 22, 1775, he made a splash. Hearing of the Battle of Lexington and Concord, he rallied the Second Connecticut Foot Guards to go to Massachusetts to join their brethren. Hannah Arnold had raised her son aware of the past of the notable Arnold family and the future of what was expected of him. What is surprising is not that he fought for the cause of liberty or arose as a leader of men but that he was in such a rush. When he tore off to Bunker Hill, he must have supposed the armed resistance would be short and did not want to miss out. He was also arrogant, and it galled him when the local Committee of Safety told him to wait. At 14 he had yearned to join the colonial militia in 1755, which his mother blocked. He was only 16 when he enlisted and then took the unauthorized leave to go see his mother. All proving much ado as the French and Indian War ended before he could experience glory.

But as emotions boiled over into revolution in Boston, he saw a chance to prove he had the valor of his forebears, as far back as the first Arnold in America who had followed Roger Williams to Rhode Island to throw off the Puritan yoke. Therefore, Benedict told the Committee of Safety he would break into the armory on the green if they didn't give him the key. He got the key and off he and his men went to fight. Historian Charles Royster points to how sure the Sons of Liberty were that they had a mandate for revenge:

> When the revolutionaries encouraged each other to fight the British they invoked the spirit of the ancestors.... A man who went to war against the

British tyrant knew that his fathers approved his defense of what they had bequeathed him.[13]

Margaret Mansfield Arnold died in 1775 and left him in his mid-thirties with three young boys. His faithful sister Hannah now cared for them, as well having charge of the store in his absence.

2

How the General
Viewed His Treason

The great thing about having a national enemy
way back in history is that there are no longer
any political sensitivities to portraying him as a
villain in league with the devil.—J.L. Bell

Benedict's conduct in his later years, the concern of this book, would grow out of both his militarism and his ennui with revolution. He had a crisis when his experience of the war for freedom as he observed it collided with the morality that his loyalty was built on. He became a patriot to defend the rights of Englishmen in the colonies for representation in the colonial government. He yearned for glory in the colonial world and fame as a man of honor. His bold actions as a military officer expose him to have been quite deaf to the chain of command; neither was he ideologically driven. As the conflict dragged on, the "spirit of '76" was patchier. Washington needed a united front to win, while Arnold was socially and commercially in contact with the Tories in Philadelphia, who thought the goals of Americans could be achieved without more destructive warfare. He came to disrespect the new revolutionary government way before his treason. Joyce Lee Malcolm writes,

> Arnold was a moderate, not a radical, a fact that infuriated the radical Pennsylvania Executive Council. They accused Arnold of favoring the enemy because of his unwillingness to arrest the long list of Philadelphians the Council claimed were Loyalists.[1]

He was of a mind with Washington when the latter first took command of the Continental Army, to fight for liberty not independence. Partly as a result of Benedict's strength and leadership in battle, several years before peace, the British would concede more than the colonists asked for. Meanwhile Benedict threw up his hands at the politics of revolution—and inched his way to treason.

Brutality towards the captured enemy, and civilian casualties, were appalling. He had sacrificed his health in warfare and dying for glory had never held an attraction. Benedict was never going to be the same gallant officer hailed as virtually superhuman again, and there was no clear enemy or assurance that more warfare would bring peace. Arnold's viewpoint, Carl Van Doren explains, was in line with the populace he was governing in Philadelphia when he committed treason:

> In the prevailing bitterness and suspicion the zealous patriots were intolerant of opposition or dissent. The British peace offers in June [1781] and the lingering presence of the peace commissioners in New York till November, made many honest Philadelphians wonder if it would not be wiser for America to return to its old place in the Empire on favorable terms than to go on fighting bloodily for independence—and in the end perhaps fail to win it.[2]

The Carlisle Peace Commission offered self-rule but not full independence. The head of the commission, the gallant Frederick Howard, 5th Earl of Carlisle, did not have the authority to push for a deal that would have concluded the revolution. (In 1798 the Earl was commissioned with another challenge when appointed guardian of ten-year-old Lord Byron, the poet.)

Changing sides was what Benedict thought sane as the course of the war moved sluggishly on. When in February 1777, Congress declined to promote him to major general, he wrote to George Washington that he deemed this "a very civil way of requesting my resignation," and elaborated to General Howe,

> When I received a commission of brigadier I did not expect Congress had made me for their sport, or pastime, to displace, or disgrace whenever they thought proper. If this plan is pursued no gentleman who has any regard for his reputation will risk it with a body of men who seemed to be governed by whim and caprice.[3]

It was whispered when I was a child that my father would rise to the rank of admiral. He had served on battleships, done cryptography, understood machines, had not a fleck on his reputation, and was an Annapolis graduate who had played water polo. Then my father was passed over and, consonant with the "up and out" policy, was soon a civilian compelled at 43 to devise a second career (he taught math). I heard my parents talk and understood there was a "fleck," that an officer in a different branch of the armed forces, guilty for some security lapse, blamed my father. We understood that to tell his side wasn't possible by my father's code of honor; that meant lowering oneself. The choice given my father of a final billeting was between the Aleutian Islands and New York City, in those days equally unattractive to naval officers.

In terms of the tradition of the armed forces, an officer passed over was out as surely as if he fell off a ladder. Historians have verified that for eighteenth-century officers, to be passed over was a death. Arnold's reaction to the unfairness of the military brass would have made sense to his contemporaries. Gene Procknow, author of a multidisciplinary blog on the American Revolution, has studied the phenomenon of promotion of generals by the Continental Congress. He concludes that from the appointment of the first four major generals by Congress and George Washington the day after the Battle of Bunker Hill, "immediately, unhappiness with the appointments and the rank order led to rancorous and in some cases unresolvable disputes among the new military leadership."[4] On February 19, 1777, Congress promoted four brigadier generals, in so doing bypassing six brigadier generals with higher seniority. That same season, Nathanael Greene summarized to John Adams the reactions of those officers bypassed:

> I fear your late Promotions will give great disgust to many. But whatever promotions you intend to make, pray let them be completed as soon as possible, that those difficulties of reconciling discontented persons may not be at a time when harmony and concord is necessary.[5]

The distinctions in rank seem trivial, especially when the colonies were only teetering on the brink of independence. An explanation is found in what Joseph J. Ellis maintains, that whereas in England one was an officer because one was an aristocrat, in the American army one was an aristocrat because one was an officer.[6]

Of the passed over high officers, Robert Howe remained on duty, but Andrew Lewis and John Armstrong felt so snubbed they resigned immediately. William Thompson resigned later (he was legally a prisoner of war on parole), James Moore died shortly after being bypassed, and Arnold waged a campaign to get the promotion, with Washington's support:

> An incensed Arnold, with Washington's support, waged an aggressive campaign to "restore" his rank. After an eight-month dispute with Congress, Washington received authorization to backdate Arnold's major general commission to February 17, 1777, moving him ahead in rank.[7]

In Philadelphia, though, he was riding the gift of a caparisoned horse that Congress had given him and living handsomely. As soon as he was military commander it was to be expected that he entertain. He bought Mount Pleasant, praised by John Adams before his presidency as "the most elegant country seat in Pennsylvania"[8] as a wedding present for his second wife, the young patrician beauty Peggy Shippen. That it was built by a Scottish privateer who had been shot twice in the arm during his exploits must have appealed to Arnold. The Georgian mansion's showiness—it had a coach house, stable, walled garden and warehouse, and recent tenants had been the Don Juan de Miralles, the first Spanish envoy to the Continental Congress and, before that, General Howe—made an appropriate statement. Such public works took cash and Arnold asked both sides to his first big party to mend the relations of the reoccupied city. The U.S. military top brass still give and expect parties; if they have no private fortunes their wives resort to "counting the shrimp."

The chances of the freedom fighters winning the war were at a low ebb and appeared sinking. Arnold was preoccupied with staying afloat financially—so were many. A colonist observed that "'such is the Spirit to trade, that *if Beelzebub was to appear with a Cargoe—the people would deal with him.*"[9] These stricken times were the backdrop for the accusation against Arnold of Colonel John Brown that "Money is this man's god and to get enough of it he would sacrifice his country."[10] Not his country but the cause; no one knows whether the United States would have flourished, perhaps ending slavery sooner, had peace been negotiated with terms that did not separate the 13 colonies from the empire.

Moreover, Arnold's honor was offended by accusations of the misuse of funds during his highly visible governorship of Philadelphia. He believed himself the smartest person in the room, and this made him arrogant and impatient. In his military career he was especially highhanded with paperwork He was flummoxed by Congress's resolution that he should order an inventory of goods taken from Tories, and the owners' names, before trade could continue, as he had been to account for his commissary in battle. How this must have burned when, at Ticonderoga and Lake Champlain, he had spent his own money. Writes Bobrick,

> With all trade but his own prohibited, Arnold evidently took advantage of his position to make wholesale purchases at low prices, ostensibly for the army but in fact in part for himself, and later sold through middlemen a portion of what he had acquired at a large profit for personal gain.[11]

After six months as governor, Arnold resigned and Joseph Reed, president of the Supreme Executive Council of Pennsylvania, meant business. Within a short time after the British left the city, the Council prosecuted Tories, hanged two Quaker collaborators, and charged Arnold with eight counts of misconduct and abuse of power. A joint committee of Congress and the Council met and recommended a court-martial on the charge of using public property for private ends. Even those who portray Benedict Arnold as a monster acknowledge that he spent patriotically his own funds during the conflict. Considering that Paul Revere was exonerated after being court-martialed on a change of insubordination (during the failed attempt to regain Fort George from the British), one can imagine that Arnold's court-martial could also have removed blame from him.

This is when in the spring of 1779 he married Peggy Shippen. Pain in his injured leg was his to bear for life; it was particularly noted at the ceremony that he had to lean on a soldier and that his bad leg was resting on a bench, or camp stool. He was, from June, contacting British agents in New York, under the code name "Gustavus." The upshot was that after days of testimony, General Knox and his board acquitted Arnold of the charge that he closed Philadelphia stores while he made purchases himself. He was found guilty of allowing a ship from a British port to dock, and for misuse of army wagons. This was the affair of the *Charming Nancy*, a ship he co-owned that was taken over by privateers; Arnold commandeered a dozen army wagons to get its cargo returned. When the Pennsylvania legislature sentenced him to be reprimanded by George Washington, Washington issued a mild rebuke, calling Arnold's action "peculiarly reprehensible"[12] but imposing no penalties. The reprimand must have burned. Arnold could not be a great general when aspersions had been cast; collective allegiance had to be single-minded, and leaders, of course, exemplify public virtue.

When Arnold came out on the British side, searing discontent with the Congress was not his alone. Nathanael Greene, Washington's favorite major-general, led the crucial southern campaign of the war and settled on the Savannah River as a plantation owner instead of returning to his native Rhode Island. Barbara Tuchman notes that General Greene, "steadiest of them all," protested that Congress was so negligent it gave him "no more equal to his needs than a sprat in a whale's belly." Greene talked of resigning in protest when he was planning an offensive for the recovery of Savannah.[13] After the Revolutionary War, Greene did poorly with the farm he bought and took a rueful look at all he gave to his country.

In this era, generals were performers, like rock stars; they could be heroes one year and discredited the next. George Germain was trying to diminish the casualties of his cavalry at Minden in the Seven Years' War and did not give the permission of an officer to act independently and "gain glory." For this, Germain was court-martialed, and ridiculed for a decade. The risks of harm to his soldiers bore no weight in public opinion.

The battles Arnold fought saturate his life story but occupied but a sixth of his adulthood. It wasn't liberty than drew young men like Arnold or Lafayette, but the chance for glory. The fighting man's views could change, which is a partial explanation why many of the Patriots returned to their farm after their enlistment was up. Arnold fought to distinguish himself first and then wanted to put an end to fighting. The two battles at Saratoga in the fall of 1777 were a watershed because of what they cost the British under General Burgoyne. Arnold led the charges against the Hessian center which forced a British retreat. A quarter of the British army had been disabled. When Prime Minister Frederick North heard he decided on certain overtures of peace. This is when the Earl of Carlisle's peace commission arrived in Philadelphia. The terms proposed to the Continental Congress included no more taxes and a new degree of autonomy for the colonies, but not full independence—the British perspective was always "we decide."

After five years of conflict, neighbors had injured, or murdered, neighbors and many insurgents had returned to their civilian lives and hired replacements. Arnold, intending to lead other frustrated soldiers out from the messy revolution to orderly (and, it was hoped, neglectful) British colonial government, wrote three explanations of his decision to go over to the British: to the American people, to the King, and much later in a kind of job application to get a military post in Britain's war with the French Republic. In them he recounted seeing a compelling need for the carnage to end. As a merchant he had objected to taxes without representation, but the war dragged on principally to benefit the egos of the leaders. It has often been pointed out proudly that America's example inflamed other violent revolutions.

It is important to take into account that many in the colonies did not want to set alight revolutionary movements; they were not "levelers" like Thomas Paine, Patrick Henry or Isaiah Thomas. Arnold, the wounded veteran of major battles, was placed by Washington in a command where he listened to others instead of charging pell-mell. That a proper young lady of 18 made the general into a traitor is unlikely to the point of absurdity. She may well have been complicit, but he acted alone. He went ahead with the treason because he judged it correct, not to show a Lady Macbeth he was more of a man. As a sea captain and a trader, he felt linked to the empire—he had a wide perspective. Moreover, he picked no bone with the social order in which he had grown up. In any event, he made up his own mind.

He was convinced of his rectitude but knew that fury would follow his actions. In his September 25, 1780, letter to George Washington from on board the *Vulture*, Benedict asked for protection for Peggy because she had no part in his lurid scheme. His phrasing is worth a close look: "She is as good and as Inocent as an Angel, and is Incapable of doing Wrong."[14] But there was a cross out of "Ignorant" that was replaced with "Incapable." What if she wasn't culpable as a schemer but simply knew what was going on? Because it was her husband, who talked things over with her, she wasn't effectively "Ignorant." It looks as though he was going to say she was ignorant of his plans but in this letter where he is straining for sincerity he cannot say that.

Yet how could anybody betray the noble, impartial, and impeccable Washington? For Arnold this was not personal treachery but a decision of honor. He had been passed over for major-general in 1777 just before the Battle of Saratoga and in 1779, facing the court-martial for his cavalier-like governing of Philadelphia, began a secret correspondence with the British command. Parties on both sides moved cautiously. Instead of crossing over and joining the British at once, Clinton advised Arnold that he could do more for the British if he operated within the American army and worked behind the lines. Only when the plan was proposed for Arnold to "sell West Point" was the mandate in place. Arnold's *Letter to the Inhabitants of America*, published in the *London Chronicle* in October 1780, implied that patriotism had motivated his betrayal:

> You have felt the torture in which we raised our arms against a Brother—God incline the Guilty protractors of these unnatural dissentions, to resign their Ambition, and Cease from their Delusions, in Compassion to kindred blood.

He said it became an offensive war when the French joined in the fight and he had not wavered in his stand, that of many Americans, of staying part of Great Britain. This same *Letter* presaged what would be the Loyalists' position:

> With the highest satisfaction I bear testimony to my old fellow soldiers and citizens, that I find solid ground to rely upon the clemency of our sovereign, and abundant conviction that it is the generous intention of Great Britain, not only to have the rights and privileges of the colonies unimpaired, together with their perpetual exemption from taxation, but to superadd such further benefits as may consist with the Common prosperity of the Empire. In short, I fought for much less than the parent country is as willing to grant to her Colonies, as they can be to receive or enjoy.[15]

Historians go so far in Arnold's defense as to verify that he was a skilled military tactician and brave warrior who became fed up with his role in the revolution. But they infer that his public disavowals of the cause he had fought for were his making excuses. Really, he wasn't the type to make excuses for ignoble behavior, then or later. He had asked the help of William Smith, formerly the attorney general of New York, to write his 1782 "Thoughts on the American War," a letter to the King, "for answers that may be put to him." (Smith's diary noted giving this help on December 10, 1781.) Yet Benedict's apologia is just how he saw his case. The ties to the cause were frayed. Being passed over was intolerable. He could not stand by and see bad go to worse any more than he could hold his chest up to be pierced with a sword. The arrows of reputation, financial want, pride, and honor pelted him. He changed sides, period. Like the Gingerbread Man, who ran with all his might, calling out, "Catch me if you can," Arnold did not anticipate being tripped up by the disdain of less intrepid mortals for posterity.

The colonists conquered doubt to form their unified front. They justified war for civic reasons, taxation without representation. They were true subjects of the Crown until the first violence, the Boston Massacre (where John Adams averred there was cause for the soldiers to fire on the protestors). Once doubt was conquered, the royalists were attacked and driven from their homes. After the war, the losers among the colonists were to have back their property. This was not what happened; the hearts and minds of the winners shut down. If the war had been merely tactical, on the chessboard of power, having one's family members and neighbors die would lose the meaning. Arnold was cast as evil incarnate and Washington was deified—this caricature comforted pieties, and history is written by the winners.

Arnold was a practical person employed as a grocer and seafaring merchant from boyhood; the ideology of liberty while it inspired his passions did not reach his soul. Congress stabbed him in the back, so he had no dreams about the great men who would lead the liberated thirteen colonies, and the misuse of funds for which he was court-martialed was arguably a matter of carelessness. Washington supposed that Arnold could handle the protocols of dealing with citizens of all political stripes in Philadelphia. But the general did not walk the fine line of a military governor well. It only confused compatriots when he threw a lavish party to win over the Tories, inviting citizens from both sides of politics. He attended theater in the midst of war. He wooed a socialite. He opposed the execution of the two Quakers denounced as Tories. He must have felt like a chess piece with nowhere to move.

The injuries to his leg had been a crossroads. He would never again pose as a gallant sexy officer. His parties to bring together the citizens were minor affairs compared with the thrilling Meschianza, concocted by Major John André to honor General and Admiral Howe. The picture of the soldier resting his leg on the camp stool at his wedding speaks for the truth of war.

Peggy's level of complicity in his treason sparked intense debate and has worked out like a knot unraveling over the last two centuries. When Arnold fled from West Point and Washington came into her bedroom and saw her half-dressed, she had a fit and did not recognize him. I think this was no pretense, but rather, an abject denial of the predicament she found herself in. If she influenced Benedict to the British side, she did not push him over a line. He acted alone. He went ahead with the nasty treason of "selling" West Point after General Clinton said that subterfuge was the most valuable contribution Arnold could make.

When Benedict challenged Lord Lauderdale to a duel two decades after the treason, Peggy kept her countenance for a week. She told her father that if she tried to influence her husband it "would unman him and prevent him acting himself."[16] Peggy's identity was as an admired, well-behaved beauty, not a manipulating person. One thinks of Washington's jest when he sent Lafayette and others ahead to breakfast at West Point: "you young men are all in love with Mrs. Arnold." Peggy was happy with herself as a belle. To see her really passionate one has to see her as a patrician daughter and a mother. An iconic "Peggy" moment was when she went around the London shops all day in the spring of 1785, advising her brother-in-law on the selection of china for "Mrs. Edward Burn."[17]

There is doubt whether becoming a traitor was as big in Arnold's mind planning it as it became. Enough soldiers on the American side defected to make regiments. Insofar as warfare was being conducted in a civil war, it was to be expected (though direly punished as treason) that some soldiers would switch allegiance.

When Arnold left with General Cornwallis, he was hoping to present new tactics to preserve the imperial status quo to the King. Arnold did not of course imagine he was switching to the losing side—or that he would spend the rest of his life in exile. A homely account of some of the Arnolds' goods left behind when he fled from West Point suggest that they were being held until he reclaimed them at the end of the conflict.

Lieutenants Richard Varick and David Franks had official charge of them. The account is as follows. A "good feather bed" belonging to Hannah was delivered to her on November 20. "Commissions of sequestration in Duchess County" seized a "feather bed of inferior quality, small pillow, iron pot and frying pan." Tin articles (tea kettle, coffee pot, quart mug and six lamps) borrowed by Arnold were returned to the owners, possibly the army. A white counterpane, two sheets and two pillowcases were "remaining in the hands of Lt. Varick Dec. 6, 1780." A second longer list is of objects that were consigned to Varick and Franks, and included a brass teakettle and chafing dish, pewter, china, iron kitchen utensils, a trunk and mahogany servers.[18]

Like a knight of the round table, Arnold for five years was fervently devoted to the cause of liberty, capturing Fort Ticonderoga, besieging Quebec for a long winter, and delaying the British invasion of the Hudson Valley by his David against Goliath campaign at Lake Champlain. But once he lost his faith in those who led the cause, and received insult from the Continental Congress, no qualms of loyalty would stop him from avenging his honor. After he betrayed the cause of revolution, he never displayed political fervor again, unless one counts his ongoing animosity towards and kneejerk readiness to battle the French. He was now conservative. He was against revolution. He showed in letters no inclination to social justice. He would fight to subdue a slave revolt in Guadeloupe even though he surely knew about the movement for the emancipation of slaves in Europe, and the gruesome reality of enslaving people. As a young man he took law into his own hands to get the ammunition out of the New Haven town armory so as to join the Sons of Liberty in Massachusetts and led a militia without being directed by his superior. Once vilified as a traitor, chances were, even on the British side, against wielding authority on the public stage.

Heroes in our imagination do not change as he did. In retirement Benedict made scant attempt to perform to applause again on the public stage, funneling all his ambitions into the private realm. He and his trophy wife Peggy felt intense concern for their own family and wanted to be respected so the sons would not be vilified. This fit with the "revolution of feeling" of the 1790s, the beginning of exalting childhood and parental focus on the nuclear social unit.

Nathaniel Philbrick evokes Arnold as "blessed with almost superhuman energy and endurance."[19] These traits went into the mundane pursuit of wealth after the American Revolution. Furthermore, the "lissome elegance" that Philbrick describes of the man was before. The man we meet in these pages, in his middle and later years, was stout and had a heavy face. One leg was two inches longer than the other, he limped, and pain must have lined his face.

In 1781, learning of Arnold's defection, Benjamin Franklin termed it an infinitely poor deal: "Judas sold only one man, Arnold three millions. Judas got for his one Man 30 pieces of silver, Arnold got a halfpenny a head. A miserable bargain!"[20] This is Franklin, keen and incisive as usual. It wasn't only that people distrusted Arnold because of his public behavior. It wasn't that he was a monster for changing sides—as convenient as he became as an example to shore up backsliding patriots. He was, unforgivably, a money-man who hadn't behaved by the rules of a gentleman. He suffered the consequences of his actions, and so did Peggy. Interestingly, they persevered and succeeded in what really counted for them, each other and the lives of their children.

3

John Champe's Ride

We are, all of us, wandering about in a state of oblivion,
borrowing our time, seizing our days, escaping our fates.
—Maggie O'Farrell, *I Am, I Am, I Am*

In all the places he lived, Arnold circulated in plain daylight. Why didn't someone who viewed him as the devil incarnate assassinate him? According to some accounts, when he led the British raid on Virginia, he hired handpicked soldiers and sailors as guards, and armed himself with two small pistols each morning. Arnold became of no strategic value. As Michael Kranish, author of *Flight from Monticello*, remarked to me, "Most certainly they tried to capture him, Jefferson put a bounty on his head, and so on. But he eluded capture, he was protected by the British, and he eventually left for England."

The General's infamy exceeded his fame but in those days the stature of a military hero often didn't last beyond a single conquest or winning battle. The Comte de Grasse was the admiral who blockaded Yorktown, which penned in Cornwallis and his army. A year later, he lost to the English in the Caribbean one of the most powerful warships at sea, blamed subordinate officers, and was banished from the French court.

After the war was over, Arnold wasn't that special a prey. Yet, three years after the Treaty of Paris, a *New York Journal* news article (November 16, 1786) gratified readers by reporting that the inhabitants of Saint John had offered to hand Arnold over to the Americans for ten dollars. He had, the story went, escaped to Halifax. He himself kept his treason in the public eye by applying to the British government for money to remediate his losses of property and goods. Thus, like the Ancient Mariner, he was compelled by circumstance to tell his story over and over. I believe you, said a naval commander to whom Arnold applied for an assignment to fight against Napoleon, but people would not want to serve under a traitor. George Washington wanted to make a public example of Arnold. He approved a first plot to bring him back alive before Major Andre's execution, writing Henry Lee:

Hd Qrs Octr 20th 1780

Dear Sir

The plan proposed for taking A——d (the outlines of which are communicated in your letter) which was this moment put into my hands without a date—has every mark of a good one—I therefore agree to the promised rewards, and have such entire confidence in your management of the business as to give it my fullest approbation; and leave the whole to the guidance of your own judgment, with this express stipulation & pointed injuction, that he A——d is brought to me alive.

No circumstance whatever shall obtain my consent to his being put to death—The idea which would accompany such an event would be that Ruffians had been hired to assasinate him. My aim is to make a public example of him—and this should be strongly impressed upon those who are employed to bring him off.

The Sergeant must be very circumspect—too much zeal may create suspicion—and too much precipitancy may defeat the project. the most inviolable secrecy must be observed on all hands. I send you five guineas; but I am not satisfied of the propriety of the Sergeants appearing with much specie—This circumstance may also lead to suspicion as it is but too well known to the enemy that we do not abound in this article.

The interviews between the party in, and out of the City, should be managed with much caution and seeming indifference, or else the frequency of their meetings &ca may betray the design & involve bad consequences—but I am persuaded you will place every matter in a proper point of view to the conductors of this interesting business—& therefore I shall only add that I am Dr Sir Yr obt & affect Servt

Go: Washington[1]

A two-by-four inch children's book with illustrative engravings, dating from a generation after Arnold's death, *Stories about Arnold* (1831), tells the plotted attempt on his life as a morality tale. It begins in the few days between Arnold's flight from his command post at West Point to the British ship the *Vulture* and continues to the execution of Major André. The curious aspect of this telling is how the rebels are presented as exemplars of honesty when they naturally resorted to trickery and spying quite like what Arnold and André used. The reader is expected to be indoctrinated that someone entrapping Arnold by whatever sneaky means was on the side of right.

A narrator is explaining to his son that George Washington was hoping to capture Arnold, and if he could be taken, André might be released. That Washington's wish to save André would come to naught gives poignancy to the tale, as told to juvenile readers, when Washington calls Major Lee ("Lighthorse Harry") to his tent. However, Champe (at Lee's command) deserted on the night of October 20 so he could not have taken on his mission with the hope of saving André by kidnapping Arnold. Hundreds of soldiers from the region had witnessed André's hanging on October 2. The collective memory was unconsciously embellished to make Champe and indeed Washington more heroic.

Captain Cameron, a portion of whose private journal reached print

HERE WAS THE HOME OF
SERGEANT MAJOR
JOHN CHAMPE
CONTINENTAL ARMY
WHO RISKED THE INGLORIOUS
DEATH OF A SPY FOR THE
INDEPENDENCE OF
HIS COUNTRY

The obelisk is said to have been built in 1939 from the few stones remaining of the house where John Champe was born, in Loudoun County, Virginia (courtesy Charles C. Ripley III).

in segments, in *The United Service Journal* in England, and an article in a 1938 issue of *The William and Mary Quarterly*,[2] is a major source for Champe's adventure, which the author of the children's book would not have had in hand to consult. Cameron was recollecting long after the event and was borrowing from the 1812 memoirs of Henry Lee (by General Lee) as well. The details in this chapter about Champe's adventures merge the story as spun by Lee and Cameron with research articles of the twentieth century by Wilbur C. Hall and William Buckner McGroarty. Cameron's account brings a lively aspect to the story of John Champe's adventure which we can presume was quite well known in the early Republic.

Did the major have a man who could be trusted, "willing to risk his life … prudent, and yet firm and sagacious?" Lee replied that he did. He chose 23-year-old fellow Virginian, Sergeant Major John Champe, as the man for the scheme. "Tell him the danger but tell him that I will reward him handsomely."

Champe was to "insinuate" himself into some menial position in the purlieus of the British command in New York City. A confederate, Mr. Baldwin of Newark, would visit him every two days, and they would at the right moment seize Arnold, gag him, and bring him across to Bergen Woods in New Jersey. Champe's bounty would be "100 guineas, 500 acres of land, and 3 Negroes." (Why do we suddenly hope the plot will fail?) John Champe's wife Jane, born in 1752, was related to Washington's younger brother Samuel. At a moment when everybody in the army was unsure whom he could trust, this must have been a point in John's favor with the commander-in-chief.

Towards midnight on October 21, John was on his horse riding south to New York. When others in the camp heard what he had done they were aghast: honest Champe had deserted. A pursuing party was formed which Lee delayed as long as he could…. Then they were off. Champe had a ten-mile ride ahead from his regiment in Totowa. He had an hour's lead and the advantage of being in pure flight, where those chasing him had to discover his path. It had rained so that the horseshoe mark on Champe's horse's left front hoof, of the division's same farrier, showed an impression in the mud. Eventually the party spied him from the top of a hill, and Champe glimpsed them and spurred his horse. He was miles yet from the Hudson River.

Approaching it, he saw two British ships. Henry Clinton had stationed ships at that location in the river to facilitate André's escape. The look-out seaman saw through his glass a man in the well-known uniform of Lee's legion, one of the most outstanding corps in the American service, racing from the American side toward the river and called an officer to see him. The officer watched the man round the corner of the woods, enter a broad road cut through the trees, and follow it to the reedy swamp banking the Hudson at that point. Then the uniformed stranger unbuckled the knapsack from the croup of the saddle and strapped it on his shoulders. He drew out his sword and cast off his scabbard and belt. Glancing anxiously from time to time behind him, he spurred his horse and set off again at top speed.

The troops were gaining on him when he reached the margin of the marsh. They were 60 or 70 yards behind when he plunged into the dark water, at the same time shouting for help. He was swimming for his life. His pursuers reached the shore and saw him struggle through the water, urged forward by oarsmen sent out from one of the British ships. A strong man caught hold of his arm and he was saved. The captain of the ship gave Champe a welcome and sent him escorted in a rowboat, with a note explaining what had been seen, to the command at New York City. The party of soldiers chasing the deserter returned to Lee's camp at three in the morning with his horse, cloak and scabbard. They were irate that the deserter had got away, while Lee was secretly relieved that he had escaped.

Champe did not immediately join the ranks of the British soldiers. Spies were manifold, so he hung around making his discontents known. His cover was that he had been ill-treated by superiors and was tired of war. General Clinton himself questioned Champe. Sir Henry would seem credulous until we realize that desertion from Washington's army was at that point a means of filling the ranks of the British army. After a few days, Champe was recruited into a unit of deserters.

Meanwhile Champe formed his daring plan. General Arnold walked late every evening before going to bed. It seems as if he could be counted on at midnight to stretch his legs and stop at the outhouse behind his lodging. The house lay next door to the British headquarters at the base of Manhattan but had a garden at one side, along a lane from which it was separated by a wooden rail fence. Champe would rush out and grab the general, and act as though he was taking a drunken soldier to the guardhouse. Then he would secrete Arnold across the river beyond British lines.

Champe communicated with Lee in New Jersey, who recruited two men from the Continental Army to wait with a rowboat to whisk the sergeant and his captive across the river, where Lee and three horsemen would wait. Having studied Arnold's habits from the alley behind the townhouse, the time came on December 11 when all was ready. Champe loosened the boards of the townhouse's fence, and that night of the plotted kidnapping, Lee and three dragoons waited in the woods near Hoboken. But the night passed and Champe did not show up in Hoboken. A letter came from Champe explaining what had foiled the plan, that Arnold had that very night changed his quarters to get ready for an expedition south. And that very next day, Champe as a British soldier was ordered on a transport ship to go to Virginia, part of a force of 1600 troops under the command of Arnold himself, now a brigadier general in the Loyalist forces.

It is noteworthy that the "Loyalists" were not merely the opponents of the "patriots." Barry Murray, St. Andrews, New Brunswick historian, has explained that the word Loyalist had specificity. "A commander sent to the King or his highest representative that he had a certain number of men and 'May I expect you to confer Loyalist status on them?' The term is used loosely but it was an approved status that gave the right to be called a Loyalist." Captain Cameron recalled liking Champe but having some reserve about him as he was "cheerless and impassive." Then again, Cameron had been reluctant to enlist in the first place.

At Petersburg, after several weeks in the uncomfortable position of seeming to have deserted the revolutionary army, Champe managed to extricate himself from the British troops after Cornwallis arrived. He returned to the encampment of several thousand of Lee's soldiers around Little Falls, New Jersey. They were astonished to see him, and in the 1831 patriotic children's book version, Champe was beloved and respected more than ever, and General Howe said he was "more than brave—he was honest."

One feels like Alice in the looking glass. What Arnold did by changing sides and also what the sergeant major did on orders from Lee and Washington were brave but dishonest, in the manner of all's fair in war. Champe was a stout and brave hero but it seems too much protest to praise how honest Champe was. From all known of him he was a good person; he might have had every virtue, but this was war. On orders, he faked a defection from the American camp and lied when he was interviewed by a superior British officer, some say by Arnold himself. Then Champe pretended to be a British soldier, and on a person-to-person level he deceived the sailors who rescued him from peril out on the dark cold river in the middle of the night.

He also bungled the assignment. Had Champe managed to acquire better information he would have pushed up the abduction a day. He had spent weeks studying Arnold's schedule and habits, watching from an alley of the townhouse. A courier informed George Washington of the strategy; apparently the General had thought the plan had the mark of a good one. But on the big day, Champe got his facts wrong. No one had tipped him off that Arnold's force of 1600 men would shortly be leaving for Portsmouth, Virginia, in command of a big expedition Yet there must have been a bustle at the harbor, as men were preparing for so many men to board a ship, which he himself would have to do.

CHAMPE ROCKS
Near Champe Rocks is the home and grave of Sergeant John Champe who was sent by General Washington and Major Lee to kidnap Benedict Arnold, the traitor, from within the British lines. The daring plot almost succeeded.

Champe Rock. John Champe settled in Pendleton County, West Virginia, after the American Revolution and died in the Picketts Fort State Park area about 100 miles away (courtesy Charles C. Ripley III).

Then again, turning the critique away from the brave soldier, General Washington could have traded Major André, saving his life, instead of the hardline decision to hang him.

The moralism drawn in the little illustrated book is that Washington appreciated absolute obedience (given that this was not a dream assignment) even when a mission failed. Of course, Champe now would be hanged if he were caught. Lee advised him to virtually disappear into the wilds of western Virginia. He was given land and, it appears, money to make a new life with his family, as he already was married with children.

After the peace, Captain Cameron was given leave to stay behind in America to visit a family of "republicans" in Virginia with whom he had established a connection. He was traveling through Loudoun County with a servant on a summer day in 1784 when they came to a place where there was a choice of three paths. The path he took led him deeper into the woods. A storm started up, thunder clapped, and lightning caused a fire to rage in the pines. The two men made their way to an opening in the woods. Flashes of lightning revealed a log cabin, but it lay at the far side of a deep ravine. Leaving the servant behind, and guided by the flashes, Cameron found a small rude bridge that traversed the torrent in the ravine. He crossed it on hands and feet to the log cabin. Its door was open, and a man came out with a torch. He went to rescue the servant and then beckoned them both into the house. The visitors were given changes of clothes and directed to warm themselves at the fire, while their host led the horses to a shed, rubbed them down, and fed them. Then the visitors ate a hearty supper prepared by the wife. Writes Captain Cameron,

> In due time our host returned, and the first glance which I cast towards him, satisfied me that he was no stranger. The second set everything like doubt at rest. Sergeant Champe stood before me, the same in complexion, in feature, though somewhat less thoughtful in the expression of his eye as when he first joined my company in New York.

The next morning the couple was up to do the tasks of the farm while Cameron still slept. When the host heard Cameron was preparing to ready the horses, he asked him to delay a few minutes, and began to talk about the past:

> I trust you will believe me when I saw, that nothing can be a matter of more perfect indifference to me than the estimation in which I may be held by the individuals composing Arnold's Legion; for the whole of whom, from their commanding officer downward, I entertain the most sovereign contempt. But you are a British born. I found you to be an honorable and a right-minded man; and though I believe that you erred in drawing your sword against the liberties of America, I still respect you so much, that I would not willingly rank as a traitor in your eyes. I have therefore, resolved to tell you a tale, which I should not think it worth while to tell to any other man, unless I knew him to be a genuine American, in all his principles and feelings.

Lee had singled him out for courage and steadfastness, to complete a strange assignment:

> If, therefore, you find that you cannot seize him unhurt, do not seize him at all; and if the choice be between his escape and his slaughter, let him go. To kill him would give the enemy an excuse for alleging all sorts of falsehoods against us. But if you can bring him alive to head-quarters, so that he may be tried by a court-martial, and publicly executed, you will at once further the ends of justice on an atrocious traitor, and strike a salutary terror into the minds of his associates.

In this account, Champe identifies the summit from which his comrades saw him as he fled to the Hudson. This is The Three Pigeons, a landmark in North Bergen, New Jersey, of the Revolutionary War. Figuring that they would cut to the bridge over the Hackensack River, he changed his route west to the Hudson. He told Cameron that there was a very effective spy network in New York, and no trouble getting commands from Lee or messages to him. Moreover, whatever was said at the dinner table of General Clinton, Champe could convey to the American headquarters.

Arnold was a strong man so Champe needed an accomplice to go to the garden with him. He undid a portion of the fence but arranged the posts so the breach didn't show. All was ready. This is where he admits to error:

> How often have I regretted since, that I should have set thus deliberately about the business! By heavens! There occurred twenty opportunities, of which, had I been less anxious to accomplish my purpose, I might have availed myself. But I permitted them to pass, or rather, felt myself unable to take advantage of them, because I had judged it imprudent to keep less trusty agents too often on the alert. So, however, it was to be.

He described the hazards of reaching Lee and also General Greene, who had succeeded Arnold at the head of West Point and given a deciding opinion that André would as a spy have to be hanged. Champe told Cameron about being sent to Washington himself,

> From whom I received much more both of praise and recompense, than my unaccomplished services merited. But he would not permit me to continue in the army. He reminded me, that to be taken by the enemy would be followed by certain death; and presenting me with my discharge, accompanied the act by a donation so munificent, that I have never since known what it is to be in want. The winding up of it all is—that I married a wife, sat myself down in this beautiful district, and have been so fortunate as to give shelter in his hour of need, to an officer under whom I served, only long enough to be taught that even the British uniform can cover a manly and generous heart.

Captain Cameron thanked John Champe and his wife for their kindness and resumed his journey. The journal tells a heartwarming instance of male bonding, generosity, and unaffected bravery. Washington may have given Champe his reward from the secret intelligence fund, or Washington's own pocket. The tracts of land Champe received were in what was then Virginia's western wilderness. He may have returned to Loudon County with his family (the Champes had six children), but they moved several times, possibly as far as Kentucky.

Attempts on Benedict Arnold's life may have been more frequent than we know. There is one newspaper article that appeared while he was in New Brunswick a dozen years after the war that speaks of a bounty on him. It does seem though that his shame was seen as punishment enough after the war. After Champe's failed attempt there were just two more notable attempts, both during the war.

When Arnold marauded in Virginia, George Washington ordered Lafayette to hang the now British brigadier general if caught. Thomas Jefferson instructed a general to hire frontiersmen to seize Arnold; Jefferson also endorsed the plan to crash into his vessel by means of a fire ship. (It grounded on a sandbar.)

It must have struck Lafayette viscerally when Arnold became a traitor because Lafayette was there, in the house with Peggy, in the first hours after the revelation. Lafayette is a character of history who never faltered from chivalry. Whether it is his eating Maine's first ice cream at a public dinner in 1825, or Adrienne's writing in the margins of books with toothpicks when they were imprisoned by Napoleon, the Lafayettes embody unadulterated glamor. Lafayette could have had Arnold assassinated but did not.

A man enslaved in Virginia, James [sometimes called James Armisted], was assigned to spy on Arnold and gained the trust of both him and General Cornwallis. In the 400th anniversary *History of Portsmouth*, Virginia, James is introduced as follows: "While in Portsmouth Arnold acquired a slave named James Armistead, or he was somehow insinuated into Arnold's service."[3] Although the information James conveyed was valuable, no attempt was as a consequence made on Arnold's life. After the war, James, who took the surname Lafayette, was not eligible for emancipation because he had been a spy not a soldier, a technicality that makes one's blood boil today. He petitioned for and gained freedom, however, and became a farmer in Virginia and raised a family.

One can surmise that no one hunted down, and killed or captured, the General from the time he escaped to New York because he was surrounded by the British. Even when he sailed out of New York he went in a vessel that was part of a military convoy. Secondly, he had the reputation of a fearsome superman who would be hell to catch. But there was also the psychology. He may have been a big fish but the stench of a traitor was stronger alive than buried. A lady in Norwich might have shot at him (September 1781 during the Connecticut raid) from her virtuous anger but that was personal vengeance.

Once the war was over, it would have been tacitly evident that no prize money for his head would be forthcoming from the American government. At that point it would have taken someone personally scarred by Arnold to hunt him down.

Model of the SS *Vulture* (courtesy West Point Museum Collection, United States Military Academy).

The Escape of Arnold on the British Sloop-of-War, Vulture by Howard Pyle (1853–1911) (courtesy the Stapleton Collection/Bridgeman Images).

When the treason was exposed, the two elder Arnold boys, Benedict, age 13, and Richard, 10, were at school in Maryland while little Henry, age seven, was at home. It must have been disruptive for Benedict and Richard to be yanked from school with their father suddenly a criminal. Benedict thought highly of the school, in the Needwood Forest of Burkittville, near

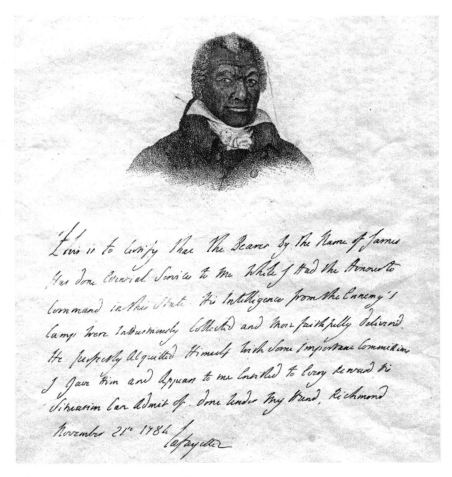

Broadside made from Marquis de Lafayette's testimonial to James's service during the American Revolution, probably created during Lafayette's farewell tour of America in 1824–1825 (courtesy Marquis de Lafayette Memorabilia Collection, Skillman Library, Lafayette College).

Hagerstown in Frederick County, run by the Rev. Bartholomew Booth. Aunt Hannah took Henry to New Haven and the older boys were sent to her. All three would grow up in the care of their Aunt Hannah.

Reverend Booth's School[4]

About six weeks after wedding Peggy Shippen, Benedict dispatched his two older sons from Philadelphia to a school in Maryland. With them went a letter to the schoolmaster, The Reverend Booth, laying out what Benedict expected of his sons' education and enclosing three hundred dollars for their expenses and to buy the boys suitable clothes (which Benedict's own tailor, the father explained, would not have had time to complete).

Benedict had resigned as military governor of Philadelphia in May and this was also a few weeks after Benedict had opened up secret correspondence with the British also in May. The nuptials or the subversion brewing in the house could be the explanation for removing the boys to boarding school post haste.

He wrote Booth on May 25, 1778, that he wished for the boys to have a useful rather than ornamental education and that they were being influenced badly: "Life is too short and uncertain to throw away in speculation on subjects that perhaps only one man in ten thousand has a genius to cut a figure in. I want my sons to become useful members of society."

Booth, who was also rector of the local Anglican church, came to the U.S. and took up a land grant in Maryland in about 1764. Accompanying him were his two older sons, William and Robert, and two ladies, one of whom, Miss Mary Valens, an heiress from Liverpool, would help fund

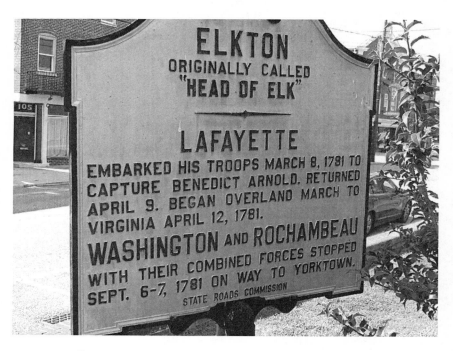

Elkton, Maryland plaque (courtesy Charles C. Ripley III).

the revolution, consequent to being wooed and wed by the widowed General Horatio Gates, whom she met in Booth's house's parlor. According to the WPA Guide to Maryland, "The fortunes of nearly half a million dollars that she brought to the general was generously spent in aiding his indigent comrades in arms."

Booth, an ordained Oxford graduate, had a wife who stayed behind in England. They did not get along. He wrote and asked a friend in Liverpool (April 25, 1783) to go to a village to visit his youngest son, "whom his mother has always detained from me. This part of her conduct was one principal reason for my leaving the Kingdom." He also asked the friend whether Mrs. Booth, a wealthy woman, was going to provide for the son, and "how far that unhappy and ill contrived woman his mother may have prejudiced him against his father."

The school had the luster of an aristocratic education—Latin, fencing and dancing were in the curriculum—that Arnold was aware of even if he cautioned against too many refinements for his son. Booth's students included Robert Morris, the financier of the revolution, Robert Shippen, mayor of Philadelphia, General Charles Lee, George Washington's brothers Samuel and Charles, Henry "Lighthorse Harry" Lee, Dr. James Craik, surgeon to Washington, and Washington's nephew Bushrod Washington.

Later neighbors threatened to burn the school as a suspected indoctrination center for Tories. The Reverend Booth moved his school to a different location, in Washington County, calling it Delamere after his family seat in England.

4

Peggy's Nerves[1]

Was Arnold's young wife, Peggy Shippen Arnold, complicit at any time in her husband's treason? Opinions differ, even today. In a 2018 biography, *The Tragedy of Benedict Arnold*, author Joyce Malcolm writes:

> In his desperate gamble [Arnold] was not likely to take his beloved wife into his confidence. It was far too dangerous for her. He certainly would not ask her advice, priding himself on making his own decisions.[2]

Yet, on May 29, 2018, four weeks following publication of Malcolm's Arnold biography, another Arnold biography, *Turncoat* by Stephen Brumwell, appeared, stating, of Peggy, that "It is now clear that she not only knew of his designs but was involved in the conspiracy from its inception. Her participation was first uncovered in 1941, when Carl Van Doren published papers from the headquarters of Sir Henry Clinton including [British spymaster John] André's careful record of his interview with [Arnold's messenger Joseph] Stansbury."[3]

So Brumwell accepts— while Malcolm rejects—Peggy's guilt, in these latest two biographies of Arnold, published during the same month of 2018. Malcolm anticipates, but rebuts, Brumwell's conclusion that Peggy conspired in her husband's treason:

Margaret Shippen Arnold; pencil drawing circa 1778, by Major John André (courtesy Yale University Art Gallery).

40

Carl Van Doren and others have assumed Margaret Arnold was a party to the conspiracy from the start.... Van Doren writes his conclusion that "André's plans for a correspondence with Peggy Arnold make it impossible to doubt that she was perfectly aware of the Conspiracy from the beginning." ... On this and other highly speculative evidence of Margaret Shippen's involvement in the plot, and contrary to all evidence of contemporaries and her own behavior,

Ticket to the Meschianza. The May 18, 1778, festivities' impresario was Major Andre. The crest on the original invitation was that of the departing British general Sir William Howe (courtesy The Library Company of Philadelphia).

Van Doren's book made its reputation. His conclusions have been accepted uncritically by all later authors.[4]

Mark Jacob and Stephen Case, coauthors of a 2012 biography of Peggy Shippen Arnold, for example, do accept Van Doren's contested conclusion of her complicity—hence their book's title, *Treacherous Beauty: Peggy Shippen, the Woman behind Benedict Arnold's Plot to Betray America.*[5] Jacob and Case, the only modern biographers of Peggy Shippen Arnold, are convinced she conspired in her husband's treason: "We hope the reader will not consider it a repudiation of the Bill of Rights and the concept of 'innocent until proven guilty' if we issue our own extralegal verdict: Peggy Shippen was guilty."[6] However, as Jacob stated in a recent book talk, the evidence of Peggy's complicity in her husband's plot is both circumstantial and speculative:

> She was probably the most dangerous teenage girl in American history. A century after her death, British papers in General Clinton's archives are finally studied by American scholars [initially, by Carl Van Doren], and they figure out, well, there was all this really important circumstantial evidence that Peggy Shippen Arnold was certainly part of the plot. I mean, there's no smoking gun, but there's tons of circumstantial evidence, enough that I think any reasonable person would agree that she knew all about it.[7]

Mount Pleasant (courtesy Charles C. Ripley III).

The phrases "circumstantial evidence" and "no smoking gun" bring to mind a great (fictional) summation by the British actor Derek Jacobi in the television series *The Jury*:

> The Crown has produced only circumstantial evidence of guilt, evidence from which my learned colleague would have you draw only damning inferences. Well, there's another word for inference, and that's speculation. And there's another word for speculation, and that's guessing. And there's another expression for guessing, and that's "I don't know." I don't know, and they don't know, and none of us will ever know for certain. And "I don't know" isn't good enough in a court of law.[8]

In the case of Peggy Shippen Arnold, even under a standard of guilt by "preponderance of the evidence" (easier to establish than guilt "beyond a reasonable doubt" in a criminal trial), the case against her is best described as "not proven," as shown in this chapter.

"Not proven" is a verdict that currently exists only in Scotland, and even the Scots have been trying to get rid of "the Scottish verdict" for some time now. As a good Wikipedia article notes, the "not proven" verdict is used "when the judge or jury does not have enough evidence to convict but is not sufficiently convinced of the accused person's innocence to bring in a 'not guilty' verdict [and today] approximately one third of all acquittal verdicts by Scottish juries use the formulation *Not proven*."[9]

There is a lot we don't know and will never know now about what transpired between the Arnold couple in 1789–90. As historian Sylvia Prince writes, "historians, when faced with the reality of incomplete sources, have to create their own narratives to explain what happened in the past. And just like a fictional narrative, it has to be persuasive and logical."[10] Yes, it is possible that Arnold chose to involve his wife Peggy in his plot to commit treason. But as physicist Richard Feynman once pointed out, in a different context, "the problem is not to determine whether it [was] possible or not, but whether it [was] going on or not."[11] He was talking about flying saucers, and reached a negative conclusion, reasoning as follows:

> …from my knowledge of the world that I see around me, I think that it is much more likely that the reports of flying saucers are the results of the known irrational characteristics of terrestrial intelligence rather than of the unknown rational efforts of extra-terrestrial intelligence.[12]

In the case of Benedict Arnold, the 2018 biography by Joyce Malcolm cited above seems to be the first time in the past 100 years that the "Peggy-noncomplicit" hypothesis has been advanced in opposition to the "Peggy-complicit" hypothesis endorsed by every other modern historian. Why has it been so hard for those writing about Arnold to accept that, in

Malcolm's words, he "was not likely to take his beloved wife into his confidence. It was far too dangerous for her"?

Several answers suggest themselves to this question. First, as two articles appearing in the 1990s point out, while "writings have become more sympathetic to [Benedict Arnold] with each decade,"[13] he remains to some extent subject to the rule that "construction of villainous reputations depends upon society's ability to negate positive actions and characteristics and to see *only* those deeds and qualities that confirm the malefactor's transformed identity" (emphasis added).[14] In other words, we like our villains to be complete. It is, therefore, hard, even more than two centuries later, to entertain the idea that Benedict Arnold would have wished to protect his wife by insulating her from guilty knowledge of his treason.

Second, there seems to be a confluence of narrative forces, one from a sexist perspective and the other from a feminist perspective, both favoring the Peggy-complicit version as "too good not to be true."

The older, sexist, "cherchez la femme" approach to Peggy Shippen's story is illustrated in the final sentence of a lengthy 1932 *New York Times*

George Washington's council of war attended by Arnold transpired in Mabie's Tavern in Tappan, New York on September 6, 1780. Major André was detained here before his trial and as he awaited execution. Built in 1754, the Dutch-style building is now a restaurant, The Old '76 House (courtesy Charles C. Ripley III).

article titled "The Fatal Web Spun by Peggy Shippen": "Perhaps, with the whole truth now available, Arnold will in future be treated differently by historians. Traitor he was; but he was also betrayed, and by means of an influence to which many of the great of the earth have been susceptible—the lure of a beautiful woman."[15]

The 2018 film *Vice* portraying the marriage of Vice-President Dick Cheney and his wife Lynne provides a modern example of the misogynistic tendency toward pinning guilt on the female: the writer and director Adam McKay "subscribes to a Macbeth-like conception of political morality. Behind every bad man, there is a woman who is even worse."[16]

The feminist approach to Peggy's story is summed up in the title of a 2008 book, *Well-Behaved Women Seldom Make History*, written by Harvard professor Laurel Thatcher Ulrich.[17] Following up on this theme, historian Charlene Boyer Lewis, director of the American Studies program at Kalamazoo, has stated that "too many [women] behaved well and they're kind of boring to write about. ... I'm far more interested in the women who don't behave well."[18]

An author who stretches to make Peggy more of an interesting, villainous character than she probably actually was is Allison Pataki in her 2014 novel, *The Traitor's Wife, the Woman Behind Benedict Arnold and the Plan to Betray America*.[19] Her comparison of Peggy Shippen Arnold to Lady Macbeth begins with the novel's epigraph, which quotes Shakespeare:

> *To beguile the time, look like the time;*
> *Bear welcome in your eye, your hand, your tongue:*
> *Look like the innocent flower,*
> *But be the serpent under it.*

True, Pataki is writing historical fiction, and very popular historical fiction at that (over 1,000 reviews on Amazon), but she makes clear in "A Conversation with Allison Pataki" in the paperback edition that she truly believes in Peggy's guilt:

> Lady Macbeth is literature's consummate double-dealer. ... [T]he Arnolds' story is so salacious, you really cannot make this stuff up! And it's true. One difference, however, is that Lady Macbeth gets her comeuppance in the end, whereas Peggy Shippen Arnold makes it out unscathed.[20]

Pataki's belief in Peggy's guilt rests on an Exhibit A that is clearly "fake news," to use a modern expression; she says, "The New York Public Library has letters exchanged between Arnold and [British spymaster John] André on which you can see Peggy's handwriting."[21] But no historian of Benedict Arnold or Peggy Shippen Arnold has made any such claim of a treason letter in Peggy's handwriting.

Pataki's claim that such a document exists is traceable to a Wikipedia article on Peggy Shippen which includes an image of a letter captioned, "Peggy Shippen Arnold's handwriting is interspersed with coded writing in Benedict Arnold's hand; [his] writing would have been in invisible ink."[22] This image, alleged by Pataki to prove Peggy's guilt, bears a stamp, "New York Public Library Prints Division."

A quick visit to the room in the New York Public Library housing the Wallach Division of the library's Print Collection reveals that the Library has nothing other than a photocopy of an original letter from British General Sir Henry Clinton's papers, an archive which includes the originals of Arnold's spy letters. The Clinton papers are located at the Clements Library at the University of Michigan, having been acquired in the 1920s from a great-great-granddaughter of Sir Henry Clinton. The letter reproduced in the Wikipedia article on Peggy Shippen is dated July 12, 1780, and can be viewed online, on the "Spy Letters of the American Revolution" website maintained by the Clements Library.[23] This letter was written in code by Benedict Arnold in Philadelphia and delivered to John André in New York. But there's no invisible ink, and there's no handwriting of Peggy Shippen—those claims by the author of the Wikipedia article are simply wrong. (The Clements Library site reproduces both the coded version of the July 12, 1780, letter, in Benedict Arnold's handwriting, and also its text as decoded in New York, in the handwriting of Jonathan Odell, who was the New York–based Loyalist working for Arnold's British contact John André.)

Another 2013 book about Peggy Shippen Arnold makes a similar leap of illogic to support a conclusion of her guilt. Nancy Rubin Stuart, author of *Defiant Brides*, a dual biography of Peggy and Lucy Knox (wife of the American general Henry Knox).[24] Stuart like all other modern biographers assumes Peggy's guilt. But once again, the evidence offered is slim. For example, Benedict Arnold's first spy letter to André is written in code and dated May 20, 1779, shortly after the 39-year-old Arnold married the 19-year-old Peggy; this letter gives André information on Washington's troop deployments and on the weakness of Charleston's patriot defenses, and goes on to demand financial rewards. Arnold closes this letter with the sentence: "Madame Ar[nold] presents you with her particular compliments." Nancy Rubin Stuart interprets this statement by Benedict Arnold as proving "Peggy's acceptance, if not direct complicity, in [his] deal to serve as a spy."[25] But this interpretation seems like quite a stretch.

A more credible and nuanced interpretation of Arnold's concluding sentence in his first spy letter, "Madame Ar[nold] presents you with her particular compliments," is offered in the latest biography of Benedict Arnold by Stephen Brumwell: "This could be interpreted as a polite pleasantry [given that André had been Peggy's acquaintance and friend during the British occupation of Philadelphia]—or as a sign that Peggy was happy to play her part in the evolving conspiracy."[26]

A few pages later in this biography, Brumwell mentions another document sent by Benedict Arnold to André in July 1779, a shopping list of fabrics and other items "for Mrs. Moore" [the code name for Peggy which André had suggested earlier]. But this shopping list is in Benedict's handwriting, not Peggy's, and Brumwell in 2018 can make no more of it than did Carl Van Doren in 1941 when the latter wrote:

> Efforts have been made, with agile ingenuity, to prove that this matter-of-fact list [handwritten by Benedict Arnold] conveyed some secret message to André. It can hardly have signified more than that she thought herself on the same friendly terms with André as ever … and possibly that André was not to think of the negotiations as ended yet.[27]

Van Doren goes on to note that the items on the shopping list were eventually made up by André to be sent from New York off to Peggy in Philadelphia.

So, we begin to see a list of communications which are open to an interpretation that Peggy played a role that was entirely unwitting and involuntary on her part, consistent with the theory that Benedict Arnold actually wished to insulate her from any participation in his plot, out of a desire to protect her person and her reputation. However, as noted above, historians even to this day lean toward interpreting the above communications—and others described briefly below—as inculpatory of Peggy, on the basis that Arnold does not deserve any credit for protecting her from his dealings with the British. This "complete villain" theory may be firmly rooted in human psychology, as two psychologists have indeed written with respect to Benedict Arnold:

> [T]he commemorative process for malefactors is not identical to that for heroic figures. … While the faults of heroes can be explained away as proof of their "humanity," virtuous elements in the biographies of villains cannot be so neatly explained. Such actors must be made totally evil, and all hints of virtue must be excised.[28]

Still, there is one other factor worth discussing here to explain how two biographies of Benedict Arnold, published only weeks apart in 2018, can take diametrically opposing positions on the question of Peggy's guilty participation in her husband's conspiracy.

Stephen Brumwell's Arnold biography published on May 29, 2018, discusses—whereas Joyce Lee Malcolm's biography published on May 1 does not mention at all—the following later-published and apparently most damning evidence of Peggy's guilt. Brumwell picks up the story two days after Arnold's plot to surrender West Point to the British had been discovered, the start of the most tumultuous month in Peggy Shippen's life:

> With Washington's approval, Mrs. Arnold left [West Point] for Philadelphia escorted by Major Franks. On the second night, they stopped at Paramus, New Jersey, as the guests of Mrs. Theodosia Prevost. ... By 1780, Mrs. Prevost was conducting an affair with Aaron Burr; they married two years later, after her husband had died of wounds. ... She told Burr a remarkable story concerning Peggy Arnold's brief stay with her. When Peggy arrived at Paramus, the "frantic scenes" of her recent hysteria resumed, "and continued as long as strangers were present." But once they were alone, Mrs. Arnold became "tranquilized" and assured her hostess that "she was heartily sick of the theatrics she was exhibiting."[29]

It should be noted at this point that Alexander Hamilton, George Washington, and the Marquis de Lafayette had all witnessed Peggy's "theatrics" at West Point two days previously. Hamilton described Peggy's "mad scene" in a letter to his friend John Laurens:

> Arnold, a moment before his setting out, went into Mrs. Arnold's apartment and informed her that some transactions had just come to light which must for ever banish him from his country. She fell into a swoon, at this declaration; and he left her in it to consult his own safety. ... She remained frantic all day, accusing every one who approached her with an intention to murder her child (an infant in her arms) and exhibiting every other mark of the most genuine and agonising distress. ... We [meaning Hamilton, Washington and Lafayette] have every reason to believe that she was entirely unacquainted with the plan, and that the first knowledge of it was when Arnold went to tell her he must banish himself from his country and from her forever.[30]

Before continuing with the story of the conversation between Peggy Arnold and Theodosia Prevost in Paramus two days later, let's consider what Benedict Arnold might have told Peggy in their private conversation just before he made his hurried getaway to the British ship the *Vulture* waiting for him downriver from West Point. No one knows for sure, but the television series *Turn* (based on Alexander Rose's book *Washington's Spies*) may have come pretty close to the truth. (These lines are edited on the assumption that Turn, which takes many liberties with known historic facts, is incorrect in assuming that Peggy had prior knowledge of her husband's dealings with André.)

PEGGY: What's the matter??
ARNOLD: I must flee now....
PEGGY: You? [perhaps dawning on her now for the first time what's going on and why her husband must flee, as she sees the panicked look in his eyes]
ARNOLD: Washington will never harm a woman, especially not an innocent

one and you are going to play the innocent better than anyone ever has. We'll be together again soon, I promise.[31]

And she does play the role of the innocent convincingly enough to persuade Hamilton, Washington and Lafayette, nobody's fools, of what very well may have been the truth, namely, in Hamilton's words again, that: "She was entirely unacquainted with the plan, and that the first knowledge of it was when Arnold went to tell her he must banish himself from his country and from her forever."

But now comes the rest of Peggy's supposed confession to Theodosia Prevost, as she related it to her husband-to-be Aaron Burr, and as Aaron Burr later related it to his literary executor Matthew Davis, who published the account only after Burr's death, in Davis's 1836 *Memoirs of Aaron Burr*.

According to Matthew Davis's account, after referring to her own feigned "theatrics," Peggy went on to tell Theodosia Prevost that "she had corresponded with the British commander, that she was disgusted with the American cause and those who had the management of public affairs; and that, through great persuasion and unceasing perseverance, she had ultimately brought the general into an arrangement to surrender West Point to the British."[32]

If Peggy's statements to Theodosia Prevost have been correctly reported—by Theodosia to Burr, then by Burr to Davis, and by Davis to us—then the case for Peggy's complicity with Benedict Arnold is iron-clad, of course. But while Peggy's confiding to Theodosia that her hysterics were feigned—so as to convince Washington and the others of her innocence—seems credible, Peggy's going on to confide that she was guilty of full-blown treason, a hanging offense, seems unlikely. It is hard to see what motive either Davis or Burr might have had for getting the story wrong as it has been passed down to us. The idea put forth in 1901, by a collateral descendant of Peggy's, that Burr might have concocted the whole Paramus confession story to get revenge on Peggy for refusing Burr's advances to her appears to be made up out of whole cloth.[33]

A better candidate for getting Peggy's story wrong is Theodosia Prevost herself. Peggy could very well have been somewhat incoherent in her still-panicked state, telling Theodosia of her concern that certain prior events might appear in a bad light on Peggy's return to Philadelphia, whereas Theodosia's perception of Peggy's narration may well have been colored by her relation with Burr, such that Theodosia interpreted Peggy's recital as an admission that these suspicious appearances did not allow for any innocent explanation.

Let us consider the position of the two women at this point in their lives. Theodosia and Burr, if not lovers in the fall of 1780, were extremely close, with Burr paying frequent visits to her home, The Hermitage (which can still be visited today as an historic site). For example, Burr wrote his sister Sally in the summer of 1780 of Theodosia sitting at his elbow, "at this moment pinching my ear, because I will not say anything about her to you."

But Theodosia was a married woman in 1780, with five children, and she was ten years older than Burr, who at age 25, had no career as yet, still studying law after retiring from a distinguished military career in Washington's army. Across from Theodosia was a young woman, a damsel in distress if there ever was one, later called by King George III "the most beautiful woman he had ever seen," and four years younger than Burr. Peggy was not single, of course, but Burr was known to have an eye for the ladies, and Peggy, given the choice by Washington of either reuniting with her husband in New York or returning to her family in Philadelphia, had chosen Philadelphia.

Peggy may very well have expressed to Theodosia her concern that a 1779 so-called "millinery" letter from André to Peggy would be discovered—as indeed it was during a search of the Arnold household in Philadelphia on the same day the two ladies were talking in Paramus. Now that André's role in the plot was known as was that he was soon to be hanged by Washington, Peggy might have expressed to Theodosia her concern that this letter could cast suspicion on her, as indeed it did, leading to her expulsion from Philadelphia only a month after her return.

Could Theodosia—perhaps colored by a perception of Peggy as a romantic rival—have misinterpreted Peggy's reference to this letter, and misreported to Burr that Peggy "had corresponded with the British commander"? (The British commander in New York was of course not André, but rather his immediate superior General Clinton.) And could Peggy also have expressed to Theodosia her concern about the possible perception, and not the reality, that "she had ultimately brought the general into an arrangement to surrender West Point to the British"?

There were indeed some grounds for such a perception. For example, as related in the biography of Peggy, *Treacherous Beauty*, Peggy believed in the summer of 1780 that her husband would be assigned by Washington to command West Point, rather than to a new battlefield command, But then, at a dinner in Philadelphia, a guest congratulated Peggy on her husband's appointment by Washington to command the left wing of the army on the battlefield. As authors Stephen Case and Mark Jacob go on to describe this scene,

> That was the first Peggy had heard of it. She reacted with what were described as "hysteric fits," and refused to be consoled. Some of the other diners may have viewed Peggy's behavior as an understandable reaction by a wife worried about her husband's safety in battle.

> Of course, it is impossible to know the meaning of Peggy's outburst at
> the Morrises' dinner or at other times in her life. Were they manipulative
> attempts to get her way? Or were they sincere and uncontrollable expressions
> of emotion?[34]

Well, exactly! Every known action of Peggy's is susceptible to an interpretation that she was innocent of her husband's plot up until the day of his flight from West Point in the autumn of 1780.

And what do Case and Jacob have to say about the "millinery" letter André wrote to Peggy in 1789, offering to be of service to her in procuring and sending her from New York items which she could not find in Philadelphia, such as "capwire, needles, gauze, etc."? They note that Peggy took two months to reply, and then only with a brief "thanks but no thanks" note.[35] If either Peggy or Arnold himself had viewed André's "millinery" letter as sent to further Arnold's treasonous plot, or susceptible to being so read by any third person, the letter would have clearly been destroyed upon reading, which it was not.

So what this all seems to add up to is a verdict for Peggy of "not proven," which was the verdict stated by the jury in the treason trial against Aaron Burr in 1807, despite the presiding judge, Supreme Court Chief Justice John Marshall, having asked the jury to render a simple verdict of "guilty" or "not guilty."[36] (Marshall also mentioned in his instruction to the jury the rule that "in treason, all are principals," meaning that mere accessories before or after the fact would not be subject to any lesser punishment than hanging.[37])

The United States Supreme Court Historical Society, in March of 2006, conducted a mock reenactment of Aaron Burr's treason trial in the U.S. Supreme Court, before the late Justice Antonin Scalia, who rendered the clean "not guilty" verdict that Burr had sought 199 years earlier.[38] The reenactment of Burr's treason trial was conducted with the approval of the Aaron Burr Association, several of whose members were in attendance. There is, however, no corresponding Peggy Shippen Arnold Association to defend her reputation by seeking a similar contemporary adjudication of her own case.

Movie deals have been rumored for both the Case and Jacob book *Treacherous Beauty* and for Allison Pataki's novel *The Traitor's Wife*, so that—in addition to the television series *Turn*—we may eventually be presented with a large screen film or two assigning a verdict of "guilty" to poor Peggy Shippen Arnold.[39]

Treacherous Beauty co-author Stephen Case is an attorney who spent many years doing exhaustive research on the case of Peggy Shippen. One wonders whether he truly believes that she was, as he states in his book's preface, deserving of his own current "extralegal verdict: Peggy Shippen was guilty ... and she was fascinating, too."[40]

On the other hand, as a lawyer, Case may have come across the book *Legal Fictions*, by the Harvard Law School professor Lon Fuller. Fuller opens his book by stating that "Probably no lawyer would deny that judges and writers on legal topics frequently make statements they know to be false. These statements are called 'fic-

Old postcard of Dickerson's Tavern site. Arnold was tried in Morristown, New Jersey, December 26, 1780. The tavern was also known as Norris Tavern since Captain Peter Dickerson leased it to a man named Robert Norris during the war (courtesy Charles C. Ripley III).

tions.'" Fuller goes on to ask, "Are there good and bad fictions? If so, how are we to tell the one from the other?"[41]

Could it be that attorney Stephen Case, in rendering his "guilty" verdict, has done Peggy, and womankind in general, a useful service in promoting a benign legal fiction, one of female empowerment and agency extending back into history?

To take a more recent example from popular culture, the film *The Man Who Shot Liberty Valance* concludes with Jimmy Stewart—playing a lawyer out West whose lengthy political career began after he supposedly killed outlaw Liberty Valance—finally revealing to the local newspaperman that it was actually the John Wayne character who killed the Lee Marvin outlaw character. Whereupon the reporter tears up the notes he's been taking, Stewart remarks, "You're not going to print the story?" and the reporter answers: "No, sir, this is the West, and when the legend becomes fact, we print the legend."[42]

Let us leave it there, thinking that Stephen Case may have justly made up his mind to "print the legend" of Peggy as an active co-conspirator with her husband, thus going with the flow of Peggy Arnold historiography—and so doing in a good way, not in the pejorative sense of "even a dead fish can go with the flow," nor in the sexist "cherchez la femme" sense of whatever the problem, there is a woman to blame.

5

Maneuvers in the James River Valley and New London, Connecticut

According to Willard Sterne Randall, General Clinton sent Arnold to Richmond after four and a half years of war, supposing that this foray would persuade local people to come to the British side and give the British army an edge in the South. Arnold, as will be seen, shared that hope. But, of course, Virginia had an active militia and the charisma of Founding Fathers including its first and second governors, Patrick Henry and Thomas Jefferson, and George Washington himself.

Although Thomas Jefferson experimented with animal husbandry and with various crops, for the first 25 years at Monticello, until 1780, like other Virginian gentry, he grew tobacco as his cash crop. Tobacco had brought European settlers to the Chesapeake region, and the colonies of Virginia and Maryland were founded around the cultivation of tobacco. It could be successfully grown on a small farm, but eventually the farms were displaced by plantations, where enslaved people replaced the indentured type of servitude. In the mid–1600s, the Caribbean islands switched from tobacco to the more profitable sugar as their staple commodity. This left the Chesapeake as the world's leading tobacco-producing area. During the conflict with Britain more flour was grown and less tobacco, but the output was still upwards of 15 million pounds per year, sent directly to Britain.[1] As the war continued in the Southern theater, British decided to lay waste to Virginia's economy, while additionally taking their military stores and horses.

In May 1779, Admiral George Collier had destroyed the Patriot naval yard at Portsmouth, Virginia, and had established the remainder of Fort Nelson, a timber and earth fortification, at the harbor as a base. In the fall of 1780, Lord Cornwallis was advancing from South Carolina to North Carolina. Part of his army was defeated by frontiersmen while the "Swamp

Fox," Francis Marion, led attacks on Loyalists. Under orders from Sir Henry Clinton, General Alexander Leslie arrived the following fall with 2200 men to destroy the magazines at Newport News and Hampton. In December, Sir Henry Clinton ordered Brigadier General Arnold to sail from New York to Portsmouth, Virginia, with mostly Loyalist troops. His instructions were to improve a base at Portsmouth for defensive operations (revamping the timber and earth Fort Nelson), strike at rebel supplies without carrying out risky raids, and in all stratagems get the accord of the two colonels who accompanied him, John Simcoe and Thomas Dundas. Not taking Arnold's advice to establish a base away from the coast, Lord Cornwallis arrived May 20, 1781, and took command at Portsmouth. In the summer, Arnold was stricken with gout and returned to New York and Cornwallis evacuated. Then, on October 19, 1781, Cornwallis's army was boxed in by American and French forces and surrendered in the decisive Battle of Yorktown.

Now we focus on Arnold's personal involvement in the invasion of Richmond—how he was judged, how his performance was received by Cornwallis, and how he returned a success yet disappointed.

Arnold left from Sandy Hook, New Jersey, across the bay from New York City, in a fleet of approximately 30 vessels. Six days out the fleet was beset by gale winds and rough seas that persisted throughout their journey. Several vessels went off course and others anchored off Newport News, awaiting the other warships. Meanwhile Arnold, waiting for no man to start his mission, with other ships of war and transport ships made his way up the James River. To lighten loads, many cannons were heaved, and horses pushed into the sea. A ship of Hessians went adrift and until they opened their orders they did not know where they were bound. Yet as Arnold sailed into Portsmouth, he had high expectations that the arrival of British forces would inspire the people of Virginia, and that thousands would return to the fold. It was his personal quest.

Of the 2500 men who had left New Jersey, due to one ship's being separated, the raiding party was reduced to 1600. They were mostly veteran troops of American Loyalists. A hundred or more were from a small regiment Arnold himself had raised, of deserters from the rebel forces and Tories. There were Hussar Jaegar, trained for scouting and skirmishes, Scottish artillery men, and infantry from Colonel Simcoe's Queen's American Rangers.[2] The largest group of 600 belonged to the Loyal Americans. This regiment was made up of tenants of the exceedingly wealthy New York landowner Beverley Robinson, commanded on this expedition by his son Lieutenant Colonel Beverley Robinson. On December 31, 1780, right after the difficult voyage, Arnold seized boats loaded with tobacco and pressed on to the mouth of the James River. On New Year's Eve day some

Historic site plaque (courtesy Charles C. Ripley III).

of the British force commenced a march inland through the woods, taking people into custody so as to keep the invasion secret. Meanwhile the General sailed up the river towards their destination, the little capital of Virginia, Richmond.

Meanwhile, on the Patriot side, General Nathanael Green had dispatched Baron von Steuben to stay in Virginia and send supplies and Continental Army troops south. Also, from November 1780 on for a year, Steuben commanded a garrison regiment of 900 troops, under General Muhlenberg, and the ill-equipped but willing state militia solders of Virginia, this by order of Governor Thomas Jefferson. Peter Muhlenberg was a Lutheran minister in Pennsylvania who married a Virginian and went to England where he was ordained an Anglican minister, as this was Virginia's state religion. He had decided that there was a time for peace and a time for war (Ecclesiastes 3:8).

Arnold took a brig and communicated to the local people that they should allow him his prize, or he would land and destroy their village. This was a sustained tactic, state historians Mark Lender and James Kirby Martin, while Arnold led the expedition. He aimed for the local people to know his intention was not to provoke unnecessary violence: "He wanted to avoid pointlessly making enemies or to initiate needless fighting. Such a restrained posture would mark his behavior throughout his independent command in Virginia."[3]

On New Year's Eve, Jefferson received a note from Jacob Wray, a member of the Committee of Safety for Hampton and Elizabeth City County,

Boulder meeting place of André and Arnold, Haverstraw, New York (courtesy Charles C. Ripley III).

that an armada had arrived. There was some confusion over whether that consisted of French ships come to aid the Americans or of ships of the British enemy. Only two days later, as January 4 dawned, a messenger would awaken the Jeffersons in Richmond to tell the governor that Benedict Arnold, the newly commissioned British brigadier, and his raiding party, had overtaken the militia at Hood's Point and anchored nearby. Jefferson called out the militia from various counties and sent his wife and daughters 14 miles up the river to Tuckahoe.

There were skirmishes before on January 4 the fleet of small river boats disembarked troops on the north shore of the James River at Westover Plantation. Instead of pushing on to the capital when the fleet departed, the troops encamped at Four Mile Creek, 12 miles away.

For a half-day on his way to Richmond and for several days on his return trip to the coast (from January 9), Arnold thus enjoyed the sanctuary of the red brick mansion of his wife's first cousin, Mary Willing Byrd. One of Mary Byrd's godfathers was Benjamin Franklin. She married William Byrd III in 1761 when, like George Washington, William was serving in the French and Indian War. From gambling he had run his fortune into debt and, in 1777, had committed suicide. Mary, a woman of fortitude, cleverness and sociability, was left to manage the estate that remained her property. Writes Michael Kranish,

> According to family lore, Arnold galloped up the riverfront lawn on his horse and urged his steed up the steps and into the hallway, where he pulled out his sword and slashed two large gashes in the mahogany banister. The story left subsequent owners of Westover to wonder whether Arnold slashed the banister to scare Mary Willing Byrd into submission or to provide her with a cover story—"evidence" to try to convince authorities that he took the house by force.[4]

Westover was a plantation of 1200 acres about 30 miles from Richmond. It had 40 outbuildings. With hundreds of soldiers milling about it must have looked like a garrison.

Arnold was received politely, despite the clear inconvenience to Mary Byrd of having hundreds of soldiers trampling the wheat, knocking down fences, butchering milk cows and using her plant nursery as a stable. According to Sara B. Bearss' article in the Encyclopedia Virginia, the widow Byrd "received Arnold tactfully and at one point offered one of her younger sons to the distrustful British as a hostage for her good behavior."[5] She is reported to have served the general a good breakfast. Then, despite heavy rains, he began a march to Richard in late afternoon.

One of America's most elegant houses, the Byrd estate must have seemed like an illusion to the soldiers who disembarked from the transport vessels directly offshore from Westover. Jefferson himself admired especially the library of 3,500 volumes that had belonged to William Byrd II, sold off by the son. A friend of Thomas Jefferson, Mary Byrd had no choice, naturally, but to extend a welcome to Arnold. In addition, she saw to it that Arnold had reliable guides for the 25 miles remaining to Richmond. But Benedict did not linger. He set off the same day he arrived with his men in a heavy rainstorm and arrived at the plain outside Richmond the next morning.

Jefferson's family was in safety while he remained in the largely undefended state capital. Apparently, Arnold hesitated to lead an assault on Richmond but Colonel Simcoe, his second in command, urged a rapid strike. The advantage was surprise, as the Americans would expect the troops to remain at Westover for several days and recover before launching an attack. The Hessians led Arnold's army, followed by Colonel Simcoe and the Queen's Rangers, sharpshooters and finally rangers on horseback. Michael Hamish notes that the militia who pulled planks out of a bridge at Four Mile Creek (a dozen miles from Richmond) made a mistake in assuming the Queen's Rangers were brother militia men, as they were clothed in green jackets rather than the red coats that usually identified British soldiers.[6]

While Steuben waited on the south side of the James River, Arnold approached Richmond from the north. Arnold's troops rebuilt a bridge that the Americans had destroyed and reached Richmond at one in the afternoon. Arnold and his soldiers had two encounters, one with the party that had disabled the bridge and another with an American patrol. When they arrived in Richmond, midday January 5, they found only 200 Virginia militiamen, many not armed. Colonel Simcoe sent dismounted soldiers up Church Hill, scattering the militia into the woods. The troops looked for the governor, but Jefferson was nowhere to be found. He had left a few hours before Arnold arrived, as had most of the other Virginia legislators.

According to Lender and Martin, Arnold's troops avoided the plunder of private goods and did not touch valuable stores of tobacco or vessels which might have belonged to Loyalists. Rather, they burned public buildings and warehouses with quartermaster's stores.

An account prepared for Virginia's bicentennial gives a sensible evaluation of the British invasion of Richmond:

> Arnold and Simcoe spent the evening at Galt's Tavern, later known as the "Old City Tavern," a two story frame structure on the corner of Nineteenth and Main. Many of the Rangers and Germans, too exhausted to sleep, went out on the town. Since these troops were "special forces," they were given more lee-way from the usual British discipline. Arnold and Simcoe knew the success of their mission depended on the high-spirits of their troops, and neither officer dampened morale.[7]

The author of the bicentennial booklet, Professor Harry M. Ward of the University of Richmond, also explicates the matter of looting:

> Even though the British rummaged through the vacated dwellings, there was no large-scale pilferage of property. The British soldier had scant opportunity to conceal any plunder, which was strictly forbidden by both the British and American armies. Yet it seems there was some looting by "straggling parties" of the British as they marched from Richmond to Westover the following day. Arnold himself left the tobacco untouched.... Whatever the reason, leaving the tobacco untouched was not an oversight.[8]

Arnold wrote a letter at the City Tavern on Main Street which made its way to Jefferson at his hideaway. It advised the people of Richmond to surrender certain supplies, the typical war prize goods—"Tobacco, Rum, Wine, Sugar, Molasses, Sail Cloth and Coffee." If they complied (they would have to supply a few hostages as well), instead of just confiscating goods, Arnold offered half-market value for them, "one half of the current price at Richmond."[9] He was thinking as a merchant in a businesslike if somehow also unrealistic way.

The merchants of Richmond applied to the governor, and on January 6 Arnold received Jefferson's reply flatly rejecting the proposed terms.

Whatever the full panoply of Jefferson's motives, as a patrician he would not deal with the "parricide Arnold." The die was cast. At this point Colonel Simcoe led the destruction of public buildings, and after sufficient rum it is possible the soldiers looted. Sources concur that Americans did the greater part of any looting after the British troops withdrew. Writes one historian, "There were reports that some hogs drank the rum that was dumped in the street and got drunk."[10]

The same day, Colonel Simcoe's troops left Richmond for the Westham Cannon Foundry about seven miles away. Again, instructions were to destroy only war-related targets. They dumped barrels of gunpowder into a stream, and destroyed guns, and stocks of oats. Before they got there, Jefferson oversaw an operation to try to remove official papers, and fill wagons with arms and gunpowder that went to a court and church far from Richmond. Jefferson himself rode to Tuckahoe, rested, and shortly after dawn took his family to a more remote location, Fine Creek, on January 7.

Twenty-four hours after Arnold and his men came to Richmond, they were on their way back down toward Westover—a two-day journey in torrential rain. Simcoe fought with militia at Charles City Court House. The British troops encamped at Westover January 7 through 10. Captain Johann Ewald, a Hessian from Denmark, wrote in his diary that Arnold came away with abundant stolen goods that ended up packed into 42 vessels. "Terrible things happened on this excursion: churches and holy places were plundered."[11] Michael McMillen Decker writes, "Arnold left behind a town covered by a great cloud of smoke, with provisions and liquor strewn about the streets.... Only the desire of General Arnold not to overextend himself and his overriding intention to return to Portsmouth before he could be captured saved Virginia from depredations."[12]

In his history of Chesterfield County, Francis Earle Lutz includes an intriguing incident that occurred soon after Arnold withdrew from Richmond:

> Governor Jefferson was infuriated to learn that Arnold had left 20 guineas with James Buchanan a Richmond merchant, "for the relief of the poor" and he sent a letter to Steuben at Chesterfield Courthouse directing him to order Buchanan to return the money to the donor. Records show that Buchanan was a leader in Masonic circles and as Arnold was a member of that order it is probable that the donation was left with the Richmond lodge. This cannot be verified because the lodge records for 1781 are missing. However, Jefferson was an enemy of Arnold long before the latter's desertion of the American cause and he was unwilling for the traitor to be credited with an act of generosity.[13]

Arnold led raids into the nearby countryside and attacked the courthouse at Chesterfield. All through the Revolution an advantage of the American rebels was that their warfare was less choreographed. The Virginia militia in the face of large British troops scattered like marbles from a pouch and the Loyalist/British troops had to split up and go after them.

It is recorded that when Arnold returned with his troops to Portsmouth he fortified it with a long brick arc. During this time George Washington instructed the French fleet under their admiral the Comte de Rochambeau, and also Lafayette from the land, to hem Arnold in and capture him, but the French fleet did not give Lafayette the required naval support and Arnold was safe. Invitations Arnold sent out as the commanding officer evidence he had a social life. This one was found behind a drawer in a chest purchased at a Virginia Beach auction in the 1960s:

> Brigadier General Arnold presents his compliments to Col. Edward Moseley, Sr., requests the pleasure of his and Mrs. Moseley's company to dinner and pass the evening on Wednesday next.[14]

During this period of his life Arnold wore several small pistols and slept with a gun. He was eager to leave the interior, where he could be captured quite easily, and to return to fortified Portsmouth. George Washington had put a bounty on his head. He wrote Lafayette that if Arnold "should fall into your hands," Lafayette was to deliver a punishment "in the most summary way."[15]

The British command was congratulatory: Frederick Mackenzie, Clinton's deputy adjutant general, said that Arnold's reputation had eclipsed the other generals.[16] The views of historians differ as to how Arnold performed as the leader of the expedition. Decker faults John Simcoe for the plundering of Richmond while Milton Lomask in an *American Heritage* article states that Arnold not only ordered his soldiers to burn the warehouses but "gave them carte blanche to plunder the city."[17] Lender and Martin, biographers of Arnold, have taken a 180 degree turn in their opinion:

> Portrayed in patriot accounts as a rampaging operation featuring pillage and desecration, Arnold's raid into the Old Dominion in January 1981 was anything but. Arnold actually displayed considerable forbearance. The turncoat hoped to draw Virginians back to the King ... and he issued unambiguous orders against unauthorized plunder and gratuitous harm or insults to noncombatants. He reprimanded his own officers when they threatened civilians, and he was indignant when patriot authorities violated a flag of truce. Arnold's men hit public facilities and war-related economic targets hard but there was no general sacking of Richmond or any other Virginia town.[18]

Ewald spoke of the plundering of holy places and quantities of merchandise as booty. By contrast, Arnold wrote in a jocular manner to Henry Clinton,

As Mr. Jefferson was so inattentive to the preservation of private property, I found myself under the disagreeable necessity of ordering a large quantity of rum to be stove [and] several warehouses of salt to be destroyed.[19]

Regarding shops and private homes that were burned in Richmond, Benedict blamed his soldiers: "Private property was burnt without my order by an officer who was informed it was public property."[20]

That spring, before the British surrender at the Siege of Yorktown, Mary Byrd was accused of treason for hosting Arnold and later Cornwallis at Westover. In August, Thomas Nelson, Jr., Virginia's governor after Jefferson, allowed her to fly a flag of truce and to recover her 49 slaves, three horses and two ferryboats that had left with Arnold's troops. A trial of the widow Byrd was scheduled to take place that spring, but it was postponed and did not eventuate. In fact, she would seek restitution from both the United States and British governments; Cornwallis supported her application.

Captain Ewald disapproved of Arnold's military tactics and clashed with him but obeyed orders, fighting as commander of the jaegers in Richmond, Portsmouth, Norfolk, York, and Gloucester Heights. He commented wryly on how chagrined Arnold was not to be welcomed by the

Westover Plantation (courtesy of Rob and Andrea Erda).

populace. Going from Portsmouth to York and Gloucester, Ewald wrote, "We had hardly arrived when we found a loyal-minded subject, which was regarded as a miracle, although General Arnold had asserted that when he made an appearance the people would change their minds in droves."[21]

Arnold convoked an assembly at Kemp's Landing, now part of Virginia Beach, on February 21. He told the 400 inhabitants who came to take a new oath to George III. There were refreshments and many of the gentry, men and women, complied with Arnold's request. Arnold judged the event a success if it proved ineffectual. Addresses like this to drum up support for the Crown were not unusual, although Arnold's was unique because he used his name to advertise a mass meeting.[22]

Those people who might have rallied to the British side typically questioned whether Arnold would soon disappear as had the other officers who had promised to protect Virginian Loyalists Lender and Martin write,

> Late March saw the abrupt end of Arnold's deliberate outreach to Virginia Loyalists. Loyalist volunteers were not rallying to his standard. Whigs were not recanting. Virginians were not changing their minds "in droves," and the military situation was anything but under control. Arnold would attempt no more mass assemblies of Loyalists and issue no further proclamations to return to the king. His mission of reconciliation was failing, so was his attempt

Westover Plantation (courtesy of Rob and Andrea Erda).

to champion Loyalist resistance to what he had come to believe was a failed revolution. Any exoneration he sought for his treason would not lie in persuading Virginians to abandon their Patriot cause.[23]

After retiring to the base camp from Richmond with prizes and slaves from plantations between Westover and Richmond, Arnold sent a message to the people of Virginia, offering "such Negroes, Horses, & etc. as can be given up consistand with my duty shall be delivered to you if my conditions are agreeable."[24] A letter to General Muhlenberg elaborated that known rebels would not recuperate their slaves, but Arnold would consider requests from "widows, orphans, or persons" with no Whig connections if under oath. Jefferson flared in words that in retrospect appall. He would not bargain for returns of "'property'": the slaves were property and had to be returned—that is, without "political conditions."[25] "[A]pparently there was no time to arrange bargaining and Arnold and his soldiers confiscated the Byrd slaves and sailed to Portsmouth but left the horses and moved south."

Reprisals soon came for the assault on Richmond. Writes Kranish, "As word spread that the invasion was being headed by the despised traitor, the militia was inspired to turn out in large number. The very name Arnold did more to galvanize Virginians than the state's leaders could otherwise have hoped to accomplish." The British were harried by 200 Virginian militia under Jefferson's friend Sampson Matthews. Once in Portsmouth, the British set up defensive fortifications and awaited reinforcements.

When General William Phillips arrived with reinforcements (2000 soldiers), he took command of the British forces and Arnold had subcommand. From April to June, they burned large quantities of tobacco stock, took Williamsburg, and "concentrated on fighting Patriots, not trying to reason with them." Much of the destruction was in Chesterfield County and Manchester, now a part of Richmond. Phillips and Arnold seized Williamsburg for two days, and they marched against Baron von Steuben in late April. In the Battle of Blanford, April 25, where 2500 British regulars fought 1000 militia men, the action of the militia bought time for General Lafayette to arrive to defend Richmond. Arnold and Phillips turned back to their headquarters in Portsmouth, but Phillips fell ill and died on the journey (fraught with militia attacks), and Arnold took command until Cornwallis arrived.

Under Phillips, one unforgettable maneuver occurred on June 4, 1781. This day Colonel Tarleton's cavalry broke into Monticello (drinking Jefferson's French wines but not destroying his house) on the heels of Jefferson's flight by horseback to avoid capture. Jefferson, who had decided not to run for a third one-year term as governor, now followed his family to Poplar Forest, his retreat in the Piedmont region.

In May Arnold left Virginia and returned to New York. He was suffering from gout in his hands and feet, tedium, and disappointment that Lord Germain in London ignored his request for promotion. Arnold's mission had been accomplished but the British were losing ground. Typically for Arnold, there was a quarrel over money on his exit. Thomas Symonds, newly the supreme commander of the British naval force, had made a secret agreement with Arnold over the disposition of captured tobacco and other war prizes. Arnold understood this as a 50/50 division, but Symonds refused to share. As a result of the quarrel, which became public, Symonds pulled out his patrol of the Chesapeake and General Lafayette and his army crossed the bay unchallenged. This was another nail in the coffin of Arnold's reputation as an opportunist who put money before honor. Captain Symonds co-signed the Articles of Capitulation with Lord Cornwallis at Yorktown, October 18, 1781.

It is not clear who ordered the military expedition to destroy the patriot privateering base of New London, Connecticut, which Arnold led on September 6, 1781. This mission was his second and final command as a British brigadier in America. From the British vantage it was a success—the privateer haven was devastated. Arnold's troops of Loyalists, many Continental deserters in his own Loyal American regiment, were in and out in the course of a day, everything to do with privateering operations was in flames, and more than 80 Patriots died to fewer than half as many of Arnold's men.

The raid of the important port town got terribly out of hand when the British stormed Fort Griswold, not realizing that those within had surrendered. The damage to New London and the course of that day have been recounted in many sources, most notably *Homegrown Terror* by Eric D. Lehman. The scholarship that interested me for this book is a single article by Mark Edward Lender and James Kirby Martin, whose research has already been cited regarding the James River expedition. Whereas previous historians interpreted Arnold as having slaughtered his own people in the New London raid, Lender and Martin in "Terror Reconsidered" (the *Journal of Military History*, January 2019) examine the principle of *jus in bello*, or "fighting justly," and demonstrated that Arnold's leadership was within the limits of allowable conduct during war.

That Arnold led forces against a town that was less than 20 miles from where he grew up highlights the fact that the Revolutionary War was effectively a civil war. Since the whole town was involved as a support infrastructure for privateering it was first of all not feasible to separate all military targets from other public ones. Another factor responsible for the trail of ruin was a wind that carried flames in from a burning ship in the harbor. But the great loss of lives resulted from the tragic confusion during the forty minutes of battle at Fort Griswold.

Eight hundred soldiers with Colonel Edmund Eyre assaulted the fort. Arnold saw that taking the fort would only bring carnage and called off the attack. When the British shot through a flag on a pike, the lanyard of the fort's colors, they believed that Colonel William Ledyard had surrendered: he had not. When he did surrender it didn't communicate to all the militia, some of whom kept firing. Two-thirds of the Patriots were killed or wounded and the cost to the British was heavy as well.

According to Lender and Martin, the town was sacked, and damage included 31 mercantile establishments and warehouses, 18 mechanic's shops, 20 barns, and 9 public buildings, all wharves and 10 to a dozen ships, and Arnold himself reported destroying cargos of East and West Indian goods. To what extent did Arnold ignore the theory of "fair play," a rule that he upheld in the Virginia raids? Lender and Martin note that "He never reprimanded any officers when troops under their command engaged in pillage or failed to prevent others from pillaging."

Yet it would have been a lapse of leadership and out of character for General Arnold to shrug off the pillage that occurred. After the Battle of Ticonderoga in May 1775, Arnold and Ethan Allen clashed when Arnold complained about Allen's soldiers plundering and destroying private property, including the British commander's stash of 90 gallons of rum which Allen and his Green Mountain Boys proceeded to drink to the lees.

There is also the paragraph at the end of Arnold's report to General Clinton on the New London raid:

> I am greatly indebted to Captain Stapleton, who acted as Major of Brigade, for his spirited conduct and assistance; in particular, on the attack upon Fort Trumbell, and his endeavors to prevent plundering (when the public stores were burnt) and the destroying of public buildings.[26]

Did *soi-disant* appropriate warfare fall apart in a chaotic situation, was Arnold bathed in shame over attacking people he had grown up near to, or did the course of events tragically escape his control? The story of a brave New London woman suggests that Arnold was a victim of his own actions.

Abigail Dolbeare Hinman was the wife of Captain Elisha Hinman, an officer in the Continental Navy and privateer during the Revolutionary War. His privateering adventures include rises and falls in fortune, time in an English prison and escape to France, where he may still have been in 1781. Their daughter, Ann Hinman Kellogg of Fairfield, Connecticut, lived until her nineties and at her death a story of her mother's hitherto unrecorded heroism appeared in the *New York Times*:

> At that time Capt. Hinman's ship was hourly expected to arrive at New London, and it was hoped that he might come in time to save the town. Mrs. Hinman was well acquainted with Arnold, as he had often dined at her house,

Daniel Huntington, *Portrait of Abigail Dolbeare Hinman,* **circa 1853–1856 (courtesy Lyman Allyn Museum, New London, Connecticut).**

and had been a friend of her husband. Induced by anxiety for her husband's safety, she remained after all others had fled, and watched the entry of the British from the doorway of her house. As Arnold rode up he saw and saluted her, and said that if she would point out her own property it should be spared. She pointed out the houses of several of her neighbors as her own, and thus saved them from destruction. Arnold remained on horseback near her house nearly all day noting the battle that was raging at Fort Griswold…. Mrs. Hinman,

Charles Ripley visited seven cemeteries, in New London, Groton, Stonington and Ledyard, Connecticut and photographed 14 gravestones. He states that "All have the look of being carved by the same person. All have the phrase 'died 6 Sep 1781 in Fort Griswold by traitor Arnold's murdering corps.'"

having witnessed these outrages ... became so incensed against the traitor that she hurriedly descended from the roof, took a musket from a closet where it had ben left the day before by an American soldier, and leveled it at Arnold as he sat on his horse in front of the house. Taking a long steady aim, she pulled the trigger, but the piece missed fire. Hearing the snap of the lock, Arnold turned and asked her what the noise was. With great presence of mind she had dropped the gun, so that he did not see it, and she answered that it was the breaking of a chair.[27]

For his distinguished service, in his mid-sixties Elisha Hinman was given command of a federal revenue cutter. The episode of Abigail's defying the General inspired a beautiful and dramatic painting by Daniel Huntington, now in the Lyman Allyn Art Museum. The artist's wife was Abigail Hinman's grand-niece.

A story was passed down connected with the New London raid of another courageous woman, which demonstrates not only valor but what a small world it was, where local people in New London had personal acquaintanceship with Benedict Arnold. Eunice Forsythe Latham was the wife of a Patriot captain, William Latham, who was wounded but recovered. He removed his uniform and was placed in a cart with other wounded but when it hit a rock was able to roll out unremarked. The Lathams' young teenage son was taken prisoner and his mother walked to British headquarters and asked for his release. The story goes that Arnold asked lightly whether this was a request. No, a demand, she replied…. "Well, take him, but do not bring him up as damn rebel." As Eunice hurried out with her son, she retorted how she was not bringing him up as a traitor.

At the other side of the Thames River from New London is the Fort Griswold Battlefield State Park with remains of Fort Griswold, as well as a Revolutionary War museum. The Ebenezer Avery House which sheltered the wounded after the battle has been restored on the grounds of the park.

Charles C. Ripley III of Methuen, Massachusetts, who has studied the sites relating to Arnold's life for three decades, visited seven cemeteries, in New London, Groton, Stonington and Ledyard, Connecticut, and photographed 14 gravestones. He states, "All have the look of being carved by the same person. All have the phrase 'died 6 Sep 1781 in Fort Griswold by traitor arnold's murdering corps.'"

6

Ups and Downs in London

Life could begin anew, thought Hornblower.
—C.S. Forester, *Admiral Hornblower in the West Indies*

In October 1781 Lord Cornwallis surrendered to the combined American and French forces at Yorktown, Virginia. The Arnolds were in New York City which had remained British from the landing of General Howe in 1776 all through the war. By 1783 80,000 Loyalists had immigrated in. Two weeks later, General Clinton gave Arnold permission to leave for England with his family as soon as the French fleet departed and a ship became available. Arnold was bent on persuading the King that the British should fight on. He carried a letter of recommendation from Clinton to Lord Germain.

The Arnolds left New York harbor in January in the same fleet but different ships. Peggy, now 25, and her three children boarded a civilian packet. The two sons by Benedict's first wife came home to the New Haven house with Hannah (they had been in Maryland at school), and General Clinton arranged that Benedict VI be commissioned as an ensign in the British Army. Benedict sailed on a warship, the *Robuste*, with Lord Cornwallis, who had been a prisoner of war on parole after the Yorktown surrender, freed in an exchange of prisoners for Henry Laurens, the president of the Continental Congress, who had been confined in the Tower of London. Cornwallis's storied protégé Banastre Tarleton and Colonel Dundas were on the same ship. Eleven days out of New York, the *Robuste* was disabled in a violent story and had to bear away for repairs in Jamaica. Tarleton and Dundas boarded the *Grey Hound* with Cornwallis and Arnold sailed on the *Edward*. The convoy, a fleet of 100 ships landed in Falmouth on January 21, 1782, this being a safe port to avoid confrontation with the French navy.

By this accidental circumstance, Arnold's friendship with the powerful Lord Cornwallis was struck, and set the keynote for the third of Arnold's life after the treason. Just when his reputation was sullied, he let people into his life, networked, and formed friendships. He bonded with, sometimes did business with, grieved and joked with his friends from the time he left New York after the defeat of the British at Yorktown on. There is something of outsider kinship and humor often about his friendships as his letters and comments by other Loyalists about him reveal them. His affection for and attachments to other men seems to have gone beyond self-interest. For example, he took with him on the *Robuste* two "memorials" or applications of friends as to why they should receive more remuneration for their losses. Later, when he left

Lithograph by Max Rosenthal, after Daniel Gardner's 1783 painting executed in England. The child is Peggy's firstborn, Edward Shippen Arnold, born March 19, 1780, in Philadelphia (photography @ New York Historical Society).

North America permanently in 1791, Arnold was concerned about the health of his old friends in Canada (as this book sometimes will identify Britain's post–Revolutionary War colonies in North America, viz. by the name of the land after the dominion was confederated). That Arnold had long-term friends meant in that era as now he could be a friend, despite his putting self-interest first.

Arnold and Cornwallis kept in touch in England. Cornwallis spoke to William Pitt the Younger, when he was prime minister on behalf of Arnold's elaborate proposal to capture Spanish possessions in the West Indies and Central and South America. Cornwallis accepted Arnold's fifth son (Peggy's second), James Robertson Arnold, as a gentleman cadet in his artillery, and through Cornwallis's influence George went to the New Royal Military College.

For two hundred years, the occasional exotic American had been introduced to the courts and cities of Europe and toured England or the Continent, as object of wonder. By the Revolution many Americans had visited Europe but a noteworthy colonial still had the sheen of a curiosity from being from afar. A contemporary diplomat said that "Arnold was received with open arms by the King, caressed by the ministers, and all imaginable attention shown him by all people on that side of the question."[1]

The Arnolds were very well received at the British court. George III called Peggy the most beautiful woman he had ever seen. Queen Charlotte told her ladies to pay attention to polite and pretty Peggy. The day before the fall of the Lord North government, an annuity was arranged for her and for each of the children. Benedict was received at court "leaning on the arm of Sir Guy Carleton."[2]

It was fortunate for Benedict that he had Peggy's second cousin. This was Sir Walter Stirling, a naval officer who had married Dorothy Willing, daughter of a rich merchant in Philadelphia. George III admired Stirling's bravery. He had been engaged in combat with an American privateer off Charleston, and the King offered to make him a baronet, but Walter refused. There is an unverified story that Sir Walter convinced the father of Lord Nelson to let him join the Royal Navy. In his portrait at the Royal Museums Greenwich he looks every bit the commander of a ship.

Often mistaken for his son the banker having the same name, Stirling presented Arnold to the court. The son, born in Philadelphia, was independently wealthy and claimed the title his father had spurned. He had an ardent ambition to be a baronet; how it must have galled him that his father had refused one for distinction as a naval captain. Walter the banker's ambition was fulfilled in 1800 when, during the second term of William Pitt as prime minister, he became Sir Walter.

The elder Stirling would not have done the American any favors unless the King was keen on conversing with him. According to *Drake's Historic Fields and Mansions of Middlesex*,[3] Benedict was much consulted about American affairs by Lord Germain and the Cabinet. Sir Benedict conferred several times with King George and was seen strolling in the park with a brother of the king and the Prince of Wales. It must have been music to their ears that the thirteen colonies need not be lost. Arnold related to King George a clever idea of a peace commission of ranking statesmen, plus a policy of accommodation including a civil authority involving Loyalists, more troops along the Hudson, and sea power concentrated along the coast.

In any event, through early 1782, King George was often spied in the park conversing with Arnold and Lord Germain. Isaac Arnold, a descendant of the general, states that "The king saw the treason as an honest change of opinion. The King took Arnold at his word." This author cites the King's "active aid in placing Arnold's sons in the way of obtaining a military education, preparatory to commissions in the British army."[4]

Ben Franklin wrote "We hear much of audiences given to the latter [General Arnold], and his being present at councils. He seems to mix as naturally with that polluted court as pitch with tar."[5] Despite their exciting start, the Arnolds soon became like any other displaced persons, if immigrants rather than refugees per se. Furthermore, the war in a distant land had been costly and the Whigs were inclined to disparage General Arnold.

When Arnold led his patriot militia the flag had the motto *Qui Transtulit Sustinet*, "he [who is] transplanted sustains." In England Arnold turned to his first trade of sea merchant and threw himself energetically into action. According to an early biographer, Arnold straightway built ships with his own funds and sent them to the West Indies: "It is believed that the government granted him facilities, in the way of contracts for supplying the troops in Jamaica with provisions."[6]

The Arnolds moved to Portman Square, along New Street (now Marlybone Road)—the most fashionable address they would have in the years in London. It was beyond their means and would eventually be sold to pay for Arnold's trading voyages. Some former officers from General John Burgogne's army which Arnold had helped defeat at Saratoga lived in the Portman Square neighborhood as well as a colony of American Loyalists. (Burgogne had resumed playwriting in England.)

While the Arnolds would have to downsize from Portland Square in the times they lived in London, they had a comfortable lifestyle until Benedict's death. What mattered to him and Peggy foremost was that the sons be well placed in their careers, which, with the influence of friends, notably Lord Cornwallis, occurred. As the independence of the U.S. became manifest and then an old issue, the Arnolds lost their cachet, but, on the other hand, counted friends among the Loyalist refugees. When Clinton made an introduction for the Arnolds to a friend of his, the report came back:

> She was well dressed and had an ease in her behavior which astonished everybody, and novelty made everybody desirous of being presented to them. He played at high whist with the Duchess of Bedford, and 'twas the same at St. James, for they both seemed quite at home when they were presented to the King.[7]

Georgiana Byng, born 1768, was the first wife of the sixth Duke of Bedford, a Whig politician, and mother of a prime minister, John Russell. Where did Benedict learn to play the fashionable game according to Hoyle? It could have been in Philadelphia from the Shippens' social set, or seaboard, where gaming passed the time. The indication is that Benedict had the confident air of a high personage. A diffident manner curdled lords and ladies, where his bold affect bespoke quality when he mixed in London society.

Peggy conceived and lost two infants who were born in 1783 and 1784, but the next little step, Sophia, the Arnolds' surviving daughter, became a model of filial and domestic piety.

Arnold had changed his motto when he came to England, from *Gloria mihi surgum*, "All I seek is glory," to *Nil desperandum*, "Never despair." This surely had to do not with his own person so much as his clinging to hope that the British would crush the rebellion and return the colonists to the empire. In 1782, writes Ruma Chopra, "Many Loyalists still refused to believe that the empire's focus on the Caribbean and other regions represented a complete abandonment of the North American colonies."[8] *The Daily Advertiser* of February 3, 1782, reported that Arnold was "shortly to return back to America and to have command of the Loyalists, a prosecution of the war having been determined upon."

I sat in the café of the beautiful provincial museum in Fredericton (NB) with scholars orienting me to a picture of the refugees of two and a half centuries before. Gail Campbell summarized the status quo of the Loyalist evacuation of which Arnold, despite his fighting spirit, was a part:

> About 60,000 left the United States. A third of the colonists had been patriots, a third wanted to stay citizens of the Crown, and a third were in the middle. Families were split. Sometimes women's choices were made for them, some left for economic reasons or were runaway slaves. So when many drifted back when they thought it safe for themselves, some had not been ideologically anti-patriot anyway.

Bonnie Huskins, of the University of New Brunswick, elaborated on the statistics to me:

> There were multiple evacuations—Boston, New York, Savannah, Charleston and east Florida. Of those uprooted 35,000 made their way to Nova Scotia (soon split into the two provinces). Tens of thousands of Loyalists were wartime refugees living close to the bone in the Maritimes. Some were from the colonial elite; merchants loaded up what they had in their warehouses into ships they chartered.

Sir Guy Carleton had granted the evacuating Loyalists "particular permissions" to make whatever profits they could with their goods when they left New York.[9] Professor Huskins summarized the situation,

> Sometimes they liquidated property, so they had cash. The New York City docks were laden with furniture, four-posted beds, and portraits. On April 26, 1783, Guy Carleton said to settle debts first. This may explain that a tenth of the Loyalists went on private ships, taking pigs, cattle, nails, hinges and so forth.

More than 5,000 "American sufferers" filed claims for the property and jobs they had lost. They had expectations that would rarely and only partially be fulfilled by the government, as they curried attention to their "memorials," and rather than being welcomed they were seen as opportunistic by the populace. In 1783 a commission was appointed to adjudicate their claims, which would take seven years to sort out. Arnold's claims in 1785 for his service, disability, and recompense for his lost property of £16,000 is considered to have been unrealistic; it may well have been a bargaining strategy not a matter of greed. The Loyalists wanted to be paid back for what their loyalty took away, and have their dreams reinstated. Arnold estimated Mount Pleasant, his Philadelphia home, to be worth £5,000.

What the Arnolds did in London was commented on; one author states that Benedict "was almost universally referred to as 'that man Arnold.'"[10] Earl Bacarras, who was with General Burgoyne at Saratoga, refused to shake Benedict's hand one evening. He and Benedict were in the drawing-room of King George, which made the slight worse. A Loyalist and former New York lawyer Peter Van Schaack saw the Arnolds at the Poets' Corner of Westminster Abbey reading the inscription of the new marble cenotaph ordered by the king "Sacred to the memory of Major John André." Van Schaack observed: "What a spectacle! The traitor Arnold in Westminster Abbey, at the tomb of André, deliberately perusing the monumental inscription, which will transmit to future ages his own infamy."[11]

Now that he had taken off his epaulets, Arnold even made friends with his previous enemy Sir Guy Carleton. Carleton "introduced him to all the right families and took him to the House of Commons."[12] But he had a checkered reputation that even a gracious spouse could not erase. What occurred in the Commons was truly embarrassing, when one member asked that the traitor be thrown out of the chambers. Arnold stalked out before any further insult. Caustic newspaper articles under the signature "R.M." appeared in the London *General Advertiser* and *Morning Intelligencer*. One called him a "mere mercanery" while another said he should be hanged as a common criminal.[13] But in that era gossip about well-known people was the spice of life. Overall, the Arnolds' problem in London, then and after their years in New Brunswick at the very end of the century, was how to live like aristocrats on inadequate funds. They were ever downsizing but kept up socially. When General Clinton made an introduction for the general to a friend of his, the report back was as follows:

> She was well dressed and had an ease in her behavior which astonished everybody, and novelty made everybody desirous of being presented to them. He played at high whist with the Duchess of Bedford, and 'twas observed how little of the mauvaise honte he had about him. Indeed it was the same at St. James's, for they both seemed quite at home when they were presented to the King.[14]

There exists a document at the Clemens Library of the University of Michigan, dated August 13, 1783, with a scheme for privateering which Arnold submitted to the new British secretary of state (after Lord Rockingham died suddenly), the Earl of Shelburne, at the tail end of the Revolutionary War. It was filed but there is no evidence of its having been read. All the same, it reveals Benedict's impetuous nature. He had a grandiose idea and was confident. Having made his request, he had more thoughts, and submitted those, but vaguely, like his first plan, sketchily formulated.

The government, he proposed, would furnish him with £30,000 with which he would build a frigate of 40 guns that he would man and sail with no expense to the government. At the end of the war it would belong to the government unless taken by the enemy. If building the frigate cost more, his friends would make up the expense.

A week later he added he would build the frigate in a private yard in Liverpool and man it mostly from Ireland; it would be a "nursery for seamen" as the crew would be Irish "landsmen." Arnold laced the proposal with a mention of the sacrifices he had made of "Country, Friends, Fortune and Prospect." His postscript attested that only part of the money for building the frigate was due at once, the remainder not for four to six months.

He tried to use his connections to get a high command from George Johnstone, the newly elected director of the British East India Company. It took Arnold but a day to answer Johnstone's request to submit an account of his political conduct—which was he stated, never to wish independence from Britain. I only switched sides stated Benedict, when General Clinton reassured me that Americans would suffer no more taxation. The answer came rapidly too:

> Under an unsuccessful insurrection all actors are rebels. Crowned with success, they become immortal patriots … although I'm satisfied of the purity of your conduct, the generality do not think so.[15]

This was Arnold's final attempt, after four years in London, to get employment.

When the trial balloon failed, Arnold decided to strike out for a new life in Canada. A great booster of the importance of Canada for British power in commerce and territory was John Graves Simcoe, the colonel who had carried out the raid on Richmond with Arnold. Eventually Simcoe would be appointed lieutenant governor of Canada but from before the Revolution he had focused his expectations on Canada. Arnold himself had fair prospects, as he had his bounty for changing to the British side in the Revolution. He asked for his papers (the "memorial" that was a Loyalist's justification for a grant) back from the government He said that

Sir Henry Clinton had given him compensation "in great measure" for his personal estate. It helped the Arnolds that Peggy was receiving her pension from the Queen. He also expressed another reason for withdrawing his claim: "the expense of remaining in London to prosecute it." The memorial was returned to him, but a copy was kept at the Public Records Office. He set sail in a brig, the *Lord Middlesex* in October 1784, which carried a shipment of butter, flour, beef and pork to start his business in Saint John.

The journey took five weeks. He stopped over in Halifax to see acquaintances, and this occasioned a sarcastic yet bouncy note from Loyalist Sampson S. Blowers to his Harvard classmate over in Saint John:

> Dear Chipman: … Will you believe General Arnold is here from England in a brig of his own, as he says, reconnoitring the country. He is bound for your city, which he will of course prefer to Halifax, and settle with you. Give you joy of the acquisition.[16]

7

Sanctuary Province

"Gentlemen, I wish you all well. I wish you may go to
Heaven, but you must go there by way of Nova Scotia."
—George Washington

The British government had their eye on Nova Scotia for Loyalists
while the war was going on. The Crown needed lumber and fish from the
Colonies, and the rich farmland, once Acadian, was promising econom-
ically. Nova Scotia also offered a location to reproduce the hierarchical
society of gentry and commoners that was dear to the hearts of the British
ruling class. Ever since the evacuation of Boston, certain "Tories" had gone
a few days' sail north, to Nova Scotia, or returned there after a spell in London currying contacts.

The big push however was of Loyalists who fled the stronghold of New
York in the spring of 1783. Benjamin Thompson, Lieutenant Commander of
the Kings American Dragoons and Edward Winslow, chief muster-master
of the Provincial Forces drew up a "memorial" to the government which
they presented a month before the articles of peace were officially received.
The articles stated that no further confiscations would be made, people
would be released from confinement, and prosecutions discontinued. But
a dozen or so officers including Thompson and Winslow expressed appre-
hension over whether the Loyalists would be allowed to return home and
live at peace. These officers who were close to the action of war asked for
grants of land in some American provinces of the Crown, as well as pensions for the disabled, the widows and orphans, permanent rank in America for the officers and half-pay when the regiments were disbanded.
Eventually the requests were granted and both Winslow and Guy Carleton,
the commander in chief, immediately set about granting land to the provincial forces that were willing to resettle elsewhere in British dominions.[1]
The American Legion of 140 were on the *Elizabeth*, the Loyal American
Regiment of 187 on the *Apollo*, both large vessels of about 350 tons.

The Provision Muster at Fort Howe in 1783–1784 had 60 men, 18 women,
21 children and 13 servants (112 persons) in the American Legion, and Loyal

American Regiment had 108 men, 46 women, 89 children, and 18 servants (345 persons). Robbie Gilmore, an archivist of the University of New Brunswick Library at Fredericton, notes that the return of the state of troops under Benedict Arnold's commission (July 1781) was American Legion rather than the Loyal American Legion—i.e., the two may be one and the same.

Nova Scotia was an asylum for "Tories" fleeing persecution during the war for independence up until the Treaty of Paris—all told nine years. New Brunswick was separated from Nova Scotia in 1784. Half of the refugees who made their homes in the new province were disbanded soldiers from the provincial regiments and their families from, or who had settled around, New York City and Long Island at the close of the revolution. The first-generation upper class would be formed of dispossessed elite, many of whom had first gone to England and Halifax, who saw an opportunity for government jobs and the pursuit of the life of a gentleman on estates under British rule.

Some merchants were hopeful of profit in adversity while others, including the rich, feared for their families. Joshua (latter Judge) Upham wrote his Harvard classmate Edward Winslow:

RECEPTION OF THE AMERICAN LOYALISTS BY GREAT BRITAIN, IN THE YEAR 1783.

Reception of the American Loyalists by Great Britain in the year 1783, an engraving by H. Moses (courtesy Lewis Walpole Library, Yale University).

If war is ended I shall suppose in defining my own affair I am drawing in Some Sense a Picture of yours.... Should the War terminate at this Moment and as it ought, I shall find it Uphill work to extricate myself from pecuniary embarrassment, and before over-taken by old age, to procure anything sufficient for the decent Education of my Children.[2]

Ward Chipman wrote from aboard the *Tryal* off Staten Island to Winslow how ashamed he felt over the defeat: "I have been a Witness to the mortifying scene of giving up the City of New York to the American Troops."[3]

The voyage took twelve days from New York City to New Brunswick. For a week after the first fleet anchored, the Loyalists stayed on board the vessels, awaiting the report of scouts. Saint John, at the mouth of the St. John River, was the point of debarkation. The first settlement began on what became King Street although most of the Loyalists intended to settle on lands further up the river. Conditions were primitive. The disposition of essentials to each refugee was fair, sparse, and carried out by the military. Refugees received most of their relief in building supplies—boards, shingles and weatherboard. Those soldiers who arrived in the summer of 1783 were encamped in the St. John River Valley, while those who arrived in the fall spent their first winter in Saint John in tents around the coves of the harbor, looking southwest to the great Bay of Fundy and their former American homeland.

According to Robert Dallison's *Hope Restored*, 112 officers and their families and servants from the American Legion embarked for the St.

Reversing Falls, Saint John, New Brunswick (courtesy Charles C. Ripley III).

John River Valley.[4] A legion was smaller than a regiment. Benedict Arnold raised this legion mostly of deserters from New York and Long Island Loyalist camps and led them on the raids in Virginia and New London.

Twelve-year-old Richard and nine-year-old Henry Arnold received commissions as lieutenants of cavalry when the regiment was formed. The prominent Loyalist Edward Winslow, whose path would cross with Arnold's, tried to have one of his infant sons commissioned as an ensign: this ploy was not of Arnold's invention. By such a means a father ensured a son half pay for the rest of his life.

Block Number Ten lay in the parish of Wakefield northwest of Fredericton, bordered by the St. John River at the east and the United States on the west. Benedict Arnold knew some of the soldiers in the American Legion personally. For example, Andrew Phair, an Irish Protestant who left Ireland at ten, was recruited by a regiment of light dragoons, stationed in New York in 1782 and appointed adjutant in the American Legion under Arnold. Dr. William Stairs retired out of the same legion and became first pay clerk for the Fredericton garrison and then Fredericton postmaster. It seems, however, that soldiers in Arnold's legion did not cluster in a group. They fanned out to wherever they saw the best future, leaving Block Number Ten a mere notation of the first organization of a beautiful town.

Just as tales of Norumbega, with columns of gold and buckets of pearls tantalized Europeans after the earliest explorations of North America, so New Yorkers on the Tory side at the close of the Revolution were lured to the northernmost British colonies by flowery prospectuses. In January 1783, Amos Botsford and other representatives of the private New York agency charged with evaluating the area for future settlements sent their report back to the Agency that the St. John River was equal in magnitude to the Connecticut, or Hudson, and had a harbor at its mouth accessible year-round, and above falls with ice that could bear boats. Having gone into the woods and 70 miles up the river to a blockhouse that was a British post, they wrote a cheering report: "It is navigable for vessels of 70 or 80 tons burthen, for about 80 miles up the river, and for boats much farther." Fertile soil on the banks from the overflow of the river "produces crops of all kinds with little labour; and vegetables of the greatest perfection; parsnip of great length, etc."[5]

Although more sophisticated than to suppose that the flight was to paradise, Ward Chipman, from New York, wrote his friend Edward Winslow in a jocular tone:

> If it is practicable to have me included for a tract or lot or share or whatever it is called, among those that will be of your party, don't forget me. I should admire a very romantic, grand-water-river-falls-lake prospect with a good cold spring of water near my house.[6]

It is believed that few of the soldiers were experienced farmers, unlike the thousand colonists who came from Yorkshire twenty years before, or the 300 New Englanders from Essex County, Massachusetts, who immigrated during the American Revolution and brought their own stock and equipment.

Landing of the Loyalists, 1783 after Sandham Henry (1842–1912) (Private Collection @ Look and Learn/Bridgeman Images).

General Carleton granted provisions—clothing, food, medicine, building materials, farming tools, and weapons—through the board of agents while the Nova Scotia civilian governor, John Parr, granted surveyed lands. Three persons had charge of the civilian refugees from Lloyd's Neck, Long Island: Benjamin Thompson, born in Woburn, Massachusetts, the inventor who became with Benjamin Franklin the most famous American in Europe after the Revolution; Edward Winslow, born in Plymouth, Massachusetts, who would spy out the land around Saint John; and S.S. Blowers, who became an important official in Nova Scotia. Before the fleets of Loyalists arrived, Governor Parr wrote London to ask how to handle land grants. Instructions did not come back for ten months, and when they came there was a dearth of surveyors or boats to transport them. Considering this, the settling of refugees proceeded peaceably. Civilians were allotted the lower St. John Valley and the disbanded Provincials the more remote regions above it.

The Loyalists held in common a sense of being ground down by the imperial powers, an ethos which go-getting Arnold did not seem to share. Writes Professor Bell:

> They came not as heroic founders of a new nationality but as sufferers and exiles. They saw themselves as victims—the inexpressibly unfortunate casualties of three decades of British ineptitude, culminating in the ruinous terms of peace. "Was there ever an instance," demanded one devastated Refugee, … "can an history produce one, where such a number of the best of human beings were deserted by the government they had sacrificed their all for?"[7]

Initially two towns flanked the harbor; these were joined to make Saint John. According to David Goss, author and veteran guide of the city, people were ferried across in gondolas: "A lot of boats were for hire; Judge Ludlow rowed to the mercantile area from his home every day." Goss describes its forbidding geography (the hills he cycles on):

> It was a difficult city to develop. The terrain was solid limestone cliffs or swamp. The clearing away of rocks which were dumped in the harbor went on until the 1930s. Men drew lots and even 300 feet was too far from the water. By 1784 there were habitable buildings around Market Square, but that year fire burned everything they had built. The house Arnold bought on King Street had a water path. No one expected the city to grow. As it did the harbor was pushed out.

The lots for land in Saint John, St. Andrews or elsewhere were drawn during the settlers' transport. First engineers surveyed, then the Loyalists took up their grants. Two decades before, the British government held a lottery for lots in Prince Edward Island, taken from the French. Absentee landlords turned out not to develop the farms, however.

By contrast, the grants for the Loyalists were organized with exactitude. Barry Murray explained to me:

> You had two years to build a house. Some did not, and their land revoked to the officials, who often would give it away to someone waiting, or they might sell it. Meanwhile the King sent shiploads of supplies. Supplies even included window glass.

Yet conditions were harsh and soon some died, and some left for warmer climes. Ironically, the Loyalists' landing (spring to fall 1783) coincided exactly with the greatest eruption of the Laki volcano in Iceland, which began June 8. Ninety percent of the lava flowed during the first five months, effecting bad weather and extra frigid conditions. It was a very cold, foggy summer in the Maritimes as in the entire Northern Hemisphere. Tree rings in Alaska prove this. Anecdotal testimony comes from what the Loyalists wrote back to the former colonies about the hardships they faced, as well as Ben Franklin's report of a "constant fog."

The gentry brought pleasant features of their New England culture with them. The first issue of the *Royal Gazette* had notices of butchers, bakers and sailmakers, lately of New York, on King and Prince William streets. Mr. Evans sold perfumes and cosmetics from Paris, London and Milan, and in the back room of his shop completed the towering coiffures (at their zenith before the French Revolution), until he left for New York. A tailor named Matthew Partelow took over the shop and geared his high-style clothes to men. Mr. Partelow imported fabrics from Britain and provided fashionable men with pantaloons, wide coats, and sprigged silk or velvet waistcoats.

The Loyalists dressed up to gather at public occasions and private balls, where several dozen did the waltz and minuet. The society season started just when Arnold arrived, Christmastime, and went on through the winter. Provincial Secretary Jonathan Odell, Chief Justice George Ludlow, Attorney General Jonathan Bliss, Surveyor-General George Sproule, and three junior judges, Isaac Allen, Joshua Upham, and James Putnam, were a phalanx of the elite who had sought patronage successfully in the year before Arnold, with his commercial ambitions, sailed into the province. The prominent families defined the official life for the generation when Arnold was in the province, while the representative assembly gradually became more assertive and gained power from the executive council.[8]

Professor Huskins commented to me: "They tried to recreate communities in their new world. They used sociability, including taverns, Masonic Lodges, parties and dances. These were ways to hang together."

They were the genre of people it behooved Arnold to befriend. Two other notables, Edward Winslow and Ward Chipman, came with unsalaried titles (surrogate general and solicitor-general) but still belonged to the ruling class of the province. The Loyalist elite was not a revered pantheon of marble statues though. Early on, there were conflicts between influence groups, corrupt officials, and tensions between haves and have-nots. The tumult was quieting right when Arnold arrived, because those who were most unhappy with the oligarchical set-up, work the government wanted them to do free, other politics or their land grants, left the province. A disturbance had flared up at the very first, over blankets.

The government issued blankets to the refugees when they fled New York. Then, hole-ridden blankets arrived in Saint John, as someone thought it better to send them up there than to incinerate them. This charitable donation to the Spring Fleet was misunderstood. The refugees felt ill-used, as though the government believed them only deserving of cast-offs. The actual plan was for one good and one damaged blanket to go to each family and naturally to the settlers this felt like being Cinderella. Irate settlers signed petitions to the Army and Saint John was on the brink of a riot. According to Valerie H. McKito, the difficulty the government had in managing the ordinary people over the blanket incident was a factor in the establishment of the new province of New Brunswick, breaking off from Nova Scotia. Meanwhile the government feared a revolt, and the army sent no more blankets at all.[9]

Edward Winslow, whose first winter was the same as Arnold's, was the chap to make merry despite bleak conditions. He wrote to John Wentworth, former governor of New Hampshire (who governed Nova Scotia after John Parr's death), "Till this winter I had no idea of the jollity and sociability which a good neighborhood may enjoy in the coldest of weather."[10] The social season went from Christmas through the winter.

Benjamin Marston, a businessman and sea merchant from Massachusetts, fled to Nova Scotia in 1776 at age 40. He became a surveyor first in Shelburne while gearing up to present his claim for restitution for having spoken out as a faithful Tory back in his hometown of Marblehead. For several years he floated around New Brunswick with different jobs. One was an assistant to John Wentworth, formerly governor of New Hampshire. But Marston wasn't stringent enough about reserving all the best white pines for masts for the Royal Navy, and displeased Wentworth (then Superintendent of the King's Woods).

Marston was by education and birth part of the Loyalist clique. He was cousin to Edward Winslow and admired but did not marry one of Edward's sisters. His career as a Loyalist—which in New Brunswick included operating a trading post and a sawmill, and sea trade with the West Indies—like Arnold's was a variegated, energized, and problematic winding path. Marston died in 1792 in a tragic accident at sea and left Edward Winslow his diary. Descriptions he gave shed light on Saint John of between a year and six months before Arnold moved there. In *Loyalists and Layabouts*, Stephen Kimber used archives like Marston's diary to build a vivid panorama of the early Maritimes. The following portrait of Benjamin Marston from Professor Kimber's book gives a different, brighter side of the elite in Saint John when the Arnolds settled in.

Saint John Frolics
By Stephen Kimber[11]

Socially, Saint John—though physically still a "rude little town of frame houses and log cabins scattered amid stumps"—proved more to Benjamin Marston's taste that either Halifax or Shelburne, Nova Scotia, largely because most of Saint John's leading citizens had "numbered among the gentry of the old thirteen colonies."

Marston shared lodgings with the new province's young socialite solicitor general. Ward Chipman—Chippy, as he was known to his friends—had been born in Marblehead and, like Benjamin, was a Harvard grad. He's spent most of the war in New York as Edward Winslow's deputy muster master and—like Benjamin again—owed his current position to Winslow's support. The two men, along with a young army officer named Harris Hailes, lived in a party house where they often entertained the cream of New Brunswick society. The house was known among lesser locals, somewhat disparagingly, as Felicity Hall.

"Last Wednesday," Marston gushed in one letter to his mentor Winslow, "'we exhibited' at the Hall under the auspices of General Chippy." The event, declared the man who'd so recently been so disdainful of the excesses of parties in Shelburne, had been "a monstrous great ball and fine supper [with] about 36 gentlemen and ladies, such as governors, secretaries, chief justices, chancellors and such kind of people with their wives and daughters. We ate, drank, danced and played cards till about four o'clock in the morning."

While he wasn't entertaining others, he was being entertained. On the occasion of the queen's birthday, for example, Benjamin was a guest at a ball and supper at the Exchange Coffee House hosted by Governor Thomas Carleton and "his handsome and vivacious wife." The thirty to forty female guests "were of the best families only [and] the business was as well conducted as such an entertainment could be."

Saint John has been called "The City built in a day," because once the almost 1500 lots were drawn, construction began. From *Pioneer Profiles of New Brunswick Settlers*:

Men, who had never before lifted anything heavier than a goose quill pen, took off their expensive coats, rolled up their lace-frilled shirt sleeves, swung picks and axes and trundled wheelbarrows with the hardened laborers ... these people had not left their comfortable homes for a mere whim.[12]

Within a year of their landing, merchants were discussing business deals, quaffing rum and smoking their pipes at McPherson's Tavern, while The Exchange Coffee House was popular up the hill. Balls and other festivities as well as performances by traveling entertainers were held in the 50-by-25-foot Assembly Hall. Having fine houses, dressing up for musical evenings, and dancing and hobnobbing kept the displaced people's spirits up. It was less of a situation of impressing one's neighbor than in Halifax, a more established port city with army and navy officers coming, going and giving panache to the society.

No salary came with Benjamin's being John Wentworth's deputy surveyor of the woods but after six months, helped by his cousin Winslow, he was appointed sheriff of Northumberland County, the largest of New Brunswick's eight counties, and moved northeast to the village of Miramichi, where he felt truly exiled and which he left to pursue his claim for restitution in England.

What was a middle-aged immigrant gentleman to do? Arnold arrived with less of a support group and more money but how to reshape himself was as puzzling and his investments in activities capricious by necessity in the uncertain new colony. John Byles III wrote his sister of the bright social round—visits back and forth to the governor's house where he was staying, and Ward Chipman who "sent every body a laughing."[13]

Arnold came two years after the fleets carrying most of the Loyalists from New York. Like others of high status, he had gone to England first. The settlers were like archeological layers. The authors of *The Economy of British America* limn the region's settlements as New England outposts from present-day Maine to Newfoundland:

> Attracted by market opportunities in fish, timber and farm produce and pushed by the pressure of population on the land in more-densely settled regions, New Englanders flocked to Nova Scotia during the 1760s as part of the same migration that had earlier led them to New York, New Hampshire, Vermont, and Maine and that would later lead them to the Midwest.[14]

Moreover, the merchants in Atlantic Canada now had a monopoly of West Indian trade, as the British Navy had orders to block ships from the United States from its colonial ports. In his biography of Arnold, Randall states, "The man who once evaded the British trading laws now hurried to take advantage of them."[15]

Choice lots at the harbor that had been granted initially to New Englanders at the beginning of the town's settlement were reassigned to newcomers who had lost their prior property in America or were offered for sale. The second year after the landing of the Loyalists a fire burned most of the city. Even though it was soon rebuilt, it must have alarmed the elite in particular. Fredericton looked better and better—a milder climate and longer growing season, being away from the cold winds of the sea. Having the elite set their sights more on Fredericton meant more waterfront and other town lots for Arnold to purchase, although he also purchased a thousand acres of forest upriver.

The Loyalists had large families—a kind of insurance at the time, and the men became family-oriented as their scars of war healed. They built dream houses for a variety of reasons. First, the size of the family and live-ins (help was hard to find). Secondly, from nostalgia, as the Georgian style made a statement in architecture of one's belief in the type of government that the 13 colonies had thrown off: A rich Virginian built a reproduction of his brick house in wood. To show their prestige, thirdly: The prevailing architecture was plain and sturdy so one wonders why Arnold's 2½ story house on King Street was called somewhat pretentious. This view of Arnold's home may have referred to commodious size or to details that John Porteous had worked into the design; or to his presumption to having a house as nice as those of the New England aristocrats. As a merchant, by the company Arnold kept and his home he showed affluence, that he was up and coming, equipped to hobnob with the elite government office holders.

Saint John
By Ronald Rees[16]

Saint John, like most of the Loyalist settlements, was a mushroom growth. Between the spring and fall of 1783 more than four thousand Loyalists arrived to be accommodated on two rocky peninsulas on each side of a narrow river mouth and harbor. They arrived as soldier surveyors were laying out a grid pattern of straight streets and square blocks, with no concessions to slope or contour, and dividing the blocks into building lots on land that had been recently cut over. Tree stumps thrust through the rough ground. Arrivals fortunate enough to be assigned lots began putting up makeshift shelters, often "half-worn" tents donated by the military, while others "hutted" in crude log and brushwood shelters in the woods or on open ground where they wouldn't interfere with the surveyors. Still others stayed on the transports. As one sailor described Saint John: "numerous huts and houses scattered over the hills and rising grounds near the entrance of the river ... and great numbers of new wigwams, framed and log houses ... continually beginning as the settlers arrived."

The first winter was chaotic and inevitably trying but the Loyalists, having supported the Crown in the Revolutionary War, were due help. Once assigned lots they could, as wards of the British government, draw on the king's provisions for food, clothing, tools and building supplies. All of these were usually inadequate. Sawn lumber was so scarce that many houses were framed with logs, the available lumber being reserved for floors, partitions, windows and doors. Anticipating shortages, many brought door frames and windows with them, and a few even brought bricks. Several far-sighted Loyalists from Castine and Fort George in Maine, learning of the shortages, dismantled their houses, numbered the main parts, loaded them onto skiffs, and towed these behind the transports to St Andrews, a port sixty miles down the Bay of Fundy from Saint John.

In spite of shortages, rates of building were remarkable. Most of the Loyalists were tradesmen, disbanded soldiers, craftsmen and farmers, accustomed to physical labor and adept at basic carpentry, and not the pampered gentry of once-popular myth. As the survey took effect a planned town began to emerge. By the middle of July 1783 about 400 hundred houses had been built and by the end of September about 700. In November 1784 James Putnam, writing to his brother in Boston, was surprised to find "a large, flourishing town regularly laid out, well built, consisting of about two thousand houses, and many of them handsome and well finished."

Handsome, well finished houses may not have been common in 1784, but once settled on lots those with funds and access to government supplies began building with intent. House design was a matter for the owner but there were few departures from accepted norms The Loyalists were unusual refugees. Unlike later immigrants, they had come to British North America to replace a world they had lost, not build an experimental one, and as people of a common culture they were subject to unspoken restraints that prevented great deviations from what was considered normal or respectable. To these instinctive restraints they attached official ones designed to enhance safety and appearance. Lot sizes were generous and owners of lots who ignored the conditions of clearing, setbacks, fencing and building were subject to forfeit. This was well-ordered British North America, not the lawless, in their

One of a dozen chairs advertised by John Chaloner in the Saint John newspaper for his auction of Arnold's household effects (on September 22, 1791) as "A set of elegant CABRIOLE CHAIRS covered with blue damask." Ward Chipman bought the chairs but was slow to pay for them. Known as the "Traitor's chair." In a Louis XV French style where the arm slopes to the back, the chair is made of painted birch, brass and silk velvet. Later the Gilbert family bought the chairs and this chair was given to the provincial museum (courtesy New Brunswick Museum).

eyes, volatile republic they had left; and in an environment that at every turn reminded them of their frailty and limitations, a well-planned town or even a well-proportioned house was reassuring.

The standard dwelling, whether cottage or grand house, had classical proportions: a central doorway with well-proportioned windows evenly spaced on each side. On second floors, three or more windows were usual. Trim, if any, was restrained and economical; doorways were unadorned except for fanlights, and eaves and gable ends were spare and plain. Rooms were well-proportioned and arranged symmetrically on each side of a central hallway or staircase. In the larger houses, doors, window cases, mantles and stair rails were usually delicate and finely made. Dreading the loss of creature comforts, the more affluent Loyalists often embarked with accoutrements, so their houses might have had fine mahogany chairs, tables and desks, silver and glassware, imported English wallpapers, books and, in a few cases, extensive libraries. A gloss of civility and refinement not only put the wilderness in its place but served to foil the republican distrust of finery and polite society. Coming from England, Benedict Arnold might have arrived without many possessions but the auction list prior to his departure from Saint John suggests that he did not live austerely.

When planning a town house in 1787 George Sproule, a native of New Hampshire, and New Brunswick's surveyor general, issued these directions. The ground floor was to consist of three rooms and a hall, seven feet wide, through the house. At least two rooms were to open from the hall: a dining room on the right, connected to a kitchen, and on the left a drawing room connected to a bedroom. Each of the ground floor rooms was to have a chimney and to

The mahogany clock case displayed at the Morehouse House at King's Landing Historical Settlement in New Brunswick once belonged to Arnold and passed to the family of a Dr. Skinner, who bought it from Arnold at the 1791 auction (photo by Evelyn Fidler/courtesy Kings Landing Corporation).

have papered lath and plaster walls. The first floor was to be fitted up with two bed chambers, each with a fireplace and chimney. Winters were cold. Their walls, too, would be lath and plastered and papered and each was to have sash windows and paneled doors with knob-locks. A passage lighted with a dormer window would run between the bedrooms and would connect, via a short flight of steps, to two garret rooms for servants at the back of the house. With a gambrel-roof and dormers at the front, Benedict Arnold's two-and-a-half storied house on King Street in Saint John, if not of the same design, would probably have been built to the same standards of construction.

The first forty-some houses of the Penobscot Association who came to St. Andrews from Castine were built immediately with the materials they brought with them. Robert Pagan, Arnold's acquaintance and fellow merchant, had the first store in that town (now moved to 75 Montague Street) which he later added to, and the Pagan/O'Neil House at 235 Queen Street is there today. "They took chimneys, fireplaces, roofs, and floors in bundles on the ship, then the furniture, livestock, and themselves," states local historian Barry Murray. "The tax collector brought his houses from New York and Philadelphia." However, constructing a house on the rocky hills of Saint John harbor must have been the most challenging in the new province.

Arrival in Saint John

This was the beginning of one of those periods of transition which Hornblower knew so well, as did every sailor, the strange days or weeks, between one life and the next.
—C.S. Forester, *Admiral Hornblower in the West Indies*

Having done the impossible several times over in military campaigns, as a strategist Arnold felt invincible. This made him forge ahead as real estate speculator and in business as in battle. But after the treason he was toppled from the panoply of American heroes of legend. The British shrugged when he wanted to fight the French. *Quo vadis*? Now is when a thriving family assuaged whatever shame he had. The boys would all be funneled into military academies or straight into service; they stepped into his silhouette. Even his frail daughter would eventually be dispatched to India where Englishmen of worth, officers, were on the marriage market. Ambition is the deepest of various rhythms and shapes that repeat through his story, and his thirst to extend his capital for the next generation of Arnolds is the framing point of his six years in New Brunswick.

When Arnold decided to strike out for a new life, he asked for his papers back from the government, saying that Sir Henry Clinton had given him compensation "in great measure" for his personal estate. He also expressed another reason for withdrawing his claim, "the expense of remaining in London to prosecute it." The memorial was returned but a copy was kept at the Public Records Office. And so, he wrapped up the issue of compensation for loss that obsessed many Loyalists. Including Peggy's pension from the Queen, the Arnolds' annual income from the government is said to have been stable at £1500.

His plan was to make Saint John his headquarters for a return to the trade he had learned from his father, and the site of a distillery for the sugar product he would bring up from the West Indies. He did not have to buy all the land, leasing was fine, viz., six months after his arrival, permission was granted for him to build a 160-foot wharf on land leased from the government. Benedict, now 45, bought a large vessel, the *Lord Middlebrook*.

We can suppose it to have been a classic three-mast four-sail design, to carry comestibles to start his triangle trade in Saint John.

Arnold sailed in October as a supercargo, that odd term for a representative of the owners, as cargo typically belonged not exclusively to one person. Peggy stayed behind with their children except for Richard, 16, who went with his father. The voyage took five weeks during which Arnold suffered from gout. Then the ship was wrecked on the tricky shoals of Saint John. Arnold had to be carried off the brig on a stretcher and, to add to his depression, stores were stolen. His advertisement in the newspaper mentioned missing firkins of butter and a reward for information that led to capture of the culprits but there is no evidence any goods were recovered.

Portrait of unidentified woman by William Grimaldi (1751–1830); watercolor on ivory (courtesy Library and Archives Canada).

New Brunswick was spotlighted as a colony and glistened with possibilities for a new start. Arnold sent for his sister Hannah and his three older sons—this was to be a new home. He set out for a life in New Brunswick when it had just (June 1784) become a province. He would base his trading operations in Saint John, incorporated as a city only a few months before he arrived. These new political units in the magnificent forested region south of Quebec and along the Bay of Fundy on the east were little populated and had the familiarity of New England from which Loyalists were effectively banished. Seven thousand of the province's population of about 12,000 were Loyalist refugees who had arrived in 1783 in the dozens of transports expedited by Sir Guy Carleton. Some were New Yorkers, most were people who had fled to the New York headquarters of the British forces; some had first lived in Nova Scotia, or, like Arnold, London.

In a fashion Arnold was a Loyalist officer part of a flood of immigrants. However, the fascinating aspect of his move was that he was back in North America. It would be easier for Peggy to visit her family in Philadelphia (childbearing delayed this visit, December 1789 to April 1790) and for Hannah to come to help with the boys. The region, the people and the economy were familiar to him. He wanted to make good where he had been expelled. While he did not expect to be a popular figure there was nowhere else with more of a mix of individuals who had been on different sides of the war or not caught up in the outcome. He was certainly part of a wave of adventurers hurrying to the Maritimes excited about trading prospects. Beyond these factors, he must have felt a magnetic pull to his homeland.

Not only were the British colonies given their advantage by Parliament vis-à-vis West Indian trade, but Benedict foresaw that his Welsh friend David Owen

Painting of David Owen in the Campobello Library & Museum (photo by Jessica Cline).

would be staking out a "free port" on an island he and his brothers had inherited.

A view that the Loyalists were exiled to the barren woods is inaccurate. First of all, before coming, when land was already being parceled out, the refugees heard of the fine farmland and looked forward to working it or owning it. Secondly, it is the kind of attitude cartoonist Saul Steinberg mocked in his famous 1976 cover art for the *New Yorker*, which takes its view from Ninth Avenue, and sees beyond the Hudson River a wasteland of foreign parts, with Canada and Mexico just penciled in at the edge. Looking back, it is easy to suppose that New Brunswick was immensely distant from Boston or Philadelphia, whereas even Jamaica was but a few weeks' sail, and Saint John and Halifax were in the last two decades of the eighteenth-century primary ports for the carrying trade to the Caribbean.

As was usual with persons who wanted to declare their presence, Benedict had stopped in Halifax. Here he was received in the dual fashion that he was met with in general the last twenty years of his life. First it is known that he visited a friend of high status, William Smith, a man a generation older than Arnold, Yale graduate, the father of eleven children, and chief justice of New York. In the summer of 1780, William Smith had received from an intermediary the message (but not the letter, which the intermediary kept in his pocket) that Arnold was offering his services to the British. It was to Smith that, when ordered back from the raid on Virginia, Arnold went to air his frustration over British inaction. Now a refugee in Halifax, Smith shared with his old comrade in arms his belief in the need for a strong federation of the remaining colonies. It must have heartened Benedict to see that despite some political counts against him (Smith had been criticized for being slow to join the Loyalists—to the British he had been "lying under the oars"), he was a rising star in the Maritimes.

Contrarily, Arnold was privately derided. S.S. Blowers gave his jocular notice that the infamous general was on his way and another letter was dispatched from Halifax to Saint John that was meaner than Blowers' comment. Hugh McKay Gordon, former lieutenant governor of New Jersey, wrote to Loyalist Edward Winslow: "Gen'l Arnold arrived yesterday … and I understand means to visit your province. Mr. Hake and he will be good company."[1] Samuel Hake had the reputation of being a corrupt official; and had been charged with embezzlement while acting as a quartermaster at Fort Howe, at the mouth of the St. John River.

Naturally the Founding Fathers were keenly interested in whatever was afoot with Arnold. John Adams gave his opinion to John Jay early in 1787 on what the scheming traitor was doing back on the shores of North America:

> General Arnold has gone out to America too…. From this some persons have conjectured that war is determined upon, or at least thought not improbable. He went to Halifax in a vessel of his own, with a cargo of his own, upon a trading voyage, as given out. This I can scarcely believe. It would hardly be permitted a general officer to go upon such a trade. He said himself he had a young family to provide for, and could not bear an idle life. This is likely enough. I rather think then that he has obtained leave to go out and purchase himself a settlement in Nova Scotia or Canada, that he may be out of the way of feeling and contempt in which he is held not only in the army, but the world in general.[2]

Arnold's first days in Saint John were arduous. He put an advertisement in the *Saint John Gazette* to try to recoup looted goods from the wrecked ship, including many firkins of butter, but to no avail. And he had the gout.

Members of the gentry who had lost their sway when the 13 colonies became the United States were instrumental in creating the new province. It offered them a new footing for official posts. Many of the gentlemen knew one another; having cast their lots with the Crown bound them in trust. Players in New Brunswick whose activities were important to Arnold during his stay will be discussed in the next chapter. Suffice it to say here that Arnold's first experience of New Brunswick brought him into a volatile political and social setting. The Loyalists had been jockeying for plum parcels of land and official positions for two years and the assignment of lots was being held up by the lack of surveyors.

But the situation for the settlers was no longer so dire. The tent city was a thing of the past. Naturally Arnold straightway purchased a small house, commercial wharf, warehouse and office near the harbor in the busiest part of Saint John, at the intersection of Charlotte and Broad Streets. He established a lumber yard near the old Fort Carleton He built commercial wharves on the Saint John waterfront and kept these properties, which included a house on Main Street, in the part of town known as the Lower Cove (Arnold called it Lower Town in his correspondence). He moved up the steep hills when Peggy came, to the Upper Cove, where government administrators and people of means lived. He also soon purchased property in York and other counties.

According to McNutt, the winter Benedict arrived, while the British parliament "emphasized the sacrifices of the Loyalists and urged greater compassion for them, the principal contest was for town lots, particularly those fronting the harbors of the two towns."[3] Arnold's interest was to get a fresh start for his family and to increase his assets. He had his purse of £6,000 pounds the government gave him for his service to the Crown, but he too would have to struggle for survival in the frontier economy, where everyone was short on cash. Many of the ex-soldiers in the Saint James Valley could farm, but the people Benedict and Peggy would socialize with had never held a hoe or kept any kind of shop. It would be said that black Loyalists preferred being household servants because they were unaccustomed to farming or outdoor work in the northern climate, but that could also be said of the merchants, seamen, and gentlefolk Arnold met. Black loyalists simply got the dregs of lots and no permit for commercial fishing, or franchise to vote.

Attorney Ward Chipman wrote his wife from Halifax how glad he was she didn't wear frippery and paint her face as the women there did. Property was another matter. The colonial elite preferred to establish their estates in the St. John Valley, and their needs made Saint John's craftsmen thrive. By 1785 it was home to craftsmen including tailors, barbers, hatters, cabinetmakers, goldsmiths, silversmiths, a chair-maker, a hairdresser, and an upholsterer. Bakers, tobacconists, merchants, auctioneers, tavern keepers, lodging-keepers, mantua-makers, and dry goods retailers advertised their trades. For those aspiring to gentility, there was Mrs. Cottnam's school for young ladies, giving instruction in needlework, writing, arithmetic, French, and English grammar, and dancing, piano, and sewing. Formal education for boys in the province was admitted to be lacking, but Mrs. Cottnam's for girls was universally admired.[4]

Furnishings bespoke a family's status more than anything else. It was important that the Arnolds had fine furniture, window treatments, and carpets in their home to denote their prosperity and rank. In Digby, Nova Scotia, as the crow flies opposite Saint John, New Brunswick, my relatives became hostile to an American couple they had at first welcomed, who bought a ship captain's house in the cluster of houses by a lifesaving station and did not observe age-old rules about pitching in with a fund for road gravel. It reached a point of contention where my relatives were in a stony silence. Suddenly one evening I saw six men carrying the antique carved bed which had been lent to the Americans up the Shore Road from their house. The relatives had repossessed the bed which they were returning to one of the Canadian homes. It was as solemn as a funeral cortege.

During the eighteenth century, consequent to the rise of the bourgeoisie, furnishings became a premier status symbol. John Swan, who had traded in France and had French aristocrat friends, dispatched Captain Clough from Wiscasset, Maine, to save Marie Antoinette from the guillotine during the Reign of Terror. Aiming to create a space for the queen in America where she would be comfortable, while Captain Clough waited to bring the Queen out of prison, he bought up objects that had ended up for sale in the streets of Paris, after the palace of Versailles was ransacked, and loaded them onto his brig. The escapade has been called the carnation plot, since a secret message was buried in a flower.

Some of the household objects of the failed plot are said to have ended up at the Knox Mansion in Thomaston, Maine. General Knox had been friendly with Arnold during the Revolutionary War. Benedict had asked Mrs. Lucy Knox to put in a good word for him with a lady he was enamored of in Boston. To plead his case with the unresponsive young woman, Benedict gave Lucy a fine garment to offer her. However, this ploy too failed; Lucy communicated this to Benedict and requested the finery be hers.

Some British statesmen including William Pitt had tried to establish trade reciprocity with the United States, but mercantile interests successfully lobbied to keep the Navigation Acts in place, enforced by the Royal Navy. By forbidding trade between the British West Indies and the United States, and British ships from carrying American staples like fish, meat and flour, the Navigation Acts gave special privileges to the citizens of New Brunswick. Loyalist agents from New York fastened on the sites for commerce in the estuary of Saint John. However, the Loyalists could not register their American-built vessels without petitioning the courts for special privilege. Naturally this sparked the shipbuilding industry.

Some vessels were sold to England and Scotland while others were used in local or West Indian trade. Single topsail schooners with small crews could dart very quickly, but other schooners were rigged with two or three masts, each equally tall, and each with gaff sails that were effective for the varying wind directions along the coast. Brigantines had two masts with square sails on the foremost mast and gaff sails on the mainmast. Square sails distinguished brigantines and also brigs except the brigs tended to have both masts with square sails, good for carrying cargo over the ocean, following the winds.[5] Lest one think of illegal traders making use of only the smaller vessels, we learn that a square-rigged brig could come neatly into a small harbor. It seems intrinsic to the smugglers to have small crews, which does suggest schooners dominated the border trading.

Arnold banked on his success. He had been one of the New England shippers who dominated the carrying trade to West Indies before independence so was of course cognizant of the larger scene. Lord Sheffield, who wrote an influential tract advocating mercantile monopoly, sponsored the Navigation Acts. He was the patron saint of Loyalist shipowners and merchants, which explains why Arnold named his first big (300 tons) ship the *Lord Sheffield*. All the same, when Benedict reconnoitered up the

Smugglers & Revenue Cutter, oil painting by Thomas Buttersworth (1768–1842) (**Private Collection@ Royal Exchange Art Gallery at Cork Street, London/ Bridgeman Image**).

Saint John River, he was doubtless dreaming of sawmills and distilleries, and flouting the trade regulations of both the U.S. and Canada.

Arnold's instinct was solid when he sought to establish himself in New Brunswick. He had six vigorous and exciting years based in Saint John and the surrounding Passamaquoddy Bay region. Like a Joseph Conrad character, he had moved not just anywhere but to a pulsating frontier, a location whose small ruling class aimed to outdo their former opponents at their southern borders. He was among those who wanted things as they had been when all the colonies were under the rule of the Crown, but without the custom tolls and taxes. Whatever flaws in the colonial government had galled the Loyalists in their former lives, the dissatisfaction had not incited them to war. They tended to be idealists about how they would shape the new land. In this regard, Arnold was different. He had been on both sides, status seems to have been of no consequence compared with a reputation for honest dealings, and he wanted nothing of posts from the British Crown. When a Christian organization came to convert the Indians to Protestantism, local gentry went onto their board. Arnold's name though was absent. He wasn't a patrician and it seems accurate to assume he was tone deaf to religion all his life.

The situation in Saint John was a split screen. On the one hand there were deprivation and primitive conditions, especially two hard winters when the bulk of the 15,000 Loyalists arrived. Mrs. Lewis Fisher, wife of a soldier, recalled getting through the whole first winter of 1783 in St. Andrew with very few provisions and trying to have a tea party with steeped spruce or hemlock bark. Shelter, food and water were in poor supply. People became ill and died and some pulled whatever strings they had to in order to return to their previous homes. On the other hand, this was the land of promise. The land was beautiful and there was a chance for a more sedate or less regulated society, depending on one's inclinations.

According to Barry K. Wilson, who made a thorough study of Arnold's affairs, as well as Saint John's two eighteenth-century newspapers, populist and patrician, he had within 18 months become "the most successful business man and trader in early New Brunswick."[6] The spring of 1786 found him with wharves, warehouse and stores in Saint John, agents to sell his goods in the province as well as a five-room house, with a fireplace in every room, in the Lower Cove.

Interestingly, accounts say he didn't limit his enterprise to Britain and its possessions but traded in the United States as well. To get goods to and from New England he used middlemen. According to Barry Wilson, Thomas Hanford, owner of the schooner *George,* was "a willing accomplice" who helped Arnold penetrate the American market: "On 27 December 1787 Hanford agreed to take his schooner from Saint John to

North Carolina, then to Jamaica and back to Saint John."[7] Barry Wilson explained to me how and why Hanford earned different amounts for the stages of the journey.

> Under the complicated terms of the agreement which did not involve shipping goods from New Brunswick, Hanford would be paid three pounds sterling per month during the initial test trip to North Carolina to buy cargo which he transported to Jamaica to sell, then purchased Jamaican goods for sale in New England. After a second round trip between Jamaica and North Carolina convinced Arnold that the clandestine trading tie to the United States was feasible, he committed to doubling the monthly payment and giving Hanford a percentage slice of the value of goods bought and sold in North Carolina in recognition of the risk the Saint John trader was taking by acting as a secret commercial agent for the hated Arnold. There was to be no extra remuneration beyond the monthly fee for business that Hanford conducted in Jamaica.

If he did not emerge after six years as a roaring success, he was impelled by the new place to intense activity, responding with vigor to his new life due to its opportunities and the restlessness that led him there.

In a year or so, Arnold made the strategic move from Lower Cove to Upper Cove. He must have decided he could live in one place and have his business operations down the hill in another: Warehouses and wharves and the bustle of trade was now removed from his house to which he brought Peggy. This 2½ story house at the corner of King and Canterbury streets had belonged to a Loyalist named John Porteous, who had it built on Upper Cove and left after two years. The house had large rooms and several fireplaces, a gambrel roof pitched toward King Street, and three dormer windows completing the upper story. A Scot, Porteous succeeded in the fur and West Indian trade in Detroit and New York, and in Saint John focused on herring fisheries at Saint John and Bear River. He had trouble regrouping in New Brunswick, although a daughter said she was happier in the province than could be expected of a New York–bred girl, as her father's affection compensated for the loss of bright society.[8] Porteous had cash tied up in family property he may never have seen, and when financial headaches continued, moved to the more familiar territory of Albany, New York. Like many others in the Loyalist upper crust, the Porteous family had at least one slave, "Sukey," freed in 1797.

Some of Arnold's business properties were purchased and others leased. John Wentworth, subsequent to his visit in 1783 (while he was still in charge of the King's Woods), had proposed that the government keep control of the best sites for wharves and mast-ponds in the St. John River estuary, but he did not want to dispute the city charter; therefore, Saint John was empowered to collect rents on certain properties, among them the choice spots where Arnold located a wharf, which was a thorn in his side after he left.

As in 1780, when Benedict and Peggy reunited back in New York she conceived a child (John). She conceived again when Benedict went to fetch his family. Likewise, a few weeks after he set out for New Brunswick, Sophia, the Arnolds' only daughter, was born. Peggy and Sophia accompanied Benedict to Saint John, George was born in the King Street house in September 1787. When Peggy took him to Philadelphia for five months—a much delayed trip taken in December 1789, George was two. Writes Louis Quigley in his *New Brunswick Reader,*

> The young, personable, and attractive Mrs. Arnold proved to be a popular addition to the fledgling social life of Saint John.... Early, she was lonely, and wrote during one of Arnold's absences about "being in a strange country, without a creature near me that is really interested in my life." But she was resilient and was reported to have directed her household and its affairs "with skill, prudence and success."[9]

Richard and Henry were in their teens and Peggy's children were very young. Richard and Henry were young enough to develop a Canadian identity and James is known to have had warm memories of this period of his life.

Most Upper Cove heads of household, with astonishing uniformity, held salaried government posts; some also had half-pay as former military, investments in trade or land in the British West Indies, and property they could still lay their hands on in the former colonies. Arnold was among men he had associated with in New York or London, Loyalists who aimed to create a colonial world like what they would have had without the rebels. They were setting themselves up as patriarchs, interpreting the ideas of the salient political philosopher of their generation, Edmund Burke. The landholding aristocrats, the best men, should control government. They would remodel the colonial system so the "people out of doors," the great majority of the populace, would leave government to the gentlemen and have no reason to complain.

Theirs was to be an open aristocracy inclusive of men of talent, literary figures and artists. Arnold, who had been befriended by the Court and had significant money to invest, was socially acceptable if quietly disparaged as more a money man. Entitlement is a concept that could have been invented for this influx of the Loyalists making a go in the Maritimes. They got deserved favors but the ordinary people who fled America and lost what they had did not have their connections.

The patricians were wrong that the ordinary folk would welcome rule by the elite. Governor Carleton had to impose it. The elite also must have felt alarmed that the class system they had grown up with based on property-owning and education was ceding to one based on capital.

Sir Thomas Carleton (younger brother of Sir Guy) authorized the first election just before Arnold first docked in Saint John. To prevent the Lower Covers from gaining representation in the legislature, Sheriff Oliver closed the polling booth at McPherson's Tavern by the harbor, and moved it up King Street, to a tavern called Mallard's, where the supporters of Jonathan Bliss and Edward Winslow were. Thereupon, the Lower Covers besieged Mallard's, throwing bricks and breaking windows. Troops were dispatched from Fort Howe and broke up the melee, and Lower Cove leaders were arrested. Yet Lower Covers won the election, at which point the government candidates neatly demanded a new ballot. None of the Lower Cove candidates appeared and the government's choices on the ballet were installed.

This was par for the course for Thomas Carleton. Like his brother Guy, who had overseen the evacuation from New York, Thomas was a military general quick to action and little attuned to democratic process. In January (1786) the Lower Covers asked the governor to dissolve the legislature on the grounds that the sheriff had no authority to declare the winners. Carleton made no response and the first legislature met and commenced business by sanctioning the decisions of the governor, supporting the acts of his officers, and establishing the Church of England. So as not to be imprisoned some of the democratic contingency left the province. The conflict between the haves and have nots did not devolve into the violence of Shays' Rebellion a year later in western Massachusetts, but the scenario was the same. A new government hailed freedom and a society based on reason, but the elite preferred to view the common people as helpless children. In Saint John that fall before Arnold arrived, the resentment flared because former soldiers used to action riled at inaction regarding participation in their governing. With undoubtedly high approval rating from the elite, Carleton used the military at Fort Howe to nip the civic unrest. Complete democracy for Canada would come later.

Political discord, having reached a pitch in the winter, had settled and melted away by the spring, which brought a warm season and new ventures. Henceforth there were no emergency requisitions from the King's stores at Fort Howe or elsewhere.

Arnold's grandest action in the province went both ways. He built his ship while it was still on the stocks in Maugerville 100 miles up the St. John River from the city of Saint John (where he also had land). He was in a hurry to recommence his sea voyages and trade. The *Royal Gazette* of June 6, 1786, praised his initiative:

> On Thursday last came through the falls of the city, a new and noble ship belonging to Brig. Gen. Arnold, upwards of 300 tons of white oak, the Lord Sheffield, to be commanded by Capt. Alex Cameron. The General's laudable efforts to promote the interests of this infant colony have during his

short residence been very productive to its commercial advantage and as such deserve the praise of every well-wisher to its prosperity.

Arnold was a hard-liner who asked the shipbuilder to make changes while the frame was on the stocks.

Nehemiah Beckwith was the son of a Samuel Beckwith, a sea captain who with his brother John had migrated from Connecticut to Nova Scotia in 1760. Piracy beleaguered them and in 1780, Nehemiah, age 24, moved to the Saint John River where he received a grant from the government and took up shipbuilding and farming. He and Arnold partnered for trading with the West Indies, with Nehemiah usually taking command of the ship. Arnold, impatient, found fault with the schedule, maintaining that his partner on a run was too slow. Squabbling, while not unusual, was sure to make a negative impression on the people of Maugerville and on others who built the ship or rode in it from the mouth of Saint John to Fredericton. The vessel might also make the entire triangle voyage (Saint John-West Indies-Britain). For the coastal trade and smuggling operations, schooners were used, which had rigging that allowed a small crew and smaller capital investment.[10]

Rapids run first one way and then the opposite on the St. John as the tides rise and fall. The ship was brought through soon after slack water, when the current started to flow to the sea again. There had been doubts that such a large vessel could pass the dangerous Reversing Falls. But the shipbuilder and Arnold quarreled over payment, an alienation factor for him within the province.

Arnold was in full swing, sailing up the St. John, and riding into the interior to look at land, or traveling to the West Indies. Arnold purchased a great deal of land even in the context of large land grants, mostly in Saint John, forests up the St. John River, St. Andrews and Fredericton, the village up the river chosen by the governor, Thomas Carleton, as the location of the provincial capital.

Arnold bought 12 acres in the town of Fredericton and traded lumber and provisions there. He bought land (some say a house), but authorities concur that there was only the warehouse in Fredericton, on the west bank of the river on what is now Waterloo Row. One of the oldest houses in town, built on Waterloo Road as soon as the lots were surveyed and laid out in a panned pattern, Rose Hall burned down; Arnold may have constructed a part of it. A bronze plaque at 102 Waterloo Road at the corner of Shore Street states, "The McQueen-Fergusson House circa 1790. Land originally granted to Benedict Arnold."

In Fredericton, Samuel Beckwith's descendant Lilian M. Beckwith Maxwell wrote an article about Nehemiah Beckwith's daughter Julia (Catherine Beckwith Hart), "The First Canadian Born Novelist," who published a Gothic thriller based on her family. Maxwell asserts there was both house and warehouse in Fredericton:

> In 1786 General Arnold bought a house at the lower end of the present Waterloo Row in Fredericton, and at the upper end of the Row, facing the house, the partners built their ware-house. (Later, this warehouse, with double doors on the upper floor, was changed into the present dwelling house.)[11]

St. Ursula's Convent or the Nun of Canada, the novel, was based on experiences of Lilian's family and relatives. It can be gathered from it that the partnership of Benedict and Nehemiah ended poorly. Arnold asked for alterations just before the date of delivery and Beckwith said he was fined fraudulently for completing them beyond that date. Happily, the shipbuilder traded lumber and cattle and prospered. Beckwith also built a scow that was the first water transport between Saint John and Fredericton.

As so often in their history, once again the Loyalists prove very connected, as Nehemiah wed, in Fredericton's Government House, Julie le Brun de Duplessis, who had come to Fredericton as a governess to the children of Governor Thomas Carleton. The property had belonged to Peter Clemens, a Loyalist who had been a captain in the King's American Legion.

Rose Hall
By Koral LaVorgna[12]

Rose Hall, also known as Rose Cottage, was constructed on the lower end of Waterloo Row, in close proximity to the 1783 landing of the Loyalists. Benedict Arnold purchased this lot in 1786 and had thereon constructed a simple one-and-a-half story dwelling whose appearance was "without any pretension whatever." Local mythology insists that Benedict Arnold resided in this modest dwelling before removing to Saint John. However, so brief was his stay in Fredericton, there is actually no evidence to suggest that Arnold ever resided in this house. After Arnold left the province in 1791, he sold this lot to Jacob Elligood, whose heirs in turn sold it to Colonel George Shore in 1818. About a decade or more later, Shore began construction of a large dwelling which would become known as Rose Hall. Col. Shore had Arnold's modest dwelling moved to the rear of the lot where it served as a wing of the significantly more substantial Rose Hall. Once it was moved, Arnold's dwelling house became known locally as "the old part" of Rose Hall. In 1882, fire began in the green house on the property, soon spreading to the surrounding outbuildings and barns. Within 15 minutes, the fire reached the rear of Rose Hall, likely engulfing "the old part," or Benedict Arnold's dwelling, before consuming the rest of the house proper.

Even after the property changed hands, this lot retained the name Rose Hall. When a new dwelling was raised on this lot a few years later, it too was known as Rose Hall. That building, the second Rose Hall, was demolished in 1975, and a modern dwelling fashioned to appear historic stands in its stead at 176 Waterloo Row.

Feelings about the recent war and American independence were so mixed as to soon cancel themselves out. Naturally though, Arnold's having been on both sides provoked animosity. The memory of Major André, an authority on the Loyalists observed, was "a factor that disturbed the minds of a great many."[13] But they did business with Arnold. He employed people and did not get involved in the Lower Cove/Upper Cove conflict or enter the fierce competition for provincial office. A story often recounted in histories to demonstrate how horridly people viewed Arnold concerns Captain John Shackford, who had marched with Arnold to Quebec and been taken prisoner during the assaults. Shackford loaded a ship for Arnold at Campobello Island and recounted that "when I thought of what he had been and the despised man he then was, tears would come, and I could not help it."[14]

Arnold was very far from Connecticut, but the trading scene was not so different. Dried fish and lumber were products of the Saint John Valley in demand in the West Indies, whose sugar and rum were in demand on both sides of the Atlantic. It was quite like back in Connecticut, even with the accepted pattern of dodging customs officials to pursue commerce. Hindsight suggests he would have been wiser to have focused on the trade he knew rather than have knotted himself up over debts within Saint John.

Rum had of course emerged from and fueled the slave trade. It was also a demotic beverage enjoyed at a cheaper price than wine and was more portable than beer. When General Knox wrote to General Washington in 1780 about supplies from the northern states, he underscored that "no exertions should be spared" to provide it in ample quantities: "Besides beef and Pork, bread & flour, Rum is too material an article, to be omitted."[15] He might have been speaking of Arnold's merchandise in New Brunswick, with the addition of timber.

The notice for sale on the Lower Cove house said it had five rooms with a fireplace in each room, but even if it was large enough for comfortable quarters it was not in the elite neighborhood. Wherever the family lived Arnold gave Peggy a setting of proper status where she would be well-placed to have friends of her social background. Peggy also prepared Sophia to be genteel. She oversaw Sophia's reading French, playing piano, writing, and doing needlepoint. Advertisements in Saint John's *Royal Gazette* show that the finer things were not forgotten in this part of the British Empire.

After arriving with Henry and Richard in 1787, it is unknown whether Hannah stayed for long, or whether she accompanied them as young men when they would settle in present-day Ontario. Indeed, between trips, boarding schools, and the shifts back and forth from Aunt Hannah to their father and stepmother, the extent of the brood at any time anywhere is not to be determined.

HERE STOOD THE HOUSE OCCUPIED BY GEN. BENEDICT ARNOLD, FAMOUS REVOLUTIONARY WAR SOLDIER, PROMINENT MERCHANT AND TRADER 1787 TO 1791

NEW BRUNSWICK HISTORICAL SOCIETY

Saint John home site at 20 King Street, Saint John, NB. Charles C. Ripley III.

A fund was established to improve bridges and roads in Saint John shortly after Arnold moved in. With a contribution of five pounds towards the improvement on a certain road came the entitlement to buy a hundred acres of land on it. Arnold pledged 50 pounds for construction on the Westmorland Road.

It is surprising how early a divide occurred in the settlement of the city between Upper Cove and Lower Cover. The dispossessed elite Loyalists may have lost property but fixed on reclaiming their superior social status. And they multiplied. If a man had successive wives, the number of his progeny was often eye-popping. (Long winter nights, vigorous living and the advantage to a farm of a large family are reasons cited.) Peggy herself had the five children who survived to adulthood, and two who died in infancy.

There were musicales and dances and, from 1789, theater performances, which the Arnolds surely attended. Back in Philadelphia less than ten years before, the Continental Congress criticized Arnold for going to see officers acting on stage, "in humble imitation of the example of the British Army," as Samuel Adams noted. The American Congress had introduced legislation to suppress theater along with horseracing and gaming, but the elite of Saint John did not impose such restrictions. It is also known that Peggy enjoyed horseback rides on paths around Saint John with other women in the elite circle.

Benedict's Advance in the New Province

Never had the old woman had such a great
feast, and never had she tasted such broth,
and just fancy, made only with a nail!
—*Folk & Fairy Tales; The Bookshelf for Boys and Girls*

It may be tulip bulbs, or the size of car fins, but there are certain pre-eminent status symbols in every society at any one time. Peggy required feather beds and mahogany furniture, and fine wines; but when widowed she made light of the losses of her pretty things. Therefore, if the Arnolds were living high, which biographers like to assert without convincing evidence, it was not extravagant taste but that need to look prosperous. If a merchant was away a lot, on voyages to the British West Indies, his wife and the tea parties she gave represented his prosperity to the world. And Arnold's moral standing was, naturally, disquieting, so stability had to be projected.

Sometimes it is hard to tell if being an attorney was a métier or status marker in New Brunswick, as its plethora of people in the legal profession is hard to match even in modern times. And Benedict stubbornly held that if he used a lawyer's services instead of bashing and dueling with adversaries, all would turn out well for his enterprises. Some who knew him as a soldier must have observed the change in Benedict's tactics with the shake of a head, like Rat's concerning his neighbor Toad in *Wind in the Willows*: "I've known Toad fancy himself rightfully bad before, without the slightest reason."

Courting the Law
By Barry K. Wilson[1]

Benedict Arnold's Dec. 2, 1785, return to North America after four frustrating and unsuccessful years of self-imposed exile in London did not go well.

Instead of the planned triumphant day of new beginnings, pregnant with opportunity and optimism about life starting again as a trader and businessman in the fledgling British Loyalist colony of New Brunswick, it was a series of fiascos.

An aborted docking in Saint John Harbor because of squall conditions led to an unplanned beaching in gale-force winds in a nearby rocky cove. Passengers had to be evacuated with Arnold carried ashore on a stretcher because of a severe gout attack. His cargo of goods, meant to be the primer for his retail business, was piled on shore to be pilfered later by thieves.

It was an inauspicious beginning. Still, he thought the prospects bright as a business opportunity presented itself. The community of 3,000 or more Loyalists awaiting him, transplanted from their refuge in New York City after ending up on the losing side of the civil war that was the War of Independence, needed supplies of all kinds—food, dry goods, building material and jobs. The colony's nascent resource and manufacturing export businesses needed a way to get their products to market.

As a confident, experienced and successful pre–Revolution Thirteen Colonies businessman and trader with approximately £6000 (equivalent to several hundred thousand present day dollars) in seed money remaining from his British pay-off and available as start-up funds, he could build a business that would supply what was needed.

He would have a captive market, little competition and a viable business plan. Within days, Arnold had rented a house, leased a harbor-front store and wharf and developed a business plan that involved shipping New Brunswick commodities south to the West Indies, transporting their products to British markets and then returning to New Brunswick laden with goods needed by colonists.

Building his own ships, wharves, warehouses and stores would happen in time.

A mere 10 days after arriving, Arnold made his first deal—leasing a ship from local owner James Butler to take New Brunswick lumber south to the Caribbean and bringing sugar, cotton and rum back north. Butler was hired to captain the ship for the venture that was to begin in early January. Arnold planned to go along to oversee the venture and pay the bills.

It was to be the launch of Benedict Arnold's new career as a leading entrepreneur in his new hometown. The plan was sound in theory but missing a key ingredient—a thorough and realistic understanding of the colony's economy, the people who populated it and his place in the mix.

The Saint John of Arnold's day was a cash-poor, hard-scrabble community whose citizens had forfeited almost everything by supporting the losing side in the American Revolution and who had left most of their possessions behind when they fled their homes for safety. Many had been upper class or middle class New Englanders before the Revolution—literate, ambitious and in many cases affluent enough to own slaves who accompanied their owners into exile.

The majority of the 30,000 Loyalists evacuated from New York had

Slave market advertisement from the *St. John Gazette* (courtesy New York Public Library).

been sent to the established colony of Nova Scotia in what one historian described as "the first mass movement of political refugees in modern history" but several thousand were landed in spring, 1783 at a natural harbor in what would become New Brunswick, northwest of the Halifax settlement.

The Saint John built by the newly arrived emigrants was a rough and rudimentary frontier community with a downtown slave market near the harbor, newspaper advertisements offering rewards for the return of run-away slaves and a public whipping post designed to mete out justice and punishment near the spot where the refugees had come ashore. Slavery would not be abolished in the British Empire, including the Canadian colonies, until 1834 although the sale of slaves on Canadian soil ended at the close of the 18th Century.

The community boasted almost three dozen merchants but the lack of currency meant the early New Brunswick economy was largely credit or barter-based. The paucity of jobs and income meant many citizens and businessmen became inventive at finding ways to avoid paying their bills. Unfortunately for Arnold, his blueprint for using his cash reserves to build a business empire was based on the pay-as-you-go principle. Friction and conflict were inevitable.

Arnold also undoubtedly faced some resentment from his new neighbors for his prominent role in advancing the revolution before profiting handsomely by betraying it. As a successful pre-revolution New Haven, Connecticut, businessman, he had depleted his assets in pursuit of the independence dream but then profited by his decision to switch sides for a tidy British reward. He arrived in New Brunswick wealthier than most and undoubtedly the target of some hostility and lack of sympathy when he struggled to collect his debts from those who arrived with nothing.

Arnold's take-no-prisoners style of business dealings and his abrasive personality undoubtedly did not help and he had no natural allies among the factions that made up the Saint John community. His enlarged profile and business base made him a de facto part of the elite and he counted among his close friends prominent city lawyers who added the Arnolds to some guest lists for dinners and parties at which Upper Class denizens entertained themselves. However, presumably because of his reputation and bare-knuckle style of operating, as well as his frequent absences on business travel, there is scant evidence that he was fully a part of the city's exclusive and influential insider clique with its intertwined friendships, associations, deal-making and favor-trading that was common among the community's business, political, legal, judicial and military leaders.

Meanwhile, his status as an aggressive businessman and economic player created a barrier between himself and the community members who were his customers. Working class men had shown they would follow Arnold, the brave and inventive military leader, to the ends of the earth but as a gruff and demanding businessman, he stood apart from them.

As Arnold quickly discovered, the Saint John and New Brunswick of his day was a highly litigious society in which disputes over money owing, bills unpaid and obligations not honored often ended up in the courts. As an outsider with few natural allies, those court judgments often pronounced by judges and juries of men who disliked or did not respect Arnold often ended up delivering hollow victories and little satisfaction for the outsider.

Still, during his first two years in New Brunswick, Arnold's dream appeared to be playing out. His business affairs were going well, he had moved his family from London to Saint John to live in a well-appointed home and the local newspaper heralded him as a community leader, its most successful businessman and a success story.

Beneath the surface, a different story lurked. He was spending his savings and not earning enough to cover costs. A major part of the problem was his inability to collect on debts owed. It meant that he too often turned to the legal system for redress.

The litigious nature of his new community, and particularly its small business class, quickly became apparent in his first commercial venture— the deal with Butler to begin to launch Arnold's trading business.

It was a disaster from the beginning. Butler and Arnold disagreed about almost everything including who was in charge and the pace of transactions and decisions during the much-delayed voyage. For Arnold, delay meant lost revenue. Each man sued the other—Arnold sued for losses incurred because of Butler's bad decision making and Butler sued for money he said Arnold owed him. Arnold won but received a judgment far smaller than he demanded.

A template of hollow court victories had been established.

During Arnold's more than five years in New Brunswick, he was involved in 50 court cases both as instigator and defendant. He won most and rarely received compensation he felt he deserved or the vindication he craved. In many cases, the loser found ways to avoid honoring the court-ordered settlement owed to Arnold.

In 1786, prominent Saint John lawyer Ward Chipman (who represented Arnold in some cases and also ended up fighting him in court as well) summed up the regular use of courts at the time to settle every day commercial disputes. "Really, everybody is poor," he wrote to a friend. "There is no such thing as money to be had.... (A court case) is the only way to obtain payment." History shows even that outcome was far from fool-proof as court judgments were regularly ignored. However, in principle Chipman's observation offers some perspective on Arnold's litigious history.

Most of his court cases related to current business relationships but others traced their origins back to revolutionary times in the Thirteen Colonies and grievances alleged by men he had known or who had served with him in the latter days of the fighting when Arnold wore a British officer's uniform.

An exploration of three of the 50 court cases will serve to illustrate the breadth and futility of Arnold's vexing journey through New Brunswick's legal system.

The strange case of Jabez Cables, a Saint John baker who made a deal with Arnold to provide baked goods to feed the crew on his trading ships but also to sell commercially in Arnold's stores, offers a starting point. The deal was that Arnold would sell barrels of flour to Cables and buy back the resulting baked products. He gave Cables a key to the storehouse where flour supplies were kept so the baker would have access to supplies when Arnold was at sea. In 1787 after returning from a trading voyage, Arnold discovered that according to his books, Cables was not paying him for all the flour used and withholding some cash he owed. The baker's account books were a mess.

The following year, Arnold travelled to England to do some business and to fetch wife Peggy and their children for the trip to their New Brunswick home. On his return, he found the bakery business in financial trouble and determined the money owed by Cables would have to be written off. The business association ended. Four years later, Cables had Arnold arrested for a £49 debt he said was owed for running Arnold's store. Arnold denied he had ever employed the baker to manage the store, fought the charge in court and won. Cables never paid the court judgment and by 1792, had fled to the United States. Arnold had lawyer's bills but no justice.

Jesse Lawrence first met Arnold in 1781 in the Loyalist refugee camp in New York after fleeing the victorious American army and then the two crossed paths again in 1786 when both moved to New Brunswick. Lawrence purchased goods from an Arnold store, failed to pay and was sued. He counter-sued over an incident he alleged had occurred five years previous in 1781 when General Arnold sent him on a dangerous mission through American lines to deliver letters to Philadelphia. Lawrence alleged that Arnold had not paid and sued for £50 compensation. There was no court judgment and an out-of-court settlement is possible but once again, Arnold likely did not receive what he was owed, endured a humiliating arrest and still ended up paying lawyer bills.

Dan Lyman had been a New Haven neighbor of Arnold's before the war and followed the general in 1781 as a soldier in the Arnold-led American Legion fighting for the British against the Americans. In early New Brunswick days, Arnold purchased 100 acres of farmland beside the Nashwaak River in central New Brunswick and leased it to Lyman for development. Lyman did little to develop the farm and did not pay the rent but was elected to the New Brunswick Legislature, giving him immunity from debt-related lawsuits. The fight to redeem Lyman's debt dragged on for more than a decade, well after Arnold's 1791 return to England.

Almost on principle, Arnold continued to pay lawyer Jonathan Bliss to pursue Lyman for payment. Finally, a £259 settlement was reached in 1797, minus an £11 lawyer's fee deduction, of course.

Over his years as a New Brunswick businessman, Arnold was tenacious in using the courts to try to extract blood from the stone of delinquent debtors. He was far from the only one to do so in search of financial justice but the record of litigation has given ammunition to Arnold's detractors over the centuries. There is scant historical evidence that the lawyers ever complained.

The bustling town had its first election the winter Arnold arrived. Politics were raging, and politics were an aspect of human society of which Arnold was wishing to disembarrass himself. He had his bona fides from having been befriended by the Court and having thousands of pounds to invest. The concept of the elite refugees was an open aristocracy that would let in men of talent. With optimism he put real estate at the fore. Jean E. Sereisky writes, "Soldiers with whom Arnold had served in the British Army, including adjutant Andrew Phair, postmaster, and Dr. William Stairs, were living in Fredericton and he renewed, cordially, old acquaintances."[2] (Andrew Phair was an adjutant of the American Legion. Buried in Fredericton's Old Burial Ground.)

There was a market for real estate with settlers who got grants wandering off to new locations, and the gentlemen who got huge grants of up to a thousand acres not being able to meet the requirement (for every 50 acres plantable, three ought to be cultivated). That there was a labor shortage and a shortage of capital would mean the value of land had begun to fall just as Arnold was ending his residency (1790), at which time solons including Jonathan Bliss and Ward Chipman were of a mind that wealthy men would not speculate on land in the province.

Some of the real estate Arnold acquired had dwellings; he was, Randall points out, compassionate about not evicting tenants with families, despite his going hell-bent after rents.[3]

It is possible to picture the life of the Arnolds. Benedict was afire with projects and Peggy brought gracious living. A circle of close friends suited her temperament and there was levity as well as the challenges of the household. How fancy an occasion could be in the struggling new province comes across in the description of a ball Governor Carleton and his wife gave:

> The Governor was so animated and Mrs. Carleton so anxious to please that they showered every attention on their guests' is recorded in an old diary. Our great-great-grandmothers stepped the minuet in the low-timbered rooms of Government House to the music of flutes and violins. At supper they were served "rare and delicious foods," after which they "danced again until three o'clock in the morning." [The diary entry continued with this note of Mrs. Carleton's gown.] Of elegant tea-colored satin, with a white satin petticoat embroidered in pastel shades. Her hair was dressed in light curls with a silk bandeau embroidered with "Vive le Roi," which had a pearl brooch on one side and ostrich and peacock feathers on the other.... [She] carried a large bouquet of Jasmine and Carnations.[4]

Mrs. Carleton's gown had, as aristocratic ladies' attire inveterately had, a French touch.

What was a middle-aged immigrant gentleman to do? Arnold arrived with less of a support group and more money but how to reshape himself was puzzling and his investments in activities capricious by necessity in the uncertain new colony.

Saint John was one of five ports of entry in British North America, the others being in Nova Scotia. One impetus to shipbuilding was that as of 1786 a bill was passed in Parliament requiring all vessels—ships, coastals and fishing boats—that had a deck or were over 15 tons to be registered. No foreign vessels could be registered, so the Loyalists were not permitted to register their American-built vessels.[5] They asked for exceptions to the law but meanwhile had their hands tied. It cheered people to see the first big sailing vessel built in the province.

Some were concerned that Arnold's *Lord Sheffield* would have too deep a draft to come through the (tidal) Reversing Falls. That it was feasible at high tide encouraged further shipbuilding. This may have been the first big vessel constructed in the Maritimes. Then, from 1787 until the end of the century, over 700 vessels were built, and either sold to England or Scotland, or registered in the provinces.

The big ships, according to *The Caribbean and the Atlantic World Economy*, sometimes made the triangle voyages (Saint John–West Indies–Britain), whereas for coastal trade and smuggling operations, schooners were used, because their rigging was handled by a small crew and the investment was smaller. Yet schooners, brigantines and brigs, the little vessels were actively engaged in the trading scene both as coastals and to the West Indies; the Lord Sheffield would function for either. Saint John became a port of entry with a Collector of Customs in 1782. It was reported in the Saint John newspaper as 300 tons. According to *Sailing Ships*, there was a tendency to exaggerate the size of ships, but to get a sense of the size of this vessel, it can be compared with the first large ship built in Nova Scotia, the Roseway, reported as 350 tons, which was 78 feet long, 23 feet 10 inches broad, and five and a half feet between decks. The previous vessel built in New Brunswick, by Jonathan Leavitt in 1770, was a 15-ton sloop. The *General Wentworth*, another ship built in Nova Scotia in 1792 and registered at Shelburne, was very large for the era, 325 tons with dimensions of 102 feet five inches, and 23 feet three inches breadth.

Arnold soon had half a dozen vessels that sailed from Saint John, most of them small schooners and brigandines built for the West Indian trade. There are no extant records of just what Arnold was trading from 1785 to 1791 in New Brunswick, but it certainly was related to both the carrying of legitimate cargo, and smuggled goods. The West Indies needed lumber and dried fish to feed the slaves. The trade items were sugar and rum, as some but not all distilling was done in situ, and sugar of different grades had other uses as food. It is not as though he stayed on the ship, removed from the commerce and slavery—it is reported he was on the docks handing his transactions.

A trader like Arnold had the opportunity to see the degradation of the enslavement of people and turned a blind eye. There were early glimmerings of reality that might have penetrated a business person like Arnold from New England, most of whose livelihood was closely embedded with the slave labor of the West Indies. Evidently, fighting as brothers put a crack in the willful racism. When the disbanded Loyalist troops were leaving New York for Canada, Colonel Isaac Allen wrote Edward Winslow to provide for George Black, a black Loyalist soldier,[6] and then George Ludlow freed his slaves after allowing the slave owner to keep a slave as property, as he had considered the issue on the bench and saw the light. Arnold was not however touched by the issues of social justice.

In his enterprises, Arnold met and dealt with American traders for example going himself down to Robbinstown across the border into (then) Massachusetts. Arnold was a thoroughgoing capitalist and it wasn't hard to greet his former enemies. The quartermaster general under his brother Sir Guy Carleton, who fought in the battle of Champlain in which Arnold's makeshift fleet was taken and burned, must have observed Arnold setting up an enterprise in Fredericton.

Impatience and egoism were traits of Arnold that come up again and again. Of course people were ready to have rancor against him. In this context the mid-nineteenth-century Maine historian William Kilby relayed an anecdote figuring Captain Alpheus Pine, a Loyalist from New York who was an early settler of Saint John.

> [Captain Pine] kept the old Quoddy House at Eastport, and used to tell hard stories about Arnold whom he thoroughly disliked. On one occasion he sold Arnold a quantity of wood; but not being paid for it sold it a second time. As the wood was being hauled off, Arnold appeared and a quarrel ensued. Pine caught a stick from the pile and was about to break Arnold's head had bystanders not intervened.[7]

10

A Smuggling Culture

Arnold considered himself the leading
personage in the drama that was his life.
—Nathaniel Philbrick

The caretaker of Treat Island, Deirdre Whitehead of the Maine Heritage Trust, invited me to see the monument to John Allan, the Patriot
turned merchant who calmly sold to Benedict in the 1780s. With his wife
and children and their cow, John Allan was the only resident of Treat when
Arnold was trading in New Brunswick, and the two men could have seen
each other with spy glasses, little Treat being but a mile from Benedict's
trading operation on the much larger Campobello Island. Deirdre offered
me a day's adventure looking around the unpopulated Treat Island, from
which I looked over at where Arnold had his entrepôt on Campobello.

**Treat Island viewed from the Campobello Library & Museum (Jessica Cline,
photographer).**

115

Deidre Whitehead of the Maine Heritage Trust is the caretaker of Treat Island and the monument to John Allan, the Patriot turned merchant who calmly sold to Benedict in the 1780s. With his wife and children and their cow, John Allan was the only resident of Treat when Arnold was trading in New Brunswick, and the two men could have seen each other with spy glasses, little Treat being but a mile from Benedict's trading operation on the much larger Campobello Island. From the unspoiled natural expanse of Treat one can see where Arnold had his entrepôt on Campobello.

Arnold didn't want people to be cognizant of all the comings and goings of his business, so it was natural he had wharves and structures to keep fish and lumber and other commodities in transit distant from Saint John. Campobello was one of the three Fundy Islands on the Bay of Fundy. It had a few settlers who could be employed, and two harbors for small vessels. The big vessels from England and the British navy vessels would drop anchor well out from the island, so Arnold did not have nosey civilians or customs authorities looking into his business.

The caretaker of Treat Island for the Maine Heritage Trust, Deirdre Whitehead, communicated to me her perspective on how, after the American Revolution, open these waters were to smuggling: "All the British Navy was fighting Spain and France, so you could have a little ship, go out and be a smuggler, or a pirate."

In an impression of Moose Island (now part of Eastport, Maine) in the nineteenth century, Lorenzo Sabine declared it one of the United States' most noted places:

> But its fame was of a kind which no people should desire; for the general impression was that its inhabitants were bold and reckless men, and earned their support by sheltering, and sharing the gains of adventurers, smugglers, and gamblers.[1]

Sources that reference the shady business along the official border between the U.S. and Canada in this period draw attention to how indifferent the local people were to the existence of an international border, as if it were only an occasional impediment to free trade.

The lineage of this nonchalance to authority was long. When the realm of the Sun-King included Acadia as well as France, the Baron de Saint Castin became an Abenaki, married a Native American princess and ruled as feudal lord much of Maine's eastern coast. While he traveled all the way back to Versailles to get his official land grant, he consistently defied the rules of the French administration of Acadia by engaging in fur trade with Boston.[2]

Smuggling provided the daily bread of inhabitants of the coasts of Maine and the Maritimes after the formation of the United States. The

Smugglers, **engraving by James Ward after late 18th-century painting by George Morland (Private Collection/Bridgeman Images).**

region naturally drew an opportunist like Arnold. Contraband was an accepted way of life for common people and the well-off alike. But the Passamaquoddy Bay was more rough-and-ready than that suggests. The line between piracy and privateering was thin, and Arnold conducted his trading in an economy that had the perils of a Wyatt Earp movie.

Smuggling has shades of youthful adventure but has always been allied with piracy. For instance, Joseph Conrad formed a syndicate with three friends to buy a balancelle schooner and smuggle guns from French caves to northeast Spain. His Uncle Tadeusz observed to his nephew, writing from Poland, that "staying on land has always had an inauspicious influence upon you."[3] For the Loyalists it was a survival mechanism when political tides brought them to their plight.

The smuggling population was bound together by a desire to eschew more conflicts between British and French or British and Americans. In this manner they displayed an attitude analogous to that of the Indian tribes of the region. Governor Carleton wrote Lord Germain, the British Secretary of State, that "There are among them who are guided by Sentiments of honor, but the multitude is influenced only by hopes of gain."[4]

Smugglers Alarmed, 18th century, lithograph by W. Clerk, probably 1830s (courtesy HIP/Art Resource, NY).

He wrote General Burgogne in the same vein that the inhabitants "had imbibed too much of the American Spirit of Licentiousness and Independence ... to be suddenly restored to a proper and desirable Subordination."[5]

"Smuggling, broadly speaking," writes Professor Truxes, "was trade that circumvented the Acts of Trade and Navigation. It thrived in British North America."[6] Truxes cites a pre–Revolution merchant named Cadwallader Colder who "routinely" loaded contraband tea, India goods, and spirits at the Isle of Man after clearing Liverpool for home. Connecticut sloops ferried the illegal cargoes to the East River of Manhattan.

A sense of how the law was flouted comes from an 1892 history of a Masonic Lodge in Lubec, whose author commented on "the amazing struggle which the Government had with the pirate smugglers" between the American Revolution and the War of 1812.

> The battle was to take flour and other American produce to the Provinces and bring in British manufactures contrary to law. Hundreds of thousands barrels of flour were piled upon the wharves and shores of Eastport, and, notwithstanding the Government supported the Collector ... it all found its way across "the lines." Fire arms were freely used, and it is marvelous that only one man is known to have been killed. The fact that flour was worth $5 per barrel on our side and $20 on the other, overcame all difficulties. It is said that fortunes were made in a few weeks, and sometimes lost as suddenly; and that the men who carried on the business were a hard lot from all parts of the country.[7]

Kate Gannett Wells writes that the U.S. boats donned a Swedish register and pretended to go from Sweden to Eastport in a matter of three or four hours. American vessels also would depart Lubec or Eastport in the morning with papers saying they were bound for the West Indies and be back the same day with a load of wool they were running from Canada. Silk, wool, cotton and metals were thus carried up the bays and streams, and shipped in wagons to the Penobscot, then to Portland, Boston, etc.[8]

Arnold didn't require smuggler's vaults in the cellar as he had in New Haven. The lucrative exchange of merchandise from Britain and the Caribbean for goods desired by the Americans was the primary business of the region.

North of Deer Island, Maine, and Campobello Island, New Brunswick, the Passamaquoddy Bay has high, bold shores, dramatic cliffs, jutting promontories and steep beaches. According to *A Cruising Guide to the New England Coast*, the principal deep-water entrance to the Passamaquoddy Bay is Letite Passage, Deer Island: "The tide runs through here with considerable violence, making swirls, eddies, and boils. However, with power or a fair wind, one can run through with a fair tide." The authors cite a sea captain on "either charging through with the current or plying your wits against it."[9] Another twentieth-century sailor cited in *A Cruising Guide* commented that he knew of no area he tried with more respect in a fog. Sea smoke in the winter and fog in the summer restrict visibility to a few hundred yards.

No wonder that the Passamaquoddy Bay was the center of smuggling during all the years of Arnold's sailing these waters and living in New Brunswick. The big barrels would have been in general moved across the lines in heavy-duty, flat-bottomed shallops 20–30 feet in length, with a square or sharp stern, and two-masted rig, or bateaux propelled by two to a dozen rowers, and deep and heavy. The illegal enterprise peaked when Thomas Jefferson imposed the embargo in 1808 but was lively earlier and part of Arnold's mercantile scope. It seems that aversion to regulation was the single most important part of his personality, supported by his appetence for wealth and advancement. Having prospered on contraband rum and molasses in Connecticut, Arnold fit right in to the Passamaquoddy Bay.

The products of the Maritimes were principally gypsum, timber and lumber by-products. Up to 100,000 tons a year were exported from the Maritimes in the period, employing up to 500 small vessels. Timber for British Navy vessels flowed up from America and the west of New Brunswick to the Passamaquoddy thence to the British West Indies. The territory of these borderlands (not truly bordered lands until well into the nineteenth century) was ideally navigable as waterways ran inland from the coast in parallel courses. Wherever the settlers were, they could carry out logging in the streams meandering through sandstone and limestone. The waterways the Indians had traveled in birchbark canoes now transported a commodity whose value to white people had risen above fur.

The importance of the timber (for barrels, masts, and so forth) emerges in a note Robert Pagan wrote at the time. He was a native of Glasgow, Scotland, born in 1750 and son of a wealthy sugar refiner, who emigrated to America and became a merchant in what is now Portland, Maine, and moved from Castine to St. Andrews, New Brunswick in 1784, when Castine became U.S. territory.

> I am fully convinced that the Grand Bay of Passamaquoddy alone can supply the whole British West India Islands with boards planks scantling, ranging timber, shingles, clapboards and every specie of lumber that can be shipped from any part of New England, oak staves excepted.[10]

Thus timber, brought from forests to the coves and foggy wharves of the Bay, was specifically traded for West Indian rum, molasses, sugar and salt, especially when Napoleon blocked England's imports from Sweden. Arnold's ships could carry the rum, etc., all the way to England and if he wished a New Brunswick–built ship could also be sold there. As American goods were denied access to the West Indies, flour was transferred by way of Canada, while contraband such as wool from Nova Scotia, clothing and shoes, East India tea, fine wines and brandy were contrabands secreted to the United States. The smugglers moved "out on the lines" anything that could not be legally imported to the United States from Great Britain or to Canada from the United States. This was like an athletic European court dance but of every manner of vessel and cargo crisscrossing.

Colonel John Allan had a house on Treat Island and a store. He was a gentleman born in Edinburgh Castle, Scotland, where his family took refuge during a conflict of the Jacobite rebellion. The family emigrated to Halifax. John went to Harvard College, graduating in 1762, and sided with the Patriots.

He became a member of George Washington's personal staff. His wife was imprisoned in Halifax for six months because she refused to reveal John's whereabouts. His valuables were taken; according to Allan's memoir several silk dresses were stolen and given to the wives of British soldiers. Allan's importance during the Revolutionary War was that as Military Commander of the Eastern Area he negotiated with tribes in the Passamaquoddy region to persuade them against giving the British support. He sent his two sons, Mark, 11, and William, 13, to live with the Indians, as a token of his trust; he admonished them to "Be very kind to the Indians" and to "take particular notice" of two for whom he had special respect. Meanwhile he kept the boys supplied with things from the white world they might use—"books, papers, pens & ink, wafers, & some other things."

The American government recompensed Allan with a grant of two thousand acres in Ohio which he never used. He moved to Dudley Island, part of which was Treat's Island, also called Allan's Island, between Eastport and Lubec, where he established a trading post for goods with the Indians. His account book showed that he had business dealings with Arnold. An individual reporting to a Machias, Maine, newspaper looked at the account book with Allan's descendant and noted one day's purchase was a gallon of rum, and there were also charges to him for lumber and other articles. For now, the account book has receded into the mist of time, but it was exhibited at the centennial of Maine, and a resident of Machias showed it to a newspaper reporter. The account book used the spelling "Benedick." John Allan had been as crafty and bold as Benedict Arnold during the War, with the help of the indigenous people destroying five British ships in Machias. Arnold and Allan were of equal station and used to having command. At this juncture, in this often hostile and difficult world, their ambitions and experiences matched, which promoted cooperation.

There were accounts, unfortunately not preserved, at other locations—Moose Island, little Pope's Folly at the entrance of the Passamaquoddy Bay, and Dennysville as well as Treat's Island of business transactions involving Arnold. The individuals that Arnold traded with were in at least two cases (Allan and also Mr. Pope) veterans of the Continental Army. Business was business, making a living on the Passamaquoddy took a tough spirit, and its merchants had turned a page from the war where they were combatants.

Treat also had a fish drying station. Allan was trading with native and white inhabitants, and quantities of the dried fish must have come from the Maliseets and Micmaqs. As far as the lumber, mills sprang up on streams entering the St. John River, and the timber was floated down on barges and pulled by boats across the line to the British Fundy Islands, notably Arnold's operation on Campobello, where it could be said to be from British trees. There was a great shortage initially, Ronald Rees, author and professor of historical geography, told me, but the timber industry soon developed: "Handfuls of settlers before the Loyalists had a few saw-mills, and after their arrival there would be many more. The British army commandeered what they could, and water-powered sawmills could have been built quite quickly."

The carrying trade included slaves. Some came from Virginia to the Passamaquoddy islands, and from there were taken on an English ship to the West Indies. Some were sold in Halifax or Saint John. Servants who have lived in or trudged up the hill as day workers, or slaves, are not well documented, as to be expected. A receipt for the sale of a slave is in the papers of Peggy's father Edward Shippen, in the Clements Library of the University of Michigan. Benjamin Marston for instance put in his claim for restitution the item of his loss of three slaves that he had owned in Mar-blehead. Ten percent of the refugees who fled from New York were black, and while free black Loyalists received lots, they often ended up share-croppers, and did not have the opportunities of whites. They could be a jack of all trades, a domestic servant or farm worker or work on a ship. The 1785 city charter of Saint John "prevented them from voting, practicing a trade, fishing in the harbor or selling goods. Also, Blacks could not live in the city unless they worked as menial laborers." They were in all aspects of the economy and since the word used for enslaved and indentured people was the same, "servant," they appear thus in the records when they were involved in legal disputes.

There is no way of knowing whether the Arnolds had slaves. It is sure that Benedict employed black workers in his warehouse. But slavery was dwindling as impractical in the economy and immoral. Liberated black people came from New York in the fleets. George Washington drew a hard line, where only ex-slaves who had fought with the British could leave the American territory, but Governor Guy Carleton, to his great credit, was very cavalier about who had the right papers. (Carleton also argued for the Quebec Act, that protected the French language and religion in Canada.) That former slaves had no licenses for commercial fishing in Saint John harbor or to set up as tradesmen, no matter their skills, was a most imme-diate frustration to them, and, as stated, they could not vote.

Former plantation slave Thomas Peters petitioned for black people in the Maritimes to no avail, and so went to London and met with William Wilberforce and came back and recruited in Nova Scotia and New Brunswick for the return to Africa movement. Many of the 2,000 black Loyalists who had come left, for the white settlers a critical loss of cheap labor. Two hundred black free persons from New Brunswick joined in an exodus with 1200 from Nova Scotia, and journeyed to Sierra Leone, where they were joined by Jamaican people of color and thousands of Africans freed from slave vessels after the abolition of the slave trade.

The epicenter of historic smuggling in the Maritimes, explains Joshua M. Smith, was the Passamaquoddy Bay, yet it included many persons from far away—French, Dutch, and so forth. His *Borderland Smuggling* identifies the borderland dynamic as a commonly-held set of beliefs concentrated for many years in the border region between Maine and Canada. The Americans after the Revolution captured much of the trade to the West Indies. Writes Smith, "Its great merchants who possessed overseas connections lost their business, and almost all who would presume to live by trade had to enter upon the traffic that made them satellites to a system of dubious legality."[11]

By trading flour, lumber, rum and so forth "on the lines" with the Americans, the New Brunswick settlers in the Passamaquoddy Bay region could import directly to New Brunswick and Nova Scotia, or re-export to the West Indies and Britain. Commercial forestry or distilleries were doubtless developed with a mind to circumvent the law. Legal historian Paul Craven sums up the carrying trade as follows: that "the chief business of Charlotte County's shoreline communities was illicit trade," and that Governor Carleton failed to put a stop to it. "There were too many fog-shrouded inlets, too many inducements, and too great a dependency on American flour and other goods for anything more than token or symbolic enforcement of the laws of trade."[12]

Joshua Smith observed to me, "Arnold bought and sold goods where territories overlapped. He could say he thought he was in British territory—especially in the fog it was hard to say. He had a 'plausible deniability,' using the haze to his advantage." Smuggling was not merely an accident of fortune to Arnold. It interlocked with his attitudes towards government and his ambition to support his large family—why he chose to live in a remote spot on the coast of eastern Canada. His unhappiness with state controls and government-sent bureaucrats extended from pre–Revolutionary protest (and hostility to the Continental Congress) to a personal ideology of renegadism. Items on display in his store arrived with having had duties imposed, yet he also could pursue profit as if there were free trade—business counted for more than politics.

Meanwhile the U.S. point of view was coalescing regarding the Bay of

Fundy border region. Fisher Ames, as a representative from Massachusetts addressing the U.S. Congress in May 1789, said that, "The habit of smuggling pervades our country. We were taught it when it was considered rather as meritorious than criminal."[13] Hindsight shows that smuggling was part of the transformation to economies set by market forces. Writes Joshua Smith,

> the presence of so many adventurers from distant ports indicates that smuggling was not purely a regional response, but part of a larger process that encompassed the entire Atlantic basin: the transition to a market economy.[14]

A former American customs officer for the Passamaquoddy Bay, Lorenzo Sabine, recalled in the nineteenth century:

> The Loyalists who, at the peace, removed to the present British colonies and their children after them, smuggled almost every article of foreign origin from the frontier ports of the United States for more than half a century, and until England relaxed her odious commercial policy.... I have not room to relate the plans devised by sellers and buyers to elude the officers of the Crown, or the perils incurred by the latter, at times, while crossing the Bay of Fundy on their passage homeward.[15]

President Thomas Jefferson was angry at the region's smugglers and wrote to Albert Gallatin, "I hope you will spare no pains or expence to bring the rascals of Passamaquoddy to justice."[16] On the New Brunswick side of the Passamaquoddy Bay, a U.S. cutter sometimes captured smugglers, but officials on both the U.S. and British sides were quite lax and local people tended to ignore the border altogether. According to Smith:

> Border populations could ignore the authority of distant governments with some impunity; they could also offer criminals safe haven. Passamaquoddy's isolation, low population density, cross-border marriages and connections fostered by locals, and common frontier experiences resulted in a common rejection of commercial regulations as bothersome and unnecessary restrictions, smuggling was thus tolerated, and even received approval in border communities.[17]

The U.S. customs collector of Passamaquoddy Bay from 1789 through the War of 1812 was Louis F. Delesdernier, of French Huguenot parents from Geneva, Switzerland. Delesdernier was "in sympathy with smugglers though he made seizures from time to time." Later he was jailed for malfeasance as customs collector but "for over a decade he had the privileged position as a close friend of Treasury Secretary Albert Gallatin, a Swiss who had stayed with the Delesderniers in Nova Scotia during the American Revolution."[18]

A show trial of smuggling infraction was of Gilliam Butler, a merchant originally from Boston. Butler was convicted and imprisoned for three months and given a hefty fine. He had been smuggling American whale oil out through Saint John, under the pretense it was a product of New Brunswick. Governor Carleton used the fine of 500 pounds to pay Ward Chipman's arrears of salary and improve the jails in the county. Arnold's close friend Jonathan Bliss filed suit in the supreme court case against Gilliam Butler.

Goods from America had to be transferred to vessels built and registered in New Brunswick. Small boats in the Passamaquoddy Bay were busy making these transfers at night. Paul Craven, who recounts the whale oil tale, summarizes how smuggling worked for the carrying trade: Money was to be made

Judge Jonathan Bliss of Springfield, Massachusetts while a young man, about 28. The back appears remade to hold different locks of the hair of his sons (courtesy Walters Art Museum, Baltimore).

in expediting American transactions with the British West Indies by vessels built and registered in the province, in nocturnal transfers between New Brunswick and American boats, in evading custom house rules, in burying British goods under loads of Nova Scotia plaster consigned to U.S. destinations and American manufactures in imported flour barrels, in excise avoidance of every imaginable description. The official working assumption (not unwarranted) about enterprise of any sort was that it must be a ruse. Thus when Benedict Arnold proposed to establish a rum distillery at Saint John, Carleton responded to London's concerns on behalf of West Indies planters, "I know not at present how to estimate the quantity he might be able to distill, nor how much more, under color of such distillation, might be introduced by illicit importation from the United States."[19]

The opposition to Arnold's enterprise from London, and disconnect with Beckwith who built the *Lord Sheffield*, contrasts with the freedom to try out big ideas that Henry Knox had in the District of Maine, where Knox was by 1795 opening mills, quarries, and brick foundries. Likely, one item Arnold smuggled was wool from Nova Scotia to the United States. Meanwhile Knox was importing English sheep to Maine to cross with a domestic breed for heavier wool.

The imprecision of borders was a fact of the times—not only Nova Scotia/New Brunswick and New Brunswick/Quebec but also whether an island belonged to the United States or Canada was still disputed, due to different interpretations of an article about the boundary in the Treaty of Paris (September 3, 1783). Agreement would not be reached until 1842. A seaman could maintain ignorance of the law, and it is indisputable that authorities and traders in the two countries scoffed at tariffs and were resistant to surveillance of trade.

Arnold met and dealt with American traders, for example going himself down to Robbinstown, across the border, and the gentry were after all his former enemies. In the war men had fired cannons, fought with bay-

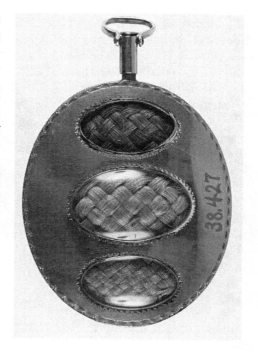

Braided locks of hair of Jonathan Bliss's three surviving sons (courtesy Walters Art Museum, Baltimore).

onets and swords, and buried their dead men and horses. It was all very recent. Yet this same person, Thomas Carleton, who established the capital of Fredericton where Arnold traded from a shop of some sort and planned a future house, had been quartermaster general under his brother Sir Guy Carleton, and fought in the battle on Lake Champlain in which Arnold's makeshift fleet was taken and burned. War heroes are romantic figures fighting for ideals who if they live on must turn realists.

The chapter and verse of the Navigation Laws for two hundred years until the mid-nineteenth century practically asked to be flouted. Only a British ship could trade with British colonies and it had to be built in the empire. Its captain and three quarters of its crew had to be British. Only certain commodities were allowed into Britain from the colonies. Most awkwardly, any goods to the colonies that came from outside the British Empire had to pass through Britain first. A factor in the scoffing of these laws was the corruption and venality of the customs collectors. According to Smith, Louis Delesdernier was in sympathy with smugglers though he made the occasional seizure. The Loyalists were committed to the Crown and a hierarchical society with an oligarchical, base but bending rules for business. Even Jonathan Sewell had acted to defend Boston smuggler John Hancock.

Of the players in the customs authorities during Arnold's years in New Brunswick there were two persons who represented different approaches. The first customs collector was William Wanton, a Loyalist from Rhode Island. His commission in 1784 was a means to recover financial losses. Smith encapsulates the attitude of this official who got very rich from 1784 to 1816:

Wanton's attitudes toward officeholding were probably inherited from his father, who as Rhode Island's governor proved remarkably tolerant of smugglers and had done his best to impede official investigations of the burning of the revenue cutter Gaspée in 1772.

> Wanton was a popular man in Saint John social circles and maintained an epicurean lifestyle on the emoluments of his office. Knowing that the province relied on trade, Wanton spent little effort suppressing smuggling. Instead he quietly collected his fees from shipmasters and merchants who were eager to pay them so long as he ignored their illicit trade. Wanton regarded his position as collector a sinecure.[20]

Contrarily, the Superintendent of Trade and Fisheries was a zealot who aimed to wipe out smuggling. George Leonard, originally of Plymouth, Massachusetts, and a childhood friend of Edward Winslow, served at the Battle of Lexington and was one of the gentleman raiders to defend Britain's interests on the American coast. He was one of the best-off of the Loyalists in Saint John, having received a large compensation, including a salary of his office and also with savings from being a New England merchant. Under Leonard a "surveyor and searcher" could enter warehouses and homes to uncover contraband. What this meant is evidenced by what Smith details of the operation of a vigilante type named Richard Batchelor, who became a surveyor at the tail end of when Arnold lived in Saint John. In August 1791, he beat a trader's watchdog to death and ordered his assistant to shoot its owner, William Comely, who sued. A few weeks later, Batchelor broke into a house on Campobello, looking for contraband goods from the U.S. Arnold must have heard that Batchelor was twitching for arrests—perhaps he was on the island when the break-in occurred. The next summer Batchelor seized a vessel for smuggling at the head of the Bay of Fundy. A crowd resisted. The hyperactivity for the law did not favor Batchelor who was, Dr. Smith relates, so unpopular, and had lawsuits against him, that he resigned and returned to England in 1793 due to ill health.

An early "Surveyor and Searcher of His Majesty's Customs for the Port of Saint John," Colin Campbell, testified about elite Loyalists as involved in contraband. Campbell testified that certain persons including magistrates were bringing in clandestine goods from the United States that they hid in in "'houses, warehouses, and other outhouses' on various islands throughout Passamaquoddy." The paths (sources and destinations) of the contraband were highly diverse. American wool could be going to Nova Scotia if there were a shortage there, while pirates could get rid of hot goods stolen from the Royal Navy.

Thus, Colin Campbell reported to New Brunswick's Supreme Court on October 19, 1795:

> That he hath good Cause to Suspect and doth Suspect that divers Goods and Merchandizes prohibited and uncustomed that is to say Wine Brandy and Tea illegally imported into this Province, are lying Concealed in the Houses or Outhouses of Thomas Jennings Blacksmith and Samuel Berry Mariner both of the City of Saint John and Province aforesaid.[21]

With similar initial wording, sounding Old Testament, Campbell made an affidavit the next summer about two individuals illegally importing brandy, tea and indigo:

> Colin Campbell Surveyor and Searcher of his Majestys Customs at St. John deposes That he had good Cause to suspect, and doth suspect, that divers Goods and Merchandizes prohibited and uncustomed Vir. Brandy Indigo and Tea illegally imported into this Province, are lying concealed in a Store belonging to Mr. James White at Portland Point, in the Parish of Portland, and in the House and Out House of Samuel B—at the same Place.[22]

The second document is countersigned by Judge George Ludlow, with whom Arnold was friends.

The local interests of particular towns and parishes, competition among business and political rivals, territorial jealousies, even conflicting ideals of honour and respectability exemplified in attitudes towards dueling all ensured a constant hum of bickering that at times broke out into violent antagonisms. The bench was not a unit but neither was it a fragmented collocation of individuals. Instead there were recognizable patterns of stable and shifting alliances.[23]

Ward Chipman, 1883, wood engraving on wove paper, Flewwelling Scrapbook No. 1 (courtesy New Brunswick Museum).

Smuggling's character naturally varies with political tides. The

Treaty of Paris had specified fishing rights and borders between British and U.S. territory, as well as allowing Loyalists to try to recover their American property. On both sides, though the borders were still imprecise, the governments were beginning to run down lawless traders and enforce duty payments.

Ronald Pesha in *Remembering Lubec* writes that smuggling deprived the federal treasury of monies to pay off $80 million in debt. Therefore, Alexander Hamilton established the Revenue Cutter Service in 1790 and petitioned Congress for armed vessels to enforce the law. The first ten tiller-steered schooners of only 51 tons displacement boasted ten muskets and twenty pistols. This was the only military surveillance, notes Pesha, until a navy was set up in 1794: "The federal government established duties for goods arriving in the new nation, but lack of enforcement paralyzed collectors and enabled the taking of contraband as spoils."[24]

Hopley Yeaton, "Father of the Coast Guard," a seaman who had served in the Revolutionary War, became the first commissioned officer of the Revenue Cutter Service. He settled his family in Eastport and then Lubec and moored his cutter at the dock. From Lubec (a mile across the Narrows from Campobello, it may have been named for the free trading medieval Baltic port), he chased and captured smugglers and collected the duties owed.

Overall, the New Brunswick economy did not benefit as much as one would think from the brisk coastal trade and ad hoc commerce. It was later that shipbuilding brought wealth to the province. Arnold lived in the province when David Owen, the grantee of Campobello island complained of his lawyers Bliss, Blowers, Chipman and Elias Hardy representing him in an eviction proceeding, that the devil was in the lawyers' fees.[25] Inhabitants were new refugees, and Britain's resources were targeting Napoleon and not bringing aid to stimulate the economy.

Elyseum:
A Potential for the Gentry

"Oh, how I long to see that place, though a strange land."
—Grandmother of Lord Leonard Tilley

Between the summer/fall of 1783 when the evacuation from New York occurred and Arnold's arrival two years later, the disbanded army was settling into their farms on the upper Saint John Valley while many of the elite of the New Brunswick immigrants were jockeying for government appointments. Many also waited for restitution; during the next five years, about 1800 cases were resolved, though rarely what was hoped for.

Assets were way down, but display was steady. Moreover, the overriding determination of prestige was where you lived in Saint John, down by the harbor, or a few hundred yards up, and whether you had means to keep servants, dress well, and show hospitality to guests at your commodious home, or whether you could barely feed your family and afford rum. Most everybody had debts to local merchants but only if the debts got a person thrown in jail were they an embarrassment. Upper and Lower Cove divided the clientele of the taverns along the same lines as real estate.

The land grants had been issued in a systematic way: for civilians a hundred acres each for heads of household and 50 more for each additional family member, and for military, grants from a hundred to 1,000 acres based on their rank. (The elite bought from each other and from those who needed cash more or wanted to move west beyond the province.) The block originally assigned to a regiment was 20 kilometers square. However, it is estimated that only four or five percent of the regiments were on their original lots at the turn of the century.[1] Government jobs were by appointment and plums on the provincial tree. Major John Coffin wrote to Edward Winslow in April 1784 asking if he could be a county clerk, saying "[Edward] Simonds is Judge of Probate and holds so many posts and has so much money that he's crazy half the time and the other [time] is vacant."[2]

Simmonds had his appointments before the mass of Loyalists arrived and Coffin knew Winslow would relish a jest.

These were sophisticates, people highly educated by the standards of the day, who knew the ways of society (often from mingling in England as well as in the colonies) and who were accustomed to the leisure to reflect. They did not forget the recent history they had participated in, and it's fascinating how much in common the exiles had of that history right back to the first public provocation of the revolution.

When the soldiers shot into the crowd that had been taunting them and throwing rocks in Boston on March 5, 1770, five persons were killed and six wounded. Thomas Hutchinson, acting governor and chief justice of the superior court of Massachusetts, declined to preside at a trial of the soldiers, and Jonathan Sewell, the attorney general refused to prosecute them. S.S. Blowers, who would become president of the council and chief justice of Nova Scotia, defended Captain Preston, along with John Adams and Josiah Quincy. It was Hutchinson who appointed Jonathan Bliss justice of the peace in Massachusetts in May 1770, but Bliss had not sought re-election to the general court and skedaddled for England early on.

It was a constellation of dispossessed patricians that moved the society forward with what political scientist Robert Michels articulated as the iron rule of oligarchy and its inevitable bureaucratization. Harvard College was a foremost spawning ground for the close-knit and conservative Upper Covers. Sewell Senior graduated in 1748, Bliss, Blowers and Upham in 1763, Winslow in 1765, and in 1770 Ward Chipman not only graduated but also delivered Harvard's commencement address. The 1763 class of three dozen also included the balloonist Tory Dr. John Jeffries, and Thomas Pickering, later the U.S. secretary of state. They believed in their formation: Chipman sent his one son all the way to, not England, but Harvard College, from New Brunswick, for what he deemed the best education.

Furthermore, Chipman articled with Sewell, came over from Britain on the same ship as Peggy and Benedict, and was deputy to Winslow. Upham's daughter married John Murray Bliss, and Blowers left his wealth to Bliss's second son. When Arnold had Bliss offered warm socks to his friends Ward Chipman and Judge Upham, after returning to England in 1791, he was offering them to Bliss's teammates. And Peggy had the society often of Mrs. Bliss, Mrs. Chipman, and Mrs. Sewell.

Ward Chipman described Benjamin Thompson to Edward Winslow as "one of the wonders really of the age."[3] His admiration shows openness to recognize a person not of his patrician circle. Thompson, born into a farming family in Woburn, Massachusetts, left with the British evacuation of Boston and became a European statesman and inventor nonpareil.

Thompson presented Winslow's and Chipman's memorials (requests for compensation from the British government) to Lord North on June 8, 1783, and wrote speedily back to his friends in New Brunswick, including Colonel Ludlow, that the task was done. The next day he wrote "My dear Chip" that he had done so and sent compliments to Colonel Ludlow among others.

The Arnolds dwelled in a twilight zone regarding their status in Saint John. Arnold was an outsider to the quintessential bastion of conservatives. Evidently he and Peggy fit in socially with the patrician crowd, as they had with friends in London, yet there was a glass wall. Arnold was an entrepreneur without the patina of advanced education, and this was more of a factor of his being an outsider than his traitorous history. Any fraternal inclination he had when a Mason in New Haven had been shed when he turned coat and was ousted from the lodge, and he never recovered it.

Peggy, however, with her acknowledged stand-out beauty and the fact that the Revolution did not shake the distinction of her Philadelphia family, expected to live *comme il faut* but her status was effectively inborn. If she strove it was for connections in the British power structure to help her sons to a reputable school and military berth. This contrasts with the other reigning beauty of the Maritimes, Fanny Wentworth, wife of John Wentworth, former governor of New Hampshire who superintended the King's Woods from Halifax. Fanny dressed in a gown of cloth of gold and wore lavish gems, as if royalty, for a ball to greet Prince William, who briefly was her lover while John trekked in the woods. Peggy, once Philadelphia's "it girl," devoted herself to hearth and home.

In short, a pretty, stylish and sociable woman like Peggy would fit in and make instant friends but a businessman like Arnold could never be one of the Upper Covers. He could employ them as attorneys, dine with them, and establish business ties with them but he was a rung down their ladder in every respect except the grants the Crown had given him.

Arnold circulated in his years in Saint John within this small coterie whose tolerance of him was essential to his progress. And as the huge wave of Loyalists came to Saint John by way of New York City, they appreciated business acumen even if most of them did not sully their hands with commerce. As in New Haven, Arnold ran a good store in Saint John, but the elite expected to be able to run up gentlemen's debts, and Arnold was a stickler.

Each player had a dramatic story of Chutes and Ladders with intriguing links to the Massachusetts or Middle Atlantic past and impressive rank in the post–Revolutionary period. All those with cameos here are a piece in the puzzle of Benedict.

The elite heads of household typically rose from one government post to another. If the first post was honorary, a man had to get by on his half-pay as retired soldiers, and investments in shipping or local stores—a gentleman could own a store but not do tradesmen-type work. It is amazing to picture Arnold among men he had associated with during the American Revolution in army expeditions, or the exodus from New York, or met in London, some as enemies, some as friends.

These were Loyalists who aimed to create a colonial world like what they would have had without the rebels. The motto on the Great Seal chosen for the province was *Spem Reduxit* ("Hope Restored"). They were setting themselves up as a ruling class, the landed gentry who would control government and remodel the colonial system so that the "people out of doors," the majority, would have no reason to complain.

Arnold was content to leave government to the gentlemen and go about his commerce after the revolution. His old friend Henry Knox, a staunch patriot, and for a time, U.S. secretary of war after an impressive service in the Continental Army, spoke for himself and many others when he turned all attention to his business projects—it was as though these men felt they had catching up to do. To Arnold's benefit, the Loyalist elite's postulation of a ruling class was inclusive of men of talent and enterprise—the wigs were coming off. Arnold had been befriended by the Court, he had significant money to invest, and he was socially acceptable. Moreover, his self-assertion was within the system. The polis saw early unrest between Upper Covers and Lower Covers, and the newcomers were disputing previous claims to land, but Arnold sidestepped both. He leased and bought land, built up businesses with ideas of expansion, and legally clamped down on those who foiled him by owing him money.

Many individuals transacted business with him that led to wrangling in court. But letters he exchanged with his friends in New Brunswick after he left let us in to his more nuanced interactions with the oligarchs. In his quest for wealth, Arnold was dealing with gentlemen originally from the 13 colonies that would have enduring importance in the history of early New Brunswick. Of those he employed to build his boats, wharves, and houses, sail in his vessels, buy his goods and smuggle for him, and the sea captains with whom he got on friendly terms, one can only conjecture, but much is known about the elite, who were known to everybody in that small pond. When the Arnolds made calls, invited people to their table, exchanged gossip and offered neighborly help, these were gentlefolk they circulated with.

Each man in the following set of cameos is presented in terms of the association with Benedict Arnold. Much of the information comes from the *Dictionary of Canadian Biography*, an invaluable and readable resource published by the University of Toronto and the Université Laval.

Isaac Allen (1739–1806)

Isaac Allen was the provincial judge who presided in a slander trial Arnold brought against a former business partner towards the end of his residence in New Brunswick. He was from Trenton, New Jersey, where he was a graduate of the College of New Jersey, now Princeton, and had practiced law, and where he raised a battalion called the New Jersey Volunteers. He was at the Siege of Savannah with them, under Colonel Campbell, and was with his battalion until Charleston was evacuated in 1782. Before New York was evacuated by the British, Sir Guy Carleton sent him to Nova Scotia to explore Nova Scotia for the settlement of Loyalists. The Allens lost their property in Trenton and on the Delaware River. Allen took his wife, mother, sister, four children and five servants to Nova Scotia. He was one of the first appointed to be a judge of the Supreme Court of New Brunswick, and because of the paid position he did not accept the one-half pay he was entitled to as a former officer. His family lived on their estate, Aucpac, a grant of 2,000 acres near Fredericton, where they also had a home, 868 George Street, described by Louis Quigley as follows: "The hand-split laths, hand-hewn beams, two fine large fireplaces in one huge chimney, interior molding and iron HL hinges tend to date this house as circa 1800."[4] It is thought that he used the high-ceilinged parlor for court proceedings.

Allen, age 61, declined a challenge to a duel by a plaintiff who thought Allen's legal opinion might lose him a slave. The plaintiff thereupon challenged one of the opposing counsels, Samuel Denny Street, and a duel ensued, killing neither. After that trial, which did not succeed in freedom for Nancy Morton, the enslaved woman who had sued for her freedom, Allen set free his own slaves.

Jonathan Bliss (1742–1822)

Jonathan Bliss was Arnold's closest friend, a lawyer for matters major and minor, the slander case and attempts to collect debts and reduce taxes owed New Brunswick, during and after the time Bliss lived in the province. Sometimes he represented Arnold with Ward Chipman in lawsuits, including the 1791 slander suit that Arnold won against Munson Hayt. Mrs. Bliss was a close friend of Peggy Arnold's.

Bliss grew up in Springfield, Massachusetts, in a family of property and status. At Harvard he was quite wild. In the *Canadian Encyclopedia of Biography*, Buckner states that young Bliss had a "disregard of Puritan mores," pointing out that he took part in a rumpus and was suspended for a term.[5] After graduating, Bliss studied law in the firm of Thomas Hutchinson. He first took sides as revolution fomented by refusing to sign the resolution in the Massachusetts legislature condemning the Townshend Acts; another who refused was his friend Samuel Blowers.

But Bliss wanted to stay clear of the conflict. In 1768 Bliss resigned from the general court of Massachusetts because he sympathized with grievances against the Crown but would not go to war over them. He arrived in New Brunswick with an appointment of attorney general and had patronage in Britain.

School ties would continue to be meaningful through his life. After the battle at Lexington, Bliss and his Harvard classmate S.S. Blowers, who had also studied in the office of Thomas Hutchinson, sailed for England. Bliss did not suffer as a refugee; he traveled to the Continent and moved in society's upper strata. Meanwhile his property was confiscated in Massachusetts. Blowers was offered in 1784 the post of attorney general in New Brunswick but turned it down and it was offered to Bliss.

Bliss arrived in Saint John on February 2, 1785, two months after the friend he had made in London, Benedict Arnold. According to Phillip Buckner, Bliss found that Governor Carleton mostly consulted the solicitor general, Ward Chipman, and the chief justice, George Duncan Ludlow. Despite being high in the class structure he became interested in farming. "Weary of this cursed celibacy"[6] at about 48, Bliss married Mary Worthington the daughter of the Honorable John Worthington, a Yale graduate and lawyer in Springfield, who was a close friend of Thomas Hutchinson. She was 20 years younger. They were a contented couple and had four sons. She was a friend of Peggy's but Peggy's friendship with several other ladies in New Brunswick, including Mrs. Sewell whom she met on the ship coming to the province, preceded it.

Bliss's wife and boys, he told Arnold, "make my Fire side happy

Portrait of a woman, 1775–1785, **watercolor on ivory miniature (courtesy Library and Archives Canada).**

even in this wretched country."[7] The marriage lasted ten years, as Mary died in 1799. Arnold, back in London, wrote Bliss a long condolence. He also suggested to Bliss that he was perplexed about the devastation of war.

The Blisses bought the Arnolds' home in Saint John after the Arnolds returned to London. Ever punctilious about sums owed him, with his establishment in Cavendish Square to maintain, Arnold, when back in London, pursued Bliss himself for a small debt.

Lest one think that Arnold was uniquely punctilious about money, in 1804–1805 Bliss prosecuted the high-toned Edward Winslow, for misuse of funds while he was "deputy paymaster of contingencies." Eventually Bliss became a judge. After his death his three surviving sons left New Brunswick.

Sampson Salter Blowers (1741–1842)

S.S. Blowers, when he sailed to Halifax in September 1783, told his friend and fellow lawyer Ward Chipman that "there is very little business in our way to be done here, and that but indifferently paid for, and there is no want of lawyers."[8] The next year he became attorney general of Nova Scotia, later chief justice. It was Blowers who notified his friends in New Brunswick that Arnold was en route from Halifax. The cases tried before Blowers were preponderantly for debt or smuggling. He was key in early steps for eliminating slavery from the Maritimes, because he demanded proof of its legality. By contrast, Judge Ludlow held that slavery was legal.

When nominated to the post of chief justice, a rival so antagonized 50-year-old Blowers that they stopped just short of a duel. Friends intervened, and an apology was made to Blowers.

Thomas Carleton (1735–1817)

Whether or not Arnold did more than tip his hat to Thomas Carleton, the two men would have been singularly aware of each other, as the Anglo-Irish Thomas was the younger brother of Arnold's nemesis at the Battle of Valcour on Lake Champlain and at Quebec City, Sir Guy Carleton. Thomas had been quartermaster at Quebec.

Arnold arrived less than two months after the first general election (October 1785), when the power of the local government still rested directly with Carleton and his council. When it was time for the general election, Carleton, who ran the show, had to take sides between the government men, patricians, and candidates put forth by the populist party of the tradesmen and small merchants. Violence erupted. A gang of Lower Covers broke the windows of a tavern in the Upper Cove, and wielded bricks. Troops were called in from Fort Howe by the governor. The Lower Cove opposition were arrested, fined and sentenced, and election gatherings were forbidden in taverns. Carleton now made sure the Bliss-Chipman ticket got the legislative posts. The Lower Covers called Upper Covers cunning New Englanders and observed that those from "the meridian of Boston" obtained the good situations. Edward Winslow termed Hardy's constituency vile blackguards.

Thomas emerged as the top administrator (Lieutenant-Governor) of New Brunswick at its founding. He sailed from England with his wife and his team, Jonathan Odell, Ward Chipman, George Ludlow and other appointed officers, in September 1784, and remained in that office, focusing on resettlement of the Loyalists, through the time Arnold was living in New Brunswick. Thomas was a strong proponent of government by gentlemen. He believed in a ruling class of Loyalists in a rural oligarchy, which became a reality in the early province. His chosen few had to be the legislature. That Thomas Carleton reversed the popular choices in the tumultuous election is remembered in Canada as an anomalous political act of oppression. The election occurred a month before Arnold arrived. Jonathan Bliss, George and Gabriel Ludlow, Jonathan Odell, Joshua Upham and Edward Winslow were all on the first council and several also in the first legislature, an overlap that embittered politically minded Lower Covers.

Thomas Carleton hated to write letters,[9] so Odell, the provincial secretary, wrote many of them. This makes the governor's personality hard to discern but certainly he was a robust individual, as he took a trip to visit his brother Guy in Quebec when Guy was ill—and snowshoed back. (Thomas had hoped to join his brother at Quebec but stayed in New Brunswick for 20 years.)

When the troops were recalled to England and the economy was in a decline that would last a generation until shipbuilding developed, with reluctance Carleton allowed the importation of commodities including lumber to New Brunswick.

Ward Chipman (1754–1824)

Known as "Chip" or "Chippy" to his old friends, Ward Chipman was Arnold's defense counsel in his slander suit against his former business partner. Chip went to Harvard and prepared for the law. When the British army evacuated Boston in March 1776, he went to live in Halifax. He also spent time in London and wrote to his friend Winslow that the Sewell

The Odell House in Fredericton with garden in foreground and slave ell at left (courtesy Provincial Archives of New Brunswick).

family was doing well (another example of the close-knit Loyalist gentry). Chip arrived in New Brunswick as an unsalaried solicitor general and recorder for the city of Saint John.

He had inadvertently when back in New York done something that dogged him to Canada, making him seem awfully snobbish. He had been among 55 signatories to a petition to maximize land grants to gentlemen, simply because they were privileged—5,000-acre grants each to be divided into tenant farms. This created consternation in New York and was recalled by Lower Covers who at election time shouted, "No votes for a fifty-fiver."

How naturally the elite put each other forward, without much acknowledging competition, comes through in a letter Chipman wrote Edward Winslow to alert him that the time was right for plucking the plums of government positions:

> I am authorized to say, in confidence, there is no doubt a separated Government at St. John's will be established, and that all your wishes will be carried into effect. Odell, who is with Sir Guy, whispers this to me for your information and desires a most friendly and affectionate remembrance to you.[10]

What a contrast to how scruffily Arnold got what he wanted after his soldier days were done. But then, he moved to Saint John to make money not to reestablish his privilege in a hierarchical society.

Chip lived comparatively high and was very popular for being convivial company. Before sailing to New Brunswick in the summer of 1784, when his income was limited to his half-pay of £91 a year, he bought a dressing box and among other toiletries 16 pounds of French hair powder. Chip had close ties within the establishment. He also married the daughter of the respected merchant William Hazen. He helped defend Judge Sewell's house in Cambridge, Massachusetts, when it was attacked by a mob.

The Chipmans and Blisses were friends the Arnolds saw socially, and Chip represented Arnold in court. He and Bliss in the first general election, held in 1785, two months before Arnold arrived, were on the "Upper Cover" ticket of six government candidates and elected as representatives, although they were handpicked by Carleton and not by the majority of votes.

Many prominent persons were trained in his law office, including Stephen and Jonathan Sewell (Stephen who was exasperated that Arnold was slandered), Robert Parker (the son of the Parkers who were the Arnolds' friends), and numerous others. In 1807, Chipman was appointed to the royal council. The Chipmans first lived in the house where Governor Carleton stayed but soon had a finer house built. When the Duke of Kent and the Prince of Wales came to Saint John, they stayed in this second house on Union Street at the north end of Prince William Street.

Chip sent his son, also named Ward Chipman, to an academy in Salem, Massachusetts, where the younger Chipman lived with his aunt and went on to Harvard College, like his father. Chip's law practice while busy did not generate enough money to bring in his son. He had a problem parallel to Arnold's as a merchant, that clients often did not pay their bills. but in 1808 when two New Brunswick judges, Joshua Upham and George Ludlow, died, Ward Chipman became a judge and his son took over the practice. Later Chipman became administrator of the colony and his son won approval for his part in the settlement of the New Brunswick–Maine boundary issue and was promoted to chief justice of the province.

According to Buckner's essay in the *Dictionary of Canadian Biography*, writing of Ward Jr., "his political and social philosophy was largely shaped by his parents' teachings."[11] This meant applying the death penalty for trivial offenses which at that time did not bring death sentences in Britain, upholding libel laws designed to stifle criticism of the government, controlling the selection of the Anglican ministers and keeping the new college (King's College, now the University of New Brunswick) under the control of Anglican churchmen.

Early in the Revolutionary War, Chip had gone to England and received a pension for his loss of property. He had then returned to New York to serve in the British forces and became a friend of Benjamin Thompson, later Count Rumford, the inventor, who at the tail-end of the war had a command on Long Island.

Chip married into another prestigious family. His wife was said to have been liked, sensible and "a perfect balance to Chipman's excessiveness."[12] With money from his sister Elizabeth, wife of a Salem, Massachusetts, merchant and the person to whom Ward had deeded all the family property at the outbreak of revolution, Chipman built a grist mill in Saint John. Nevertheless, he continued to have financial problems during the time Arnold was alive. He complained of finding himself in debt year to year, and business in New Brunswick ever decreasing.

The Chipmans entertained, since Chip was a bon vivant. When Arnold put all household goods up for sale when he was taking his family back to London in 1791, Chipman bought some of the furniture for 40 pounds, including a dozen chairs, one of which is in the New Brunswick Museum now. It took him four years to pay up, by giving the money to Jonathan Bliss, who represented the remaining interests Arnold had in the province. Arnold was not satisfied and demanded interest, which Chipman agreed to pay in March 1794. Barry K. Wilson observes that "This nasty exchange happened even as Arnold and Chipman continued to correspond as friends. Benedict Arnold was not one to concede ground generously, whether in war or in commerce."[13]

However, Chipman represented the Saint John Common Council in 1796 when it refused to relieve Arnold of taxes on harbor lands he didn't need, and which generated no income. Bliss asked Chipman to propose that, rather than charge Arnold for taxes in arrears, the city should simply take the land back. "But I have no hopes that the Common Council will listen to anything favorable to you," he wrote Arnold in mid–1796.[14] Bliss was on the mark. The Council insisted that Arnold pay back taxes, with a penalty. Chipman was Saint John's representative to the Council and he was smarting from Arnold's demand for interest after Chip had paid for the set of dining chairs he bought at auction. Alas, Benedict Arnold was a man of many parts but not a gentleman.

Nathan Frink (1757–1817)

Nathan Frink served under Arnold in the British forces. He had a lease from David Owen on Campobello, where he may have lent his house to Arnold, or at the least was a companion there. He crosses swords with

Nathan Frink's tombstone, Saint Stephen, NB (photo by author).

Owen particularly after Arnold's departure. He was living in Pomfret, Connecticut, when the Revolution began. His sister married Schuyler Putnam, the youngest son of Israel Putnam. It is said that Frink didn't make his views on separating from Britain known, because of his own marriage within the community. Nathan became King's Attorney and took on a post of deputy stamp-master of the north part of Windham County, and built an office in Pomfret. The townspeople did not, however, let him open it and he was expelled from town.

He then offered his services to the British commander in New York, serving under Arnold, as a captain in his King's American Legion.

According to the History of Windham County Connecticut, Frink's father went to his grave lamenting his loss of a son, and Lucy and the people of Pomfret were overwhelmed with grief and shame at this "mournful defection."[15]

After the American Legion disbanded, Frink left New York in 1783. It is known that he leased a house on Campobello from Squire David. This may have been the home Arnold occupied there but when the altercations of Frink and Owen heated up, Frink was in Saint Stephen, New Brunswick, where he died in 1817. David Owen told his brothers William and Arthur in Wales that building a trading was essential; shipping was his only hope. They turned a deaf ear and a few days after David wrote this to his brothers, a customs official came to Campobello to seize iron and ships' stores which Owen had illegally imported from Boston to finish his vessel. A violent altercation ensued. Owen finally got the ship off to Antigua in early 1791 but not before Nathan Frink was crown witness in an indictment against Owen for assault and battery on the customs official. (The indictment of each side against the other dragged on until it was dismissed in 1795.) The gravestones of Nathan and his wife Hester (1764–1817) are in the Loyalist Burial Ground, a picturesque small cemetery on the main road, shortly after Canadian Customs, coming from Calais, Maine.

Munson Hayt (or Hoyt)

Munsion Hayt, the Saint John business partner who famously insulted Arnold, calling him a thief and saying he had no reputation worth protecting, provoked however a court case, not a duel. In the partnership with Arnold his job was to mind the store yet he seems to have belonged to the elite. Governor Carleton appointed five commissioners to settle his provincial capital, Fredericton, three of whom had connections with Benedict— Colonel Winslow, Colonel Isaac Allen, and three lieutenants, among them Hayt. The surveys were completed, and lots assigned by these commissioners. Hayt recovered in financial terms from his tussles with Arnold.

George Ludlow (1734–1808)

Chief Justice Ludlow was a player in Arnold's legal life. When Arnold sued his former business partner for slander, Ludlow was the judge who awarded but a few shillings. Arnold would have wished more, but the idea that he was extremely disappointed, sometimes given as one reason he left the province, is unlikely. He won after all.

Not all the ascendant Loyalists had gone to Harvard. A few fled too young to go to college and several were from New York. The Ludlow brothers, George and his brother Gabriel, two years younger, were from a wealthy shipping and merchant family in Queens County, Long Island before the Revolution. In 1769, George was appointed a judge of the Supreme Court of New York. They were in the Tory stronghold of New York when the Revolution began, and their homes became a retreat for Tory gentlemen and officers. Receiving knowledge that a plan was adrift to abduct them and exchange them for rebel prisoners, the brothers sailed to England without their families in June 1783, also leaving behind their half-brother Daniel who became a successful businessman.

Both brothers received large tracts of land in Canada to make up for their property that had been confiscated in New York in 1779. They also received high colonial administrative offices. Gabriel became Saint John's mayor while George was appointed New Brunswick's chief justice; George and Gabriel's properties in New York were confiscated.

George married his cousin Francis, also of New York, and they had three children. When Carleton moved the provincial capital inland to Fredericton, Ludlow, the first chief justice went with him. He did not lay a claim for the loss of his estate on Long Island as he was well paid in his position, while his brother Gabriel, younger by two years, also on the governor's council, holding the office of mayor, stayed in Saint John and handled their commercial affairs. George acquired about 1500 acres north of Fredericton, and called his estate Springhill, after the residence of his former patron, Cadwallader Colden, in New York. Gabriel and his wife Ann were social leaders in Saint John, and Ann entertained the ladies at teas, scheduled from three to six o'clock so the slaves could have things cleared away before evening prayers at seven. The Mayor's coach met notables from abroad, who rode in stately fashion up the hill to be feted at the Gabriel Ludlows, whose house, made from of local woods such as bird's-eye maple and birch, was much admired. There he and his mild and amiable lady lived out their years.

A man of 50 when he arrived in the province, George was reactionary. In the first general provincial election of 1785, it was George who, presiding over the court, overturned the election results and proclaimed his patrician friends (including Bliss and Winslow) the winners. He also as justice charged two newspapermen with criminal activity (as members of the "rabble") and punished them by a jail sentence and fines.

Both Ludlows were slave holders. This was not unique among elite Loyalists but it seems to have put the Ludlows in a minority. Their slaves came with them from New York although they could have got them at the Saint John slave market.

George's opinions as chief justice were, writes C.M. Wallace, "more inconsistent, or more flexible, than might have been expected."[16] When Nancy Mozely, a black woman, was convicted of killing her husband with a pitchfork, Ludlow sentenced her only to a branding of the letter "M" on her left thumb, and then dismissed her.

Of great historic importance was the case of February 1800 that considered the legality of slavery in New Brunswick, where Ludlow supported the owners. Chipman wrote to his friend S.S. Bowers that

> Our Chief Justice is very strenuous in support of the master's rights as being founded on immemorial usages and customs in all parts of America even since its discovery. He contends that customs in all countries are the foundation of law, and from them the law acquires its force.[17]

Judge Upham supported Ludlow while the two other judges opposed, and the slave owner held on to his slave. This outcome sparked a controversy in the province until slavery was outlawed 1820.

When Gabriel died, George was inconsolable. He suffered a paralytic stroke a few weeks later and died later that year.

Jonathan Odell (1737–1818)

The secretary of the newly formed colony of New Brunswick was an Oxford-trained minister from New Jersey whose wife the beautiful Ann De Cou had been the intermediary between Arnold and Sir Henry Clinton during Arnold's first tentative steps towards treason. Odell and his family had a close personal relationship with Governor Carleton and his family. The Odells arrived in New Brunswick in November 1784 and Odell went 90 miles up the St. John River with Carleton a year before Arnold went up the frozen river, also to inspect the land. Odell helped choose the site of an old Acadian village as the provincial capital and established a large estate there and the next year founded the New Brunswick Academy. Arnold was keen on obtaining land in the settlement of the cultivated people like the Odells. The people of Burlington, New Jersey, a suburb of Philadelphia held clergyman Odell (also a physician) in such esteem that they didn't take him to task for being a Tory until he became really outrageous.

After graduating from Princeton (in 1754, while Aaron Burr, Sr., the father of the third vice-president of the United States, was president of the college), he studied medicine and served as an army doctor in the West Indies. Then he went to England, where he became a teacher and decided to become an Anglican priest. He returned to New Jersey and was given charge of two churches by the governor, Benjamin Franklin's son William.

He married Ann in 1770 and their only son was three when the Loyalists went to New Brunswick.

In Odell's opinion, the rights of the colonies were but murkily defined. He believed that the imperial taxation issue could be addressed by peaceful means, and personally abstained from politics. He was also a poet. In June 1776, one of his polemical poems caused a scandal when, for the occasion of George III's birthday, Odell wrote an ode that was sung by the British prisoners in Burlington, New Jersey. When a detachment of Hessians reached Burlington in December, the Reverend Odell was asked to communicate with them in French. The Hessians left, and rebel troops swooped in with orders to take Odell dead or alive.

Jonathan Odell. Watercolors miniature on ivory, 5.5 × 3.5 cm, circa 1770 (courtesy John Clarence Webster Canadiana Collection, New Brunswick Museum).

The people of Burlington would not give him up and he was hidden in a secret chamber of a Quaker woman's house. He fled to New York and his family followed two years later.

Odell made himself exceptionally useful in the British stronghold of New York. He was a chaplain of Pennsylvania Loyalists and later of the King's American Dragoons (led by Benedict Arnold). General Howe made Odell the superintendent of the printing office in Philadelphia, and when Benedict Arnold got in touch with Joseph Stansberg, a Philadelphia merchant, Stansberg in turn got in touch with Odell. Both these men wrote satiric poetry which may have been the connection between them; Odell's often virulent poetry appeared in newspapers in New York and Philadelphia.

Henry Clinton and his aide John André being naturally incredulous that Arnold was betraying the rebel cause, the communications with him were in code. Odell coded and decoded the messages in his house in Wall Street. When Odell went to England it was with Governor Carleton. He met the King and is said to have hoped to be made a provincial bishop. He received the post of the governor's secretary and clerk of the council which Winslow had wished for, but the men stayed friends.

Odell became the owner of one of the largest properties in Fredericton, which twenty years after it was established in February 1795 still had no roads, just the water route, and only 120 houses. Alfred C. Bailey, notes that "the frequency of balls and gregorys enlivened the social life of the place, the former marking events for which Odell wrote suitable songs and odes."[18]

When 1500 African Americans in the Maritimes rallied to leave for Sierra Leone, Odell was antagonistic about losing them. He spread a rumor that the leader/activist Thomas Peters would sell them in Africa. It was hard to keep the superiority of the elite without a supply of cheap labor.

David Owen (1754–1829)

David Owen was the person most like Arnold in temperament. He was in the courts as much as Arnold too and complained once that the devil was in the lawyers' fees.

Owen, the grantee of Campobello Island, arrived in New Brunswick in the fall of 1787 at the mature age of 33. Known as Squire Owen, David was the nephew of the First Principal Proprietary of Campobello Island, who gained the island's ownership, but had soon left to return to the Royal Navy so that there was a serious issue of whether the Owens were non-compliant with the terms of the grant. Certainly, local settlers on the island believed that they had cultivated and improved the land and that the Owens had forfeited their ownership. (Royal grants required a certain number of people, acres cleared, livestock and so forth.) Arnold was one of the persons who encouraged David Owen to come to New Brunswick, to take up teaching at the university then being discussed, either to flatter the grantee, because this could raise Arnold's own social position; or merely because Arnold liked to make things happen; Benedict himself never held any office or civilian position unless one counts belonging to the Masons in New Haven. David Owen was a senior fellow at Trinity College, Cambridge who had already made a sea voyage as far as the Cape of Good Hope but when he decided to defend the royal grant was at a crossroads. He had taken Deacon's orders in the Church but declined to be ordained because he objected to subscribing to the 39 Articles of the Anglican Church. What Arnold found on Owen's island is discussed in the Campobello chapter. Both Arnold and Owen were domineering, headstrong, and indifferent to diplomacy, so their hassles in New Brunswick ran quite parallel.

Robert Parker (1750–1823)

The Parkers, Robert and Jane (Hatch), were mentioned by Arnold after he left New Brunswick as a couple, good friends of himself and Peggy.

He saw Parker on the Isle of Wight in the fall of 1792, on leave from his Maritime office until spring, and noted to Bliss that Parker was "not in raptures" at returning to Saint John.

Parker, from Boston, was described in an early nineteenth-century Fredericton newspaper piece as, along with the Odells and others, "our monied people." Parker was a customs and commissary official, attorney and judge of the Court of Vice-Admiralty, a position his son Neville had after him. There is extant a bread-and-butter letter from him to friends in St. Andrews saying what a warm, wonderful time they had enjoyed one holiday.

James Putnam (1725–1789)

There are but a few degrees of separation to President John Adams from one of the two individuals Arnold hired to take care of his affairs when he returned to England

In 1755, 1756 and 1757, John Adams studied in Worcester, Massachusetts, under an attorney named James Putnam, Harvard Class of 1746, hailed by contemporaries as one of the best lawyers of the colonies, who became Attorney General of Massachusetts. Jonathan Sewall may have officiated at Putnam's marriage to Elizabeth Chandler (Sewall was changed to Sewell when he fled to London). When the war was starting, Adams refused to settle in Worcester to gain a foothold for the rebels, because he said the people he knew there were so kind to him. He declared they were worthy people and able office holders: "I envied not their felicity, and had no desire to set myself in opposition to them, especially to Mr. Putnam, who had married a beautiful daughter [Elizabeth Chandler] of that family and had treated me with civility and kindness."[19] Later the Putnams fled and their property was seized. He was made a member of the first Council and judge of the Supreme Court in New Brunswick.

Beverley Robinson (1722–1792)

The first generation of Loyalists made the fatal decision to side with the Crown and the next generation followed adamantly in the footsteps of their fathers. This point is made over and again by Canadian historians of the period.

The Beverley Robinson who figured in Arnold's treason was an unusually rich landowner in the Hudson area of New York State. A childhood friend of George Washington, he became the proprietor of 60,000 acres by marriage to his cousin Susanna Philipse, and moved from Virginia to New York. Susanna bore ten children and her dowry was a quarter of the Philipse Manor.

In May 1779, Robinson wrote to Arnold urging him to defect to the British. Robinson stressed that the French role in the revolution was increasing, which was something enraging to Arnold.

Arnold occupied Robinson's English-style rustic house, just across and south of West Point, when he assumed the command of the New York Highlands (West Point). Robinson accompanied Major André to Dobbs Ferry but the expected reconnoiter with Arnold did not occur. The next morning, September 25, the Arnolds were about to welcome George Washington and the Marquis de Lafayette to breakfast at the house when Arnold received the message that André had been captured and a warning that his treason was disclosed. Arnold fled from the Robinson house to a boat waiting to ferry him to West Point but ordered the crew to take him to the British ship instead.

After fleeing his home, Robinson created and personally led the Loyal American Regiment. He was evacuated to London where he remained. A high-placed friend wrote a letter to take to the British Secretary of State praising him as a "gentleman of distinguished probity and worth, whose possessions in this country were very large."[20] Of Beverley's five sons, the youngest was sent to England when the revolution began while four of them served in the Loyal American Regiment that the father raised and led, the eldest being Beverley Robinson born 1754. This regiment included many of the 146 tenant farmers on Robinson's land as well as African slaves who labored in the extensive Robinson estate. This regiment fought in the campaign under Benedict Arnold in the spring of 1781 and the raid on New London in September.

Beverley Robinson the younger had been a student of law at Columbia University when the war began. This Robinson had a dramatic role in removing the Royal Arms from Trinity Church in New York City, which he smuggled into Halifax, Nova Scotia. The Royal Arms had already been rescued by Edward Winslow from the State House at the evacuation of Boston in 1776. Now Winslow sent them from Halifax to Chipman in Saint John, where they hang in Trinity Church.

Lieutenant Robinson (the younger Beverley) built a large house two miles above Fredericton. He and his wife had ten children. He was clerk of New Brunswick's Supreme Court and was appointed a member of Carleton's council in 1791, which he attended for 26 years. When in 1791 Robinson was given command of the King's New Brunswick Regiment, his father was given the honorific of Colonel in Chief but died soon after.

Jonathan Sewell (1766–1838) and Stephen Sewell (1770–1832)

First of all, the Tory Sewalls became the Sewells when they sought refuge in England. Jonathan Sewell returned from exile to North America in the same ship with the Arnolds, arriving in Saint John in July 1787 to start a new life. This fact suggests that Arnold went ahead on a different ship, but it is unclear. In any event, the Sewells were well acquainted with the Arnolds and not hostile to him. Jonathan, being fair-minded, was dubious that the wreck of Arnold's brig when he arrived in New Brunswick was an act of villainy as Arnold suspected. Four years later he was irate that Benedict was accused of arson to trick the insurance company.

Jonathan Sewell had a lifelong friendship with John Adams, the third president of the United States. He is known as Jonathan Sewell Senior or II. Before they split over politics Sewall stated that in the future "when New England shall have risen to its intended grandeur"[21] Adams would be remembered among the literati as Cicero was remembered of the Romans.

The story was told by Adams of how Sewell and his wife-to-be Esther Quincy broke into the room where Adams was about to propose to Esther's sister, paving the way for Abigail, of course and the great Federalist romance. Another sister, Dorothy Quincy, became the wife of John Hancock.

Sewell was the last British attorney general of Massachusetts. Governor Bernard wished Adams to take the office of advocate general to the Court of Admiralty and Sewall carried out this purpose by calling on Adams on Brattle Street in Cambridge and announcing he had come to dine. This was 1768, a juncture John Adams would remember as being "at Antipodes in Politicks" with Sewell though their esteem for each other never abated and the warmth of friendship between them did not cool. Writing of this event Adams noted that the position was attractive because "lucrative in itself, and a sure introduction to the most profitable Business in the Province," plus it was "a first Step in the Ladder of Royal Favour and promotion."[22] This remark regarding what Adams declined adumbrates how starting up the ladder of advancement in the hierarchy of provincial appointments would be the sine qua non of the Upper Cove elite.

John Adams mistakenly for years thought that the senior Sewell was the author of the tract that Adams disputed under the pen-name Novanglus. Sewell bought a house at 149 Brattle Street from a distiller, Mr. Lechmere, the original owner. There Jonathan and Esther Sewell had lived three years when a mob of 50 men and boys came to wreck it. They got as far as breaking the windows when Esther offered them the contents of the wine cellar if they would disperse.

The next year, 1775, the Sewells departed Boston, never to return. The revolutionaries confiscated the house and the commander of the Hessian mercenaries, Baron Riedesel, and his wife the Baroness occupied 149 Brattle from 1777 to 1778. Jonathan Jr. was eight when the frightening scene occurred at the Sewall home. This section of Brattle Street became known as Tory Row.

It is often noted that Arnold received some scorn in London. However, a letter from John to Abigail puts his trials as a colonist in perspective of the plight and mood of the Loyalists overall. "By the Relation of Mr. Dana, Mr. Wrixon, and Mr. Temple. Mr. Hutchinson, Mr. Sewall, and their Associates are in great Disgrace in England. Persons are ashamed to be seen to speak to them. They look dejected and sunk."[23]

The Sewells drew three lots in Saint John but decided to build nearer to the harbor, on the southeast corner of Duke and Ludlow Streets. A sign on the front of the Georgian style house called the Sewell house identifies it as the oldest wooden structure standing in the city, built in 1791.

Jonathan Sewell, Jr. (1766–1839), arrived with Bliss in April 1785 and became a student of Ward Chipman. (Like his father this Jonathan Sewell changed his name from "Sewall" to "Sewell" when they went to England.) He married the daughter of Benedict's friend William Smith. After being admitted to the Bar of New Brunswick Jonathan Sewell, Jr., left for Quebec where he became solicitor-general.

Stephen Sewell was one of Arnold's lawyers. Writing to his brother Jack in September 1790, he characterized Benedict outstandingly. Sewell remarked that his "'notions of propriety ... often degenerates into pride and folly' such as when he insisted he was owed additional interest on debts even after a court awarded him a certain amount." Sewell said, curiously, that Arnold was often "disgusted at women, which may proceed from his bashfulness." Nevertheless, he averred that Benedict Arnold

> is modest, true to his own interest but I think not further than is perfectly right and proper.... He is by no means credulous, much the reverse, and in separating probability from improbability, his understanding is very good. He aims to have everything about him like a gentleman.[24]

Joshua Upham (1741–1808)

Ann Gorman Condon, Canadian historian, singled out Judge Upham (originally of Brookfield, Massachusetts) as a classic example of the Massachusetts Tory elite yet ready to question government policy. He and Arnold had mutual respect. As revolution fomented, Upham supported non-consumption and non-importation measures while, on the other hand, he signed addresses of homage to Governor Hutchinson and General Thomas Gage. At the end of the war he was a major in the King's American Dragoons and aide to Sir Guy Carleton. In 1782 his wife died, leaving him with five children. In the fall of 1783 he joined his patron Carleton in London, hoping to get a government position and improve his finances.

He was appointed a judge of the Supreme Court of New Brunswick and a member of the governing council. When slavery became a controversial issue in the new province, he took a regressive position in a court case involving an enslaved woman, Nancy Morton. He could have defended her freedom but instead voted with Mayor Ludlow to uphold the slaveowner's right to his property. During the time Arnold was in the province Upham was a widower; in 1792 he remarried and had two more children.

One of Upham's sons, Charles Wentworth Upham, started out as an apothecary assistant, worked on a farm in Nova Scotia and immigrated to the U.S. in 1816. He graduated from Harvard with a degree in theology, became a Unitarian minister in Salem, went into politics and was a U.S. congressman from 1853 to 1855 elected as a Whig. It is notable that Benedict Arnold too learned a lot as apothecary assistant; this seems to have been a prime apprenticeship of the era. Like many of his cohorts, Upham suffered years of painful rheumatism. Proving he had Arnold's friendship is correspondence from London to Saint John in which Arnold pressed leggings on Bliss for the judge.

In the salient family networking of the Bostonian Loyalists, Judge Upham's daughter Sarah married John Murray Bliss, son of Daniel Bliss, Harvard 1760, who became solicitor general of New Brunswick, and Judge Upham left his money to the son in law.

Edward Winslow (1746–1815)

"Ned" Winslow grew up in a mansion overlooking Plymouth Rock. He was a direct descendant of the Edward Winslow who arrived on the Mayflower, and at 23 he delivered the public address on the 150th anniversary of the landing of Plymouth Colony.

He fought with the British regulars at the Battle of Lexington and continued to have army posts throughout the war. He was scathingly critical of the timidity of the British war policy and said of Sir Henry Clinton that "The stupor which seemd to seize his Excy, & which nothing short of a Supernatural event can rouse him from—effectively prevented any military enterprise."[25]

He had a large family to care for. At the point when the issue of dividing New Brunswick and Nova Scotia was raised, he was secretary to Brigadier General Fox in Nova Scotia. They had explored the upper reaches of the Saint John River and then met the provincial army who disembarked in June 1784. Fox established 3,000 soldiers and their families up river and reserved prime lands for Winslow.

Winslow had envisioned a future when the best of American society, deprived of their West Indian trade, would move to join him and the Loyalist elite already established in the north. The new Loyalist province "shall be the most Gentlemanlike one on earth," he said.[26] A building built to mark Canada's centennial has his prophecy engraved in bronze on its façade. His letters give valuable aperçus of the times.

Partition came about when various people came on board. Winslow's friends George Ludlow and Ward Chipman got him an appointment as secretary to the commander in chief of British forces in Halifax, Henry Edward Fox with whom Winslow became good friends. Winslow had his witty and outspoken friend Chip's advice to "humor the rage of public economy, be a man of business, indulge your convivial penchant with caution."[27] But Fox left the Maritimes and Winslow lacked a patron in London to secure a high post in New Brunswick. Only after Arnold's departure did Edward Winslow get an appointment to the Supreme Court. When he interacted with Arnold he was beset with money problems—"Blast Poverty—'tis a devil incarnate,"[28] Winslow vented to Benjamin Marston in 1786, continuing:

> it's a damn shame, after recommending integrity and benevolence that a man should be prevented from exercising those virtues by the stinginess of fortune. And it is worse still that Industry cannot secure a man from starving. I'll persevere however although some late disappointments having given my heart a severe fit of the Gout.

He was concentrating his energies on farming: "our Gentlemen have all become potato farmers—& our Shoemakers are preparing to Legislate," he observed.[29] He was supporting a wife, Mary Symonds Winslow and their 14 children, two sisters and three household slaves.

If the Upper Covers were a sedate, conservative lot, Edward Winslow comes through in his correspondence as irrepressible and with a wicked sense of humor. He joked that the legislature was composed of people who three years before wouldn't have known the law from a creampuff, and when he waxed about his idea to have a fine governor's mansion with, if possible a playhouse, it was the dream of someone poor.

12

The Benefit of Friendships

"Very small things are often really larger than the large
things."—Anne Tyler interviewed by Marguerite
Michaels, *New York Times*, May 8, 1977

Widowed, my grandfather, an investment banker in New York, remarried (my grandmother) when his children were nearly grown. He commuted by train to the city to his job and sent four of his sons to Cornell, and one to Yale. Summers he packed them off to a wholesome sportive holiday in Nova Scotia. The boys stayed in a rustic Victorian-style boarding house; a photograph shows them dressed in white shirts, trousers, and bucks, hair slicked back, with gleaming smiles. From my grandfather's viewpoint unexpectedly, two sons proposed to two of the innkeeper's lovely daughters. These were my aunts who grew up in an *Anne of Green Gables* world (the elder was an itinerant teacher in one-room schoolhouses) that they shared with the extended family.

The Emerson brothers were close: they laughed loudly and clapped each other on the back and shared experiences when together. They gave handshakes that were like hugs, but also were highly competitive. Family tournaments fostered competition and individualism, while at the same time all five observed the rules of etiquette of their cast. One of the brothers argued cases at the U.S. Supreme Court. I think his proper elocution had to do with his never losing a case there: Isn't the law governed by etiquette? The only time any of my five uncles was outspoken was when they spoke out for a belief (or, Thomas Emerson, for a client) and that air of crispness of the Emerson boys caused others to attend to what they said. My grandmother could never have afforded to send her daughter to dancing school with the posh crowd in Englewood, New Jersey, but a stepbrother who considered social dancing necessary for a well-bred girl paid for it.

A preserve of cultivated and exclusive Loyalists had connections in London or Boston that other refugees from the 13 colonies couldn't conceive of having. Typically, a member of the Loyalist elite in New Brunswick had trained as a lawyer but beyond the trade he learned diplomacy and not to offend others of rank. Benedict lived in that stratified past, but he was reported as being uninterested in the social graces (except when wooing). The consummate gentleman was not Benedict at any phase of his life. Queen Charlotte gave Peggy £500 a year for her good manners but, then, she was the wife.

Manners made even some of the rituals of war, such as the duel and the surrender polite in the eighteenth century. That Benedict did not have gallant manners separated him from the elite Loyalists. As a colonial he had neither the bonhomie of Henry Knox or the elegance of George Washington. A single anecdote, which follows suggests how important it was not to appear a bumpkin. In the fall of 1777, General Gates had invited General Burgoyne and two other officers to dine. The table was only two planks laid across two empty beer barrels. The company had four plates and there was no tablecloth. They dined on a ham, a goose, some beef and some boiled mutton, and drank watered rum. The two glasses were for Gates and Burgoyne; the rest drank from basins. After dinner Horatio asked John to offer the first toast. Burgoyne toasted to General Washington and Gates to the King.

The centrality of cordiality to the Upper Covers (and soon the Fredericton elite) reduced by circumstances to little means, cannot be overestimated. The Loyalists suffered humiliation as the losers, to which for the elite was added their shame for being in tight straits. The ties of trust with other in their communities were broken. Emotional repair of their sentimental relationships with other men was meaningful to them.

Men of my father's generation, from the U.S. and Canada, had served in the Allied force in a long, terrible war. My father was rescued from the wreck of a ship torpedoed by the Japanese, and one of the uncles was part of the troops that landed in Normandy on D-Day. Like the Loyalists these veterans did what they could in their lives to create the pastoral idyll they longed for, having spent their youths in war. And a significant expression of this ambition was revealed in how their emotional attachments had practicality always mixed in. The prism from which to see the Loyalist heads of household, with whom Arnold had friendships and business dealings in the Maritimes is that community of my uncles who summered in Nova Scotia. As I read Arnold's letters to his best friend from his six years in Saint John it is like seeing a seascape of the Emerson boys. There are the bands of color of warm expressions of friendship banded by neutrals of "Don't forget to get a good price for the farm." It is not ingenuous but rather, the way for the Loyalists' friendship was based on mutual benefit in a new homeland.

The gentry were a remarkable club chasing the good life. They were proud if dispossessed, identified with one another, and had a vision of themselves as the refined squirearchy in a J.S. Copley painting. If they expected favors of provincial officialdom from the Crown, they believed they had a special role to continue the best of the colonial tradition (which included religious tolerance).

Arnold had committed an act of flaring treason; then again, Loyalists were all considered traitors by the revolutionary orthodoxy, after the Declaration of Independence. They would not condemn him but by the same token, by his dishonorable act and his mercantile occupation he could not be on their level. Take a simple letter from Blowers in Halifax to "Chip" in New Brunswick, at the time of Arnold's arrival there, to see how the Loyalist elite clung together. It is caring of the friend's practical matters, it offers something, and it goes further, inquiring in the spirit of the friend:

> And now, my dear Chip, how are you settled? Have you comfortable lodgings, and are you contented? Do you find business enough? How do you like your Province and its prospects? Can I be of service to it or you here?

Blowers enlarged the circle of his inquiring but with a little wryness when he continued with compliments to Jonathan Odell—"the Chief Justice and his brethren." As if doffing his hat, he ended on a merry note: "Write me often, and believe me always truly yours. The ladies, with me, desire compliments."[1]

Arnold as a self-made merchant did not have the collegiate inclination of the Loyalist elite yet retained the distinction of his military rank and Peggy's family. Her friendships within the Loyalist elite were sincere. She liked to ride on a horse with her friends around Saint John. After departing from Saint John, she and Benedict both expressed feelings of missing their friends there.

Returning to Nova Scotian ties of my family, in June my father would dig three feet down for each tomato plant in the rocky soil and my mother and aunts boasted that they never bought a plant in their lives—every herb, shrub and seed had the provenance of somebody else's garden along the Shore Road. But a family feud arose that showed how serious a matter the gardening, and property could be.

Two of the aunts lived in handsome houses on the cliffs high over the Bay of Fundy. One summer, the older sister discovered that one of her prize rosebushes was missing from her garden. She believed she located it down the hill in the garden of her sister. At least this is what she thought. Both sisters had flower gardens of such abundance they had to endeavor to layer the plants in plots on the knolls and hill so that they could be in view. The younger sister denied the implication of theft and her husband backed her up in a stand-off with his brother. And, so it went, the kind of discord only time heals, and a proof of the seriousness of a Maritime garden.

An appreciative and insightful article appeared in *The Maritime Advocate and Busy East* of February 1956, in which J. Russell Harper wrote of the pride the Loyalist elite took in their gardens:

> A garden for them was not just a plot of ground surrounding the house in a new land, but stood as an outward symbol of two things: it was that something which made a house into a home, and the mark which spelled quality. The flower and vegetable garden together with the orchard was a part of every English gentleman's estate. There were magnificent early gardens in New England, and the Loyalists brought with them a deep-seated love of gardens and gardening.[2]

Arnold moved so much and was always in such haste that the Arnolds did not seem to "put in roots." Yet he must have known herbs and seeds from having had an apothecary shop/general store, and his name appears in various communications of the Loyalists about procuring seed.

The first priority of the Loyalist garden was the orchard. Cider had to be smuggled in from New England to meet the needs, and cider from established orchards in Nova Scotia was expensive. Gentlemen raised apple trees to press cider. Rum and spruce beer were cheap and plentiful but in gentlemen's houses tastes ran to the more costly and scarcer wine and cider. One Loyalist bewailed the fact that only a hundred gallons of cider were available for his winter's supply since an additional forty gallons on which he had counted had been lost in transit.

To start his orchard, Ward Chipman sent to Windsor, Nova Scotia, for apple cuttings which he planted around his house in Saint John. The supplier, Joseph Gray, sent with the cuttings detailed instructions for planting them in a nursery at intervals of one yard for the first three years and then transplanting them into the orchard at 33-feet intervals. He put in for free some twigs of honeysuckle "that blows all summer" for planting around the house and for distribution among his friends.

Chipman, whose house was in the middle of Saint John, engaged its first gardener in the spring of 1788. The gardener wrote out a list of seeds of vegetables and herbs and suggestions for "as many flower seeds as your honor may please." These were to be found, Chipman learned, only at Benedict Arnold's store. Incredibly, this leads us to the rare informal comment by an Upper Cover about Arnold. Only Arnold's general store stocked flower seeds—available "to be had but English at a monstrous price at Arnolds store and so old that they cannot be depended upon." Chipman was sending Winslow (April 8, 1788) "some early Cluster Cucumber seed so called which I get from Arnold, these I suppose age, at least a few beans of it will not hurt."

Then Chipman sent to Newburyport, Massachusetts. Two pounds four pence brought him vegetable seeds for peas, beans, asparagus, parsley, cucumbers, lettuce, and turnips and herbs—balm, summer savory, sage, and sweet marjoram. He had sent up the river to his friend Edward Winslow with John Hazen a supply of early charter cucumber seeds that he bought from Arnold which he thought were still fertile, and some other seed that the commander at Fort Howe had given him the year before: "I think you can depend on them." Now he promised half his supply from Newburyport to Winslow.

The quantities being discussed were so small by contrast to what the economy of sales has become today. Men and women drank from dainty teacups, Abigail Adams longed for just a few needles when John went to Philadelphia, and even the three-story general store from which Benedict sold goods, fronting on Prince William Street, was, by modern standards, a diminutive 20 by 40 feet.

As to Winslow he was as avid a gardener as Chipman. He and his wife were from New York but their enthusiasm for horticulture began in Annapolis, Nova Scotia, where they grew fruits and vegetables, which they stored in a root house. The Winslows had "a prodigious fine green-house" a feature noted when they advertised the house for sale (Winslow arrived shortly before Arnold did in Saint John, to take up his government duties). When the Winslows moved to their estate, called Kingsclear, near Fredericton, Edward sent to Boston to his cousin for a new gardener. Isaac Winslow wrote him that both men he had engaged for the job ended up drinking themselves silly and not getting on the vessel. However, Isaac sent a box of varied seeds a gardener had prepared to which he added some "scarlet bean convolvus." He also promised the next year to buy some curious flowers, saying "there are various sorts which were unknown before the Revolution at least to me."

Among the friends Winslow called on for help were the postmaster at Quebec, who sent him hardwood cuttings for grafting in March 1790; another bundle was for Governor Carleton. Mr. Harper states:

> Some accompanying packets of seeds Mr. Joseph Chew of Montreal had collected from various gentlemen in England on a trip the previous year. As an afterthought, Finlay included a few grains of Indian corn which had come all the way from Alexandria, Egypt, and some of the finest watermelon seeds from New York.

Few of the Loyalist elite did not import gardeners from Boston. Colonel John Murray, a determined man of 6'3" from Rutland, Massachusetts, hired soldiers from Fort Howe to cultivate his garden. Arnold's best friend Jonathan Bliss named his son, John Murray Bliss, after the Colonel, his mother's father. The gardens were interconnected like the people.

That is all that is heard of Arnold's store and seeds but there is an anecdote that further witnesses the crosshatching of the elite and their gardens. Mary Tompkins Odell, the wife of Jonathan Odell who was a go-between for Arnold's treasonous letters, sent "Chip" some spinach and asparagus seeds, as well as some melon seeds for a Mr. Botsford, likely Amos Botsford, Yale Class of 1763, an attorney from New Haven who married a young widow in Saint John, the sister of Mrs. Chipman. Botsford was elected as a representative to the provincial legislature in its first election, November 1785, and chosen speaker at its first session. His two youngest sons returned to Connecticut for schooling.

In general, the Loyalists in Saint John were obliged to be practical and cultivated abundant fruit trees of all kinds in the arable interstices of the city. Chip's sister sent him some flowers from the Cape of Good Hope some years later, but flowers were but decorative edges of his vegetable garden. Chip gardened primarily as a business proposition and even exported potatoes to Boston.

The frontier town had a population that wanted the finer things. Witnessing that was the first dramatic performance in the province on March 28, 1789. That the doors were opened at 5:30 in the evening and the play began at 6:30 are indications that entertainment life was not just like at home in Boston or New York. This was unfashionably early for theater going but this was in a town with poor lighting, and, in early spring, icy streets. I am reminded of when my family was moving from New York City to Princeton and Datus Smith, the head of the Princeton University Press, told me to be ready for invitations to drinks at four in the afternoon and dinner at six. He thought it would take getting used to.

The Arnolds would have appreciated evenings of theater. Samuel Adams noted that when General Arnold governed Philadelphia, "in humble imitation of the British Army" the American officers were performing on stage, and "'one of Superior Rank' countenanced with his Presence." Arnold was courting Peggy and would have enjoyed diversions the likes of which Congress called depraved and legislated against. (Benjamin Rush made his son at Princeton sign an oath he would never go to the theater again.)

The social historian Ann Gorman Condon set out to penetrate the personal bonds of Loyalists, the mindset of the "haves" who were thrust on New Brunswick's shores. She published "the first fruits" of her research in collections of papers at the New Brunswick Museum (Saint John) and the Public Archives of Nova Scotia in Halifax, choosing the love letters of three couples whom the Arnolds knew socially—the Winslows, Robinsons, and Blisses.[3]

First of all, the parents who were refugees may have seen themselves as from refined background, but they would rather be poor and shabby and have lots of children. Benedict had eight children by two wives, the

Winslows had eight children, the Robinsons eleven and, while Jonathan Bliss had but four, he married in late middle age and his wife died while having their fifth child. (He loved his wife Mary very much and did not remarry.)

The couples who figure in the letters that are cited by Professor Condon were all in the social circle of Benedict and Peggy, and Colonel Beverley Robinson who had lived on the Hudson at The Highlands, is a figure in Arnold's escape from West Point. The quotations in the following consideration of conjugal intimacy of the Loyalists are from her article.

The Winslow household had Edward's parents and two sisters as well as the many children. He wrote Mary ebulliently from Halifax:

> what do I care whether it's the fashion for men to write long letters to their wives or no.... In matters where my own feelings are concerned I will not be shackled by any of the rules which bind the generality of mankind.... I cannot enjoy a pleasure equal to that of writing to you.

He went on (in this September 20, 1784, letter, now in the Winslow Papers) to mock the female fashions he observed in Halifax:

> Immensity of False-Tops, False Curls, monstrous Caps, Grease, Filth of various kinds, Jewels, painted paper and trinkets, hide and deform heads of Hair that in their natural state are really beautiful. Rouge & other dirt cover cheeks and faces that without would be tolerable, whilst the unfortunate neck and breasts remain open to the inclemency of the weather & the view of the world.

Edward lauded Mary for "from 16 years old to the present time" disregarding fashion: "you have only endeavored by uniform cleanliness to make yourself desirable in my eyes." Professor Condon points out that Winslow closed saying he hoped she would be able to enter the world of fashion and elegance in the future again.

Undoubtedly as disjointed as Mrs. Bliss or Mrs. Arnold might feel transported to the frontier, Mary Winslow had servants. Edward wrote Mary while in Halifax and inquired about two indentured servants or slaves: "I am vastly glad that you are satisfied with Magee and his wife and I hope they will continue to please you."[4]

Beverley and Nancy Robinson lived in Fredericton on a big farm. Condon cites letters that show Beverley chastising his wife but being romantic about her. First, in 1799, he gave her elaborate instructions on the proper way to cool down and curry horses, and then proceeded to remind her to wrap his doughnuts securely so they will remain moist. The last batch were so dry he could not eat them! Yet Beverley wrote to Nancy in January 1800 that she was "dearer to me now than when I received her with the rapture of a Bridegroom."

The Blisses are Professor Condon's third example. Jonathan went

back to Massachusetts for a bride during the time the Arnolds lived in
New Brunswick, and she became a close friend of Peggy's. Mary Worthington came from a wealthy family in Worcester and was twenty years
younger than her husband. They were married ten years until her death in
1799.

> Unexpectedly, passionately, Jonathan fell in love with his young wife. She and
> the four sons she bore became the enchanted center of his life. In his letters to
> Mary, this aging, cynical lawyer resorted to baby talk. He confessed to her that
> she had made him the "happiest man in New Brunswick"—but ruined him for
> living alone.[5]

Arnold might well have said something similar, being very close to his
much younger wife.

Professor Condon found in the correspondence of husbands and
wives that the women deferred to the men's superior education and worldly
knowledge, regularly apologizing for their "stupidity." Condon also theo-
rized a depth of feeling and mutual dependency of the Loyalist couples
whose letters she researched. She also recognized that their expressions
of caring "were also calculated performances, survival measures and personal defenses against an undeserved fate and a relentlessly cruel world."[6]
This understanding helps place Benedict and Peggy Arnold's years in New
Brunswick.

13

The Island of Welsh Squires

Have you ever known a village reputation to be wrong?
—Patrick O'Brien, *Master & Commander*

Campobello is a naturally variegated and exquisite Canadian island closer to the American mainland than to the rest of Canada. The French explorer Samuel Champlain claimed the island in 1604, calling it Port aux Coquilles ("Shell Harbor"). Later the English gave it a descriptive name for its position on the map, Outer Island. It faces Nova Scotia and (now) the State of Maine. Irregular in shape, Campobello is part of the archipelago of islands at the boundary of the Gulf of Maine and the Bay of Fundy, at the entrance to the Passamaquoddy Bay. Its sister islands are Grand Manan and Deer Island, compared to which it is middle in size, about the size of Manhattan.

The following description is adapted from a brochure on display at the Roosevelt Cottage, from the Gilded Age, when the Roosevelts were among the rusticators. Thanks to the island's being mostly provincial and international part, the scenery is the same now:

> The island is indeed beautiful. It has amazing cliffs and currents, sea life and sunsets and tides that creep up the cliffs and rocks and then recede, leaving long stretches of wide beaches, and boulders hanging like seaweed, and pebbles wet and shining like semi-precious stones. It is also wild in a storm and bitter cold in winter.[1]

Not only do thick fogs enshroud Campobello much of the year, but boats practically drift in on the strong tides, and when it was necessary to hide a boat, the caves that form in the roots of craggy vegetation on the rocky cliffs provide cover.

Nine miles long at its longest point and three miles wide at its widest point, the island has a 40-mile ragged coastline, with coves, harbors and inlets, beaches and rockbound shores, caves and chasms. It lies two miles offshore from the American town of Eastport, Maine—a trip of several hours by car. The island is separated from the mainland by the

Passamaquoddy Bay. Eastport, the eastern most city of the United States, was faced by Arnold from the part of the island where he had his depot. It would not have caused him great consternation to live in a territory of veterans of two sides of the revolution, deserters from various navies, woodsmen and fishermen many of whom had taken little. interest in the final result of the great conflict, and pirates. He may well have seen the island in his journeys as a Connecticut merchant. As for Campobello, its population of 250 was made up of Loyalists and settlers who had arrived a generation before.

For thousands of years the indigenous people came to Campobello by canoe or in the depth of winter over the ice at the Narrows. They dug for clams, hunted for herbs and wild berries, moose and deer, traded sealskins, and welded their birch bark canoes. They were Malisetts and Mi'kmaqs of the Algonquin nation who continued to come to the island seasonally. A legend tells of a young husband off on an expedition who told his bride to sit until he returned. He would, he promised, never lose sight of her. She waited and waited, and when many canoes went out from Campobello but only her lover's canoe failed to come back, she turned to stone. He saw her form in the rock across the bay, and likewise turned to stone, now called Friar's Head and the next cove up from Arnold's base.

In 1783, the Treaty of Paris fixed the border between the U.S. and Canada in the Passamaquoddy Bay at the St. Croix River, the gateway to the congeries of islands. Fixed but did not settle. Uncertainty remained over the identity of the St. Croix among various streams and rivers that flowed out to the Bay of Fundy, until after the 1794 Jay Treaty created a commission to solve the matter. Even today, people rowing down the river for recreation find themselves unsure where they may land on which banks. The Treaty of Paris awarded the islands of the Bay to Great Britain except for four islands. Ward Chipman was one of the officials assigned the task of figuring out what had been French territory. His team found the remains of the cellar that Samuel Champlain built on an island in the tidal estuary in 1604. French records of a settlement were found as well. The little St. Croix Island is also called Bone Island, probably because of the 39 men who died of scurvy that winter.

The whole Passamaquoddy Bay area of many islands and riverbank clearings was a frontier. When Captain John Shackford, a Patriot who had served under Arnold, came to Eastport in the fall of 1783, only five families inhabited it and there were fewer at Lubec. The earliest permanent European settlement in the Bay was on Campobello's Harbor de Lute (Otter Harbor), a deep and narrow bay cutting into the island, where the French built structures until the Acadians were expelled from Canada. New Englanders had settled on the Bay of Fundy coast since shortly after the Pilgrims landed at Plymouth, but the area was very thinly inhabited until a few merchants arrived on the Outer Island in about 1760. This was just before the island was granted to a British naval officer, William Owen, who changed its name to Campobello in homage to his patron. William Campbell.

Along the coast of Maine, islands have changed names like a man on the Best Dressed list changes ties. When Arnold moved to Saint John, he found settlers in the region he had mingled with already: for instance, John Allan from Massachusetts in Eastport and Frederic Delesdernier, who served under Allan during the revolution, on Dudley Island. Arnold also made purchases from a Mr. Pope, an American who carried barque, or quinine, from South America among his wares.

It was August 28, 1769, that Captain Owen met with friends at a coffee house in Warrington, England to work out a plan (shares) of settlement for the faraway grant. The Welsh "Proprietary" staked his claim in 1770, sailed to Campobello, and set an indentured team to work clearing land and building houses. He settled on the north of the island. But the Captain was a navy officer who prioritized fighting the French and died serving in Madras in 1778. About fifty families had settled on the island at that time, along with a missionary-schoolmaster, whom Captain Owen fired for improper conduct. After Captain Owen left the island, the tradesmen he had brought with him felt, in a practical sense, abandoned, and probably removed to Annapolis Royal, Nova Scotia.[2]

That the British were on their high horses about illicit trading in the colonies had fomented the war for independence. Both the U.S. and British governments took the same view in the period around 1800 in the Maritimes. Nonetheless, from a local perspective, goods passed from one ship to another ought not be dutiable. The operational theory was that if a load of gypsum (for plaster and fertilizer), some millstones, and barrels of wool came from Nova Scotia en route to the U.S., instead of off-loading on land, it was simply transferred, at sea. No law was broken because the ship receiving the plaster was an American ship that sat on the line and technically never left American waters. From the middle states came flour, grain to feed cattle, beef, and other foodstuffs. From the north (New Brunswick and Nova Scotia) came lumber and fish. The British West Indies completed the triangle as a source of sugar, molasses and rum. Lumber was being cut with sawmills functioning on water power and barges took the lumber out on the lines where it was traded for beef and flour. As opposed to a neat triangle, traders got what they could sell from wherever they could. Everything but lumber came and went up the coast in barrels. The timbers, spars and shingles were planked at tide mills on the American mainland and rafted across to Campobello from

Dennysville (Washington County) and sold to St. Andrews merchants, some destined for the British market.

The revolution was still going on and the Owens did not provide satisfaction about developing their island. Charles Morris, the surveyor general of Nova Scotia, put Campobello up for sale at a sheriff's auction, and purchased it himself. (He was an ambitious person who mapped the Maritimes, having started out as a Boston schoolteacher.) Gilliam Butler then bought or leased the parcel from Morris, and in turn sold and deeded much of the 2500 acres of land, of which he had no clear title, to Loyalist ex-soldiers. To complicate the property scene further, Butler eventually forfeited his mortgaged property. This is how the rights to the island's property got tangled.

According to local historian Mary W. Gallagher, among these Loyalists were the brothers Christopher and Hawes Hatch, and Thomas Henderson, as well as Captain Frink. All but Hawes Hatch served in the regiment that Benedict Arnold had raised and commanded. All had received land elsewhere as well as their half-pay, and the prospect of trading drew them to the island. Hawes Hatch's name appears in a letter to Sir Henry Clinton, dated January 21, 1781. Hatch had been wounded commanding the advance guard at Fleur de Hundred in Virginia; Benedict noted how Hatch "with great gallantry attacked a piquet of the enemy and rove them to the main body."[3]

Ironically, the Royal Navy continued buying beef and flour from the Americans during the War of 1812. In fact, as the warships were expected to forage for much of their supply, the Royal Navy occupied Eastport for four more years, to take advantage of the sources of smuggled food.

In olden times, the traders in the Passamaquoddy region were said not to care "what side the fish swam." Still today there is a Gray Zone around Machias Seal Island[4] which is claimed by both the U.S. and Canada, where fishermen from both countries fish. Disputes regarding these waters between fishermen and law enforcers can on occasion be found in the *East Quoddy News*. Today it requires a passport to cross the short bridge from Lubec, Maine. Someone who has spent most of his life on Campobello Island gave me an example from his experience to explain how islanders have felt about smuggling there. He had just concealed in his pickup crossing the border a pot of flowers to put on his wife's grave in commemoration of her birthdate.

A series of illustrations in *The Atlantic Neptune*, published by Joseph F.A. Des Barres for use by the British Navy, shows the extensive variety of vessels that were carrying on this brisk commerce in the Passamaquoddy Bay. The beautifully rendered views have different configurations and numbers of sails, riggings, tonnage, and so forth. A topsail schooner rig was characteristic of the period and while schooners tended to be for the coastal trade, they could also go across the sea. The boats that transferred the contraband items were among the small types of vessels. Accurate visualizations of the vessels Arnold would have seen in Saint John and on Campobello include big ships with three sails, ordinary and topsail schooners, and smaller two-masted boats with sprit sails by oarsmen. The last were the boats that served for short trips down the coast, fishing, as pilot boats, and smuggling.

When David Owen, the second Proprietary of Campobello, took over, he decided that the two countries, the U.S. and Canada, like two tectonic plates, left a crack for him to maximize profit and govern à façon. The presence of newly arrived Loyalists did not tone down his exertion of control over the islanders' life. These settlers could only be temporary residents or tenants, as the land granted to the Welsh Owens could not be granted to anybody else. The Maine State Library has David Owen's record of land contracts with settlers. That Arnold's name does not appear on the leases suggests an arrangement where he paid a tribute and occupied the house leased to another person. As the inhabitants who had settled were mostly on the north coast, where Captain Owen had settled, and hostile to his nephew David, he moved to the southwest coast to a location ideal for farming and anchorage for fishing boats. Here he built a house on a long wide slope rising up from Friar's Bay which he named Tyn-y-coed, "House in the Woods," after the Owen family seat in Wales. The house, which had a deep, sloping roof, lay at the crest of the hill, close to where the Roosevelt Cottage is today.

Colin Windhorst, who has made a long study of Campobello, observes:

> As soon as David Owen arrived the first thing he did was eject people from the land they understood as theirs. He personalized everything. His name was mud. He didn't understand how to be conciliatory and when he died his two children could not inherit, whereas William the out-of-wedlock cousin could as he had been given the Owen surname by the original grantee.
>
> By encouraging David Owen to take up the Owen family grant in New Brunswick, by setting the hook, Arnold was trying to show how capable and organized he was as a businessman. I see it as a reversion to what he learned at his father's shop. Besides the fact that Owen declared Campobello a free-trade zone, there was an ancient principle that goods exchanged over the lines were not dutiable. This was an unofficial principle, so people were in a sense just doing business.
>
> The island was an ideal trading spot. There was Eastport, in the U.S., and the Pasamaquoddy Bay, belonging to Britain. It was not a game of fox and chickens with the law because the border guards didn't want to know. Meanwhile, David Owen claimed his was a free port, wrote his own rules, and made money

from a landing fee and warehousing goods until they were picked up. It was still cheaper for people to unload here than in St. Andrew or Saint John.

David Owen feuded with everyone who did not instantly bend to his will. When Arnold arrived in New Brunswick, there were resident agents supervised the small colony on the island but within two years David Owen came out to represent the co-grantees and remained 42 years, was ever on the alert if someone, coming from Eastport in a canoe, say, had killed a pig or sheep, or cut hay on his land. He ruled the island except the peninsula around Wilson's Beach, and claimed royal privileges as far as Moose Island.

The template he offered was leases of four to seven years, which applied to fishing weirs and farmland; and settlers reaped no benefits from improving the land. An engineer who came on a visiting British military sloop 20 years after David Owen became the island's landlord, was surprised at the feudal-like conditions. Ronald Rees remarks that "It cannot be supposed that people will flock to an island where the ground is only let to them for a certain number of years, which after being cleared and improved is at the expiration to revert to the owners."

It was a predicament to have Squire Owen a law to himself. Of the families who did not recognize his hegemony of the island, viz., because in their eyes the claim was forfeited, and they had made the improvements implicit in the grants, Robert Wilson had a tidal mill on the mainland and one on Campobello. He could go back and forth once or even twice a day. Captain Owen, during his brief occupancy, had given Mr. Wilson the job to clear the top of the island. Wilson cheerfully ceded to his rule, the Captain had maintained. Captain Owen had needed Wilson's work to show that the island was settled as that was the terms of the grant—attesting that Captain Owen was not a land parasite getting the grant to resell it. In a parallel case, William Campbell, the aristocrat who had created the fiefdom for Captain Owen in the first place, did not fulfill the conditions of colonization of Grand Manan Island, and lost it.

14

Benedict's Depot

Snug Cove, Campobello, was the headquarters of Benedict Arnold's business for much of the time he resided in New Brunswick. We can call him a smuggler because he skirted the authorities as a businessman whose approach was condoned. We can assume that he did not see himself as a smuggler.

Benedict must have seen the advantage of Snug Cove's southern exposure and misty weather as well as noticing the curiosity of the occasional whales and seals sunning on the slick mud and seaweed of the rocky beach. He would have chosen not to broadcast locating the heartbeat of his trade there. For Arnold's operations the island had workers to employ, livestock for meat, springs for water, and fish delivery by indigenous people. His comrade Nathan Frink and his casual friend David Owen, among others, traded little bridled by law. Arnold may already have been familiar with the Fundy Islands from his sea trade before the War for Independence. A little over five years after his treason he saw adventurers like himself leaving the British Isles to cruise for profit in the still remote Maritimes and their islands. Several merchants besides him had big vessels like brigs or barks.

Islands spawn individualists and serve as havens for mavericks. On this island, Benedict was favored for trade yet outside the boundaries of society, away from collective decision-making and the immediacy of law. Being impetuous, oppositional, and individualistic, he found this immensely attractive. There were fishing families who lived along the shore. Their pigs, sheep and cows fed on wild grass, and cows were ordered home by eight at night. Some other Loyalists lived and/or traded there. It was peaceful.

Snug Cove was the mildest inlet of Campobello. To the United States was a bee-line that could be traversed in two round trips in a single day—less the path across the Narrows and its tides, where boats were pulled out to sea, but across the more serene Passamaquoddy Bay. Ubiquitous fog made the cove an ideal base for trading on the lines. Nature itself is stealthy here. The supreme tides of the Passamaquoddy Bay, creep up the cliffs and recede in the blink of an eye, leaving the wide beach a colorful

View of the international boundary from the site of the wharf on Snug Cove, as it snakes through the narrow channel between Campobello Island, New Brunswick, and Pope's Folly, Lubec, Maine (courtesy Colin Windhorst).

array of sand and rocks. The temperature can change 30 degrees Fahrenheit from one hour to the next. The shadow of cliffs gives shelter and a boat could be slid right up to shore on the masses of seaweed set down by the tides. On an island you can spread your arms wide and you can see who is coming. A protected cove gave Arnold a place to settle while the foggy harbors were his platform for private business.

Since the day he fled the American side on the S.S. *Vulture*, Arnold was a transient. Before he immigrated to Canada he looked to what kind of success the early settlers were having on Campobello. A little before his arrival, a merchant from New England named Mr. Curry lived for a while on the island, at an inlet a little farther up the coast from Friar's Head (just beyond Snug Cove). That was known as Welshpool, the second syllable driving from *pwll* ("pool, inlet or pit" in Welsh). This early white settler like those who followed was a trader not a fisherman. He owned two brigs and a bark and was trading in the West Indies.

According to an article in the *Eastport Sentinel* a half-century after Arnold was in New Brunswick, while he was in Saint John he spent much of his time "overseeing his business" in Campobello. It described his activities as follows:

The old wooden fish-stores that Benedict Arnold built at Campobello (on the English side) just opposite Lubec (on the American side) at the time when he was carrying on the smuggling business between St. John and this vicinity are standing yet, in good preservation. What a capital smuggler and deceiver, in both countries, Arnold must have been.[1]

Professor Craven explains Arnold's choice for establishing a depot outside of Saint John, as follows:

Campobello with its mix of pre–Loyalist New Englanders and the remnants of the Owen settlement attracted a few ex-military British and Loyalist officers interested in the profitable plaster export trade, often considered a cover for smuggling. The other settlers there and on the other islands depended mainly on the fishing for their livelihoods.[2]

Arnold did business with, and hired to load and unload goods, men who had served on both sides of the conflict. The other merchants who traded in the area were outer directed at the sea and not prone to bear their fellows ill. Pirates on the one hand and zealous customs inspectors were adversaries they had in common.

Arnold was doing business on the island before his acquaintance David Owen appeared on the scene. They would have discussed arrangements when Owen first came to Saint John and determined to live there while establishing his claim. There is no entry in Owen's notebook of his being a landlord with either Arnold or Nathan Frink as a tenant although we know they were there. Arnold must have resided on Campobello in some sort of tenancy agreement. That the Welsh lord promoted free trade, a rash course for him personally, meant little Snug Cove was a freeport for the likes of Arnold. No goods landed there would be dutiable to the Crown. Establishing himself there gave Arnold a decided advantage over all other places where customs officials might intrude in the province. While governed officially from Saint John, justice was meted out on the island by this nephew of the first grantee, or, before he arrived from England, agents of his two brothers and himself.

That prior settlers had deeds and some of them did not give up and go elsewhere—when David appeared on the island as the "Proprietary"—would continue to create a volatile situation. Incredibly, Arnold was instrumental in lighting a fire under David about the grant before he exhibited any thoughts of coming to North America.

It was in London that Benedict Arnold, the hard-hitting entrepreneur, and Jonathan Bliss, the cultivated expatriate college man, together woke up the Owen family to the reality they could lose their title. In his legal history of early New Brunswick, Paul Craven tells the story of how these two friends lit a fire under their friend David Owen:

Eighteenth-century millstone at the house of Captain William's illegitimate
Admiral FWF Owen built in 1835, now a bed-and-breakfast. The millstone
may have been brought from a stream near Captain Owen's original New Warrington settlement (Jessica Cline, photographer).

Into this legal quagmire stepped Jonathan Bliss, a Massachusetts
lawyer-politician who had been living in England since the outbreak of the
American war. In 1784 he was angling for an appointment to the newly-created
province of New Brunswick where his close friend Benedict Arnold, then also
living in England, proposed to enter the West Indies trade. Arnold had connections with the promoters of the proposed New Brunswick Academy—one
of whom, Jonathan Odell, had negotiated the general's defection to the British side during the American war—and also with Campobello, where Nathan
Frink, his former aide-de-camp, had established a trading business. Bliss and
Arnold proposed that David should come out to New Brunswick, take a position at the new college, and represent the brothers' interest on the spot while
Bliss secured their title to Campobello in the colony's courts.[3]

David Owen listened, and while he brushed the proposition of the
"New Brunswick Academy" aside, he did cross the pond. Craven quotes
two related letters from David to his brother William. In the first, two
weeks after arriving in New Brunswick, David wrote William that "The
College is a Burlesque. The Tuition he offered a sham,"[4] and "Arnold's pro-
posals seem visionary. He is not liked here. There is no College founded,
only a small School. It was well I did not come out with him."[5]

There were a lot of colleges being founded, and a lot got grants of tracts from the government. The idea of having a college in New Brunswick, similar to Bowdoin in Maine, or Dartmouth in New Hampshire, looked good on paper. As Alfred G. Bailey writes, a merchant might have money but "social position rested rather on the holding of office, church membership, and the possession of education and cultivated tastes."[6]

No documents have been found for whatever arrangements Arnold had regarding his business or dwelling on the island. David Owen must have approved of having Arnold on his island and let him build the warehouse and wharves on easy terms. Conceivably, as Owen struggled to keep a lid on his domain by sustaining pressure on the settlers on the coast of the island, he saw Arnold as a transient and took occasional tribute from him—an informal tribute, a valuable connection for each man. Joshua Smith thinks that certain white landowners including Allan and David Owen acquired prestige from their contact with the Indians; if so, one can conjecture that Arnold, given his past contact with indigenous people, was among these white men.

By a strong, multi-source oral tradition, while a merchant on Campobello, Arnold had his wharf in Snug Cove and lived on the cliff above, a stone's throw to the north. Remains of the pilings of his wharf on the beach, with a view of Pope's Folly and North Lubec, are sure evidence of his presence. A house has also been said since the nineteenth century to

Tourist china. The pitcher and plate are European porcelain that American rusticators might have bought (Jessica Cline, photographer).

have been his. Now this stretch of beach and fields is Roosevelt International Park property but a short walk from the Roosevelt Cottage. The house burned down in the 1880s and no structure has replaced it. Ancient apple trees around the clearing mark off where the house had been from the woods, but no one excavates due to the historic nature of the park itself. A draining ditch goes down to the water. Another ditch follows the

Friar's Head, Campobello, 19th-century engraving; the kind of shed and wharf that Arnold had, just around the corner (courtesy Photo@Liszt Collection/ Bridgeman Images).

edge of where the floor once was. As early houses were built on gravel and propped up later if they sank, the holes may have been for the posts that supported the floor "sitting" on the ground.

This was before pile-drivers with engines. Big wharves had ballast on the underside and cross timbers. On the beach by the remaining timbers of Arnold's wharf are boulders of a same size that may have served for the ballasts. Judging by the length of the shed or fish stage (about 20 feet) associated with the wharf in the photo, and by the boat whose oars appear in the photograph (ten to 12 feet), Mr. Gough estimates that the structure of the wharf was about 60 feet. One large timber was perpendicular to the others, which indicates the outer limit of the wharf used by Arnold.

About 100 yards beyond and 50 feet elevated above the beach with the remains of the wharf is where Arnold's house was. When you walk on the turf you stumble into the drainage ditch that ran from the house to the beach. Where now much of the hill surrounding the rise is densely covered with the growth of trees, then it was pasture for sheep or cows. The vegetation where the house was situated is thick, pale grasses rooted so deep that they cannot be mowed, unlike the meadows that the Roosevelt park rangers tend.

From the house, Arnold could wave across at John Allan but from the wharf or wharves he was gazing at Pope's Folly, at the entrance of

Timbers in beach, once in Arnold's wharf below the house he occupied (Jessica Cline, photographer).

The timbers at low tide (Jessica Cline, photographer).

the Passamaquoddy Bay, an island with another merchant who did not remain, from which direction Arnold's timber came down in barges pulled by bateaux.

For Arnold, Campobello was a refuge. He retreated there after Hayt slandered him as an arsonist and villain, thereby precipitating a riot at

Arnold's door, but might have established the wharf much earlier. He lost no time when he arrived in the late fall of 1785 in setting up business in Saint John, reconnoitering up the St. John River, and having a vessel constructed. His ideas were large, to be a top merchant in the region. He would not have delayed setting up wharves and a storehouse on a "puzzle piece" islands in the Bay of Fundy.

Ralph Dennison, a veteran sea captain in Lubec,[7] remarks,

> The southwest of Campobello had good cover to row ashore. You could moor a boat out there in the deep water and off load at the docks at high tide. The road system then was moose trails and John Allan, from Nova Scotia, and Arnold from the Connecticut coast, were mariners. The smuggled goods, for instance, U.S. flour for Nova Scotian wool could be transferred by smaller boats at places like the Campobello coves. You hardly had to paddle when coming in with the tide from Eastport. It was just far enough from Owen's property up at what is now Welshpoot, and a premier place to have a house—the Roosevelts bought the land after the house Arnold occupied burned. The wide view attracted them too.

Both an old painting and a photograph show the old house. A rumor is that he helped built it but this could be the house he "occupied" (the description on the painting uses this word) belonging to Owen or even Nathan Frink, who leased property from Owen on Campobello but lived elsewhere, in Charlottetown. Eventually Frink gave up his Campobello address, to throw off Owen's lead strings. Arnold had to live somewhere to manage his depot, just as to conduct business in Fredericton he was planning a house. Having several domiciles was practical for traders. There were no real estate taxes, or pipes to shut off in winter; but by the same token such a rustic place was not for a gentleman's family.

The house looks stark in the photograph and painting. According to the painting, it passed from Arnold to another family and was destroyed in a lightning storm. An article in the *Daily Sun* of April 15, 1903 ("The House: Where Benedict Arnold Spent His Exile, Destroyed") indicates that Arnold had the house over a period of time and lived in it before Peggy and the children came to New Brunswick:

> The destruction of the old house in which Benedict Arnold spent several years of exile has removed one of the most central figures from the Island of Campobello. Arnold lived there during 1786–1787.

A note in the *Pine Tree* magazine (August 1906) states that Arnold made trading trips from his house on Campobello, which was large, near the shore, and opposite Treat Island. When the note appeared, Campobello attracted many rusticators, and the note indicates the interest there was in Arnold, and the scavenging: "The house was destroyed a few years ago …

House occupied by Benedict Arnold during his stay at Campobello
painted by Dougald Anderson
Afterward occupied by Mr. and Mrs. Joseph Patch and their son Simeon Patch, the house was
struck by lightning and Mr. and Mrs. Joseph Patch died in the fire.
by Mrs. Raymond Hamilton

A typescript label trimmed into a lozenge on the painting reads: "The house occupied by Benedict Arnold during his stay at Campobello/ Painted by Dougald Anderson/ Afterwards occupied by Mr. and Mrs. Joseph Patch and their son Simeon Patch the house was struck by lightning and Mr. and Mrs. Patch died in the fire/ Written by Mr. Raymond Hamilton" (courtesy Campobello Library & Museum; photo by Jessica Cline).

relics of it are still to be found scattered around the island." A tourist brochure of the day, at the museum, states that "many" of Arnold's "history relics"[8] were to be found on the island.

The photograph, dating from about 1870 and identified as "the home Arnold built on Campobello after the Revolutionary War," now in the St. Croix Historical Society, is especially affecting. The pasture relieves the emptiness. Someone had lived in the big house but left. The photographer knew he was looking at a historic landmark through his lens and positioned it with care. There is a similarity to Thomas Hardy's literary recreation of Wessex, where he wrote in "Three Strangers": "Among the few features of agricultural England which remain in appearance but little modified by the lapse of centuries may be reckoned the long grassy and furzy downs, coombs, or ewe-leases as they are called according to their kind."[9] But if stark, the house had ample view of the comings and goings of maritime trading in the Bay.

Joseph Gough, whose home remains along the beach of the Roosevelt

Campobello House Location—view towards Eastport across the water from the location of the house Arnold occupied (Jessica Cline, photographer).

Park, determined with his brother the location of Arnold's wharf and house. They compared the painting now in the Campobello Library with the historic photograph.

Locating the Abode and Wharf
By Joseph Gough[10]

My brother Stephen and I found the remains of the Benedict Arnold dock in 2017, after locating the site of the Arnold house. It was common knowledge on the island that the house stood close to Snug Cove, but no one we knew could say exactly where.

Snug Cove is a U-shaped cove on the southwest side of Friar's Head. On the northeast side of that headland is Friar's Bay, where the Roosevelts' and other summer cottages lined the road to Welshpool village.

A painting in the library/museum at Welshpool shows the Arnold house down-slope form a pasture. That suggested the general area on Friar's Head where we could look. An 1883 map of the island indicates three structures on the land in that area, and it seemed likely that the one closest to Snug Cove would be Arnold's house, and a beach structure not far from it would be his dock.

Besides the map, and this turned out to be the best guide, we had an article about Arnold published by the St. Croix Historical Society. Within the text were photographs of both house and dock.

With map and photo we were soon able to find the Arnold house's location, between the present-day road leading up onto Friar's Head and the bank of Snug Cove. One can readily see the outline of the cellar and what seems to be a drainage ditch.

Then for the dock. When you walk out along the beach on the Snug Cove side of Friar's Head, the shoreline at a certain point curves slightly outward and the beach rises a bit. There we seemed to be in the vicinity of the structure marked on the 1883 map, but the beach looked bare.

We had the photograph of Arnold's dock, which was taken looking offshore at half-tide. In it, the headland on the far side of Snug Cove loosely lines up with the shoreline of Pope's Folly, an islet at the beginning of Lubec Narrows. Further in the same direction, on the American side of the border, is a notch in the horizon.

We were able to line ourselves up with the two points of land and the notch so as to put ourselves where the photographer must have been. Then Stephen spotted timbers embedded in the beach where it rises. These are few, but set at right angles to one another, and obviously part of a bygone dock.

It would seem that building the dock on the edge of that rise in the beach gave Arnold deeper water for boats on the inner side while lessening the amount of timber needed on the other side.

Might FDR have been aware that where he brought in his boats was within sight of Arnold's trading depot:

What I can say is that young Franklin knew for sure where the house was. He and my grandfather Russell Gough were the same age, their houses were fairly close, and they chummed around together. One day Franklin and my grandfather were throwing rocks at the old Arnold house when a man appeared at a window. They ran away and were later told that a tramp had gotten onto the island and was in the house.

It is more than likely that the dock was still there at that time. Its location shows up on the 1883 map, and the St. Croix Historical Society photo must have been well into the age of photography. So Franklin almost certainly knew about the dock. But it was not within sight of where the Roosevelts tied up their boats on Friar's Bay, because Snug Cove is on the opposite side of Friar's Head.

While the wharf and storehouse were firmly on the north end of the U of Snug Cove, and the house on the cliff above them, the house has a different prospect, being centered halfway down the rise. There were no fields of crops, but an unfenced grazing meadow carpeted by buttercups, cow parsnip, and other delicacies for livestock. As Benedict stepped through the thorny hedges of roses and raspberries and productive apple trees, to descend the short steep path to the rocky beach, he must have felt this was his domain. Like Mount Vernon (I don't know if Benedict visited it) this was a waterfront land holding with divine prospect and views. The Roosevelt family felt the same; they bought acreage on the ridge overlooking Friar's Bay and bordering Snug Cove when Americans flocked from New York and Boston to Campobello in the 1880s for summer recreation.

View of Snug Cove from the south. The spit of beach one-third from the left is the location of the Arnold wharf (Jessica Cline, photographer).

Regarding when Arnold started up trading from Campobello, it is clear from a letter David Owen wrote back to Wales, as Arnold's years in New Brunswick came to a close, that Arnold had a back and forth pattern of visiting the island. Whether Peggy accompanied him cannot be discerned:

According to a well-corroborated story, the tavern where Arnold hid from pursuers in a whisky barrel is on a hill near the waterfront of Lubec, Maine, a short distance across the FDR Bridge to Campobello.

General Arnold was burnt in Effigy at St. John's; and would have been killed by the Mob, unless some officers of the 54th Reg't had exerted themselves to save his Life.... Mrs. Arnold was in Fits the whole day. He was down in Camp Bello a few days, and in considerable danger when here for the people remember his exploits at New London, where many lost a Brother or some relation.[11]

The merchants made their money by judicious smuggling in wild parts and at sea, and established their families in more civilized towns. Some of the Loyalists who became refugees nevertheless added to their wealth. For example, Christopher Hatch's success as a merchant was such that he built a fine Neoclassical house in St. Andrews, which today is a museum called Chestnut Hill. Like many other Loyalists he had black slaves and indentured servants managing his extensive property. A black cook named Violet prepared sumptuous meals for the Hatches' lavish parties. Serving under Arnold in the Virginia expedition at the end of 1781, Hatch had so impressed Arnold for his leadership of the advance guard that Arnold commended him to General Clinton. Hatch's gallantry and spirit did not impress David Owen, resentful of this Loyalist who did not kowtow to him.

Arnold had himself, his wife and children to protect. The configuration of the family when the children was young is unknown—who was at boarding school or with Aunt Hannah in New Haven, or—the case of the eldest, Benedict VI, the army. It is known that the household was at its greatest size in Saint John, when Hannah brought up at least the two younger boys by Arnold's first wife, Richard and Henry, and Peggy arrived with three children and delivered another, George, straightway. This family had to be protected, and if Arnold feared it was for their wellbeing not his own person, once he was back in North America, his assassin could be any man he met.

On Campobello were some men who had served under him five years before, in the raids he led on Virginia and New London, as well as Nathan Frink, who could attest to Arnold that money was to be made faster trading lumber and fish on the lines than in the carrying trade to the West Indies.

The most prominent Patriot in the Passamaquoddy region was Colonel John Allan, whose base of trade and home on Treat Island was very close to Arnold's depot. Treat is only a mile from Campobello. Colonel Allan was born in Scotland, raised in Nova Scotia, and is thought to have gone to school in Massachusetts. His father served in the British Army and after the French and Indian War got a grant in Nova Scotia. The son, John, was a justice of the peace and farmer when the American Revolution broke out. He left Nova Scotia in August 1776 and dined with General Gates and George Washington on December 22 in Pennsylvania, just before Washington's crossing of the Delaware. During Allan's absence from Nova Scotia, his house was burned, and his wife was imprisoned for several months.

In January, John told the Continental Congress to enlist the American Indians in their cause and was asked by Washington to act as Commander of the American forces in the eastern section. Allan came back up the coast, waiting for supplies in Boston and then making Machias (now in Maine) his headquarters for the next four years. There was a price on his head; he had to be on guard.

What is known of Colonel Allan makes him a partial mirror of Arnold. First, Washington put special trust in John Allan. Secondly, Allan fought at Saratoga with Arnold. Thirdly, Allan possessed craft combined with valor. He and two sons were once on a boat when a British raft of lumber passed. They shot and broke apart a raft. Several British barges thereupon came after the little boat, which dashed out of sight. Allan sunk his boat and he and his sons swam to shore.

Another time, he was on ice skates, and Indians on the British side pursued him, but he took a flying leap from one iced portion of the river to another and escaped. And Allan was on good terms with the indigenous people. He once was in his house when a friendly Indian entered and slipped behind the front door. Another Indian came in with a hatchet poised to attack, but the first Indian knocked him senseless. Allan let the attacker paddle off in a canoe.

The Allans were on Dudley, John's name for Treat, and his aide de camp in the Revolutionary War, Delesderniers, was nearby on Frederic Island. He made Treat officially his home. He put two sons with the Passamaquoddy tribe and admonished the boys to be exemplary representatives of his family.

Eventually Allan closed his store but not until after Arnold returned to England. It may have been difficult to be paid by strangers who cruised in, the issue which may have caused the trading post on Pope's Folly to fail (*Acheson's American Encroachments* [1806] hazarded the origin of the island's name as from unfortunate business ventures). Regarding all these merchants inhabiting the wild islands of the Bay, survival had been a rationale for laying their swords for ploughshares, but to make a profit was very hard. A telling morsel of gossip appeared in the New York Packet of August 1786:

> The celebrated Mr. Benedict Arnold ... lately paid a visit, in the company
> with an English officer, to the eastern flank of the Commonwealth of Massa-
> chusetts, and in a friendly manner waited on Colonel Allan at Dudley Island
> [Treat's] but tarried only a few hours, judging it more expedient to sojourn in
> Nova Scotia, than in a country very inimical to parricides.

From a window of the Campobello Library and Museum is a view straight on of Treat Island, where Arnold would go to trade with Allan. If we can't know whether Arnold and Allan interacted as old friends, this is an indication that they were interacting as traders "on the lines" without misgivings. Despite Allan's privations during the revolution, and Arnold's having defected, Allan behaved as a peacemaker and Arnold as a capitalist *avant la lettre*.

From the Bangor *Historical Magazine,* 1887 is this note about John Allan, the most prominent veteran on the Patriots' side of the American Revolution living in the Passamaquoddy Bay region when Arnold was there:

> Among the curiosities on exhibition at the Centennial celebration of the town of Dennysville Me. May 17, 1886, was an account book kept by Col. John Alan, when just after the Revolution he was engaged in trade on the island in Eastport harbor, which afterwards was known by his name.... To this island he gave the name Dudley, in compliment to his friend Paul Dudley Sargent.... On one page of Allan's book appears an entry, "Benedict Arnold one gall. Rum," and there are charges to him for lumber, and other articles.

The *Hartford Courant* of February 16, 1888, states that "In fact, Col. Allen [*sic*] did not do anything aggressing about the traitor down the street and

The Lumber Schooner by Fitz Henry Lane (1850). The painting was commissioned by Edward Dyer Peters of Blue Hill, Maine, who by 1800 was a partner with his brother John in Ellsworth (courtesy Penobscot Marine Museum).

even sold him rum from his general store" dates Arnold's residency on Campobello to 1787. This was derived from where purchases appeared in the leather account book

The aforementioned newspaper article from The *Daily Sun* was written by a reporter from Lewiston, Maine, dated April 11. He reported on a townsperson of Machias, Daniel Smith, who had the account book of his ancestor, John Allan. This ledger mentioned several purchases of lumber, a gallon of rum, and cordage by General Arnold in 1786 and 1787:

In his quest to dominate the economic scene, Arnold turned to a specific set of people: the coterie of Loyalist Bostonians and New Yorkers who bought from him and handled his legal affairs. He also engaged with suppliers of the commodities of trade; and seamen, poor laborers including disenfranchised African American people, and ex-soldiers from both sides of the revolution in his warehouses and at the wharves. When he was down in Robbinston, Maine, for business, he might have met for instance John Boyden, who enlisted at 16 for service at Ticonderoga, re-enlisted several times, and was on duty at West Point while Benedict was in command of that post.

An anecdote exists about a former soldier under Arnold on the March to Quebec, Captain John Shackford. Born in Newbury, Massachusetts, "Jack" Shackford was the first permanent settler of Eastport, Maine (then Moose Island). He had held Arnold in awe as a commander and for long months had been imprisoned in Quebec by the British. By 1784 he had a log store in Eastport, where he traded with the indigenous people, and a fish-drying establishment. He and his wife Ester, also from Newbury, had eleven children. For a time, Frances Lloyd, the mother of the abolitionist William Lloyd Garrison's mother, who lived on Campobello and then on Deer Island, taught them.

Benedict hired Jack from Eastport to load a vessel at Campobello (Arnold hired both Americans and Loyalists). There had been a thousand men at the beginning of the March to Quebec and hundreds at the end and it seems that Arnold did not recognize Jack Shackford. Shackford said that after meals he used to sit on the deck of the ship to watch the man for whose military acumen he still held admiration. When Shackford thought back to his army days, "Tears sometimes came, and I could not help myself, he carried us through everything, and I could not help thinking of him as he was then."[12]

Like it or not, Arnold had moved on. That the former captain's eyes welled up when he thought how low his general had sunk as a traitor is an affecting story but, given Shackford's acute distress, the question is raised why he took the employment by his old commander. Curiosity or to have a good story are possibilities.

All the same, betraying one's comrades was a recipe for mistrust and unpopularity. Vesey comments: If Arnold wished to forget his past, or be among those who could forget it, he had chosen a poor place in New Brunswick. His neighbor in Saint John was Lieutenant John Ward, formerly of Peekskill, who had been in command of the escort who accompanied André up the Hudson for the momentous meeting with Arnold. And at Fredericton was one William Underhill, formerly of Phillipsburg, New York, who had been on parole when André came to meet Arnold.[13]

These were men intimately involved with the André debacle. William Underhill was a captain in the Queens Rangers, taken prisoner and on parole, when André came from Arnold. Underhill swore before the British Commissioners that shortly before André was taken, Underhill "advised him [Andre] to and they would get him within the lines."[14]

Nathan Frink had a trading business on Campobello and surely welcomed Arnold. He too had been despised for his allegiance to the Crown. Frink had served as a captain in the King's American Legion, the unit raised by Arnold, in 1781. During the raid on New London and Groton, Frink acted as Arnold's aide and guide. Frink arrived on the island before or at the same time as Arnold. When Arnold arrived in New Brunswick and made his expedition up the St. John River, Frink accompanied him.

Frink was one of the justices in New Brunswick who sought to redress some of the grievances against David Owen. In December 1790, a customs official named Richard Batchelor visited an island shipyard in search of contraband and broke into someone's house. Owen thought it an impropriety to search his island, and used that objection as a cover-up, as he had undeclared iron and ship's stores, intended for a new ship. Frink was named as a witness in the indictment against Owen for assault and battery on Batchelor. The case was dismissed five years later.

In the skirmishes that played out in the courts and government against David Owen's lordly acts, Nathan Frink was involved as a defender of the common people. Some months after Arnold returned to England, Frink requested a hearing in St. Andrews (New Brunswick) to consider the grievances of the Campobello residents. Benaiah Dow, a fisherman who was deputy sheriff, was a lodger in David Owen's house who was barred from the part of the house he lived in when he spoke out against Owen. Dow was taken to St. Andrews in the custody of a constable, but he defended his side before the justices, saying that Owen served several dozen people with arrests that were never reported to the courts. So it went. Dow continued to fish from his schooner anchored at Campobello.

In published writings that mention Arnold's six years in Saint John, authors say that a salient characteristic was his litigious nature. Yet the law was the only civilized recourse for a businessman who needed to be paid for goods sold or services rendered. Arnold should be seen more as an impatient, unpolitic, take things into his own hands sort of gent than a man overly prone to take his quarrels to the courts. Following David Owen's life, it is clear that much of his time was spent in legal tussles in the province. They seem endless. Arnold's attempts to cause debtors to pay him, by bringing lawsuits against them, do not hold a candle to the ferocious way that Owen, though a gentleman of the first order, pursued those who opposed him. David Owen was waging legal battles more than Arnold did, at much the same time. And, whereas Arnold neither dueled nor bludgeoned anybody who opposed him, the one-time Trinity College, Cambridge, Senior Wrangler (top mathematics undergraduate) and trained reverend stopped at little to trample his adversaries. He misused his office of justice, sent a posse after those whom he perceived as trespassing, and had such little regard for the legal system that, as justice of the peace on his island, dispatched a servant to make an arrest. Contrastingly, Arnold assiduously pursued debts without evicting families, and antagonized high-status citizens of the new province by lawsuits against them "equally" with anybody else for amounts large or small. In brief, Arnold was impolitic in contrast to David Owen, his vicious and autocratic acquaintance and associate.

For Benedict, Campobello must have been ideal and for Peggy a poor fit. Peggy was a city person. She liked to ride as a young woman and sought the fresh air and medicinal waters at spas in England but did not long for pastoral tranquility or other features of the countryside. Her father remarked to her in the 1790s, when the Arnold family had returned to London, that a move to the country might reduce their spending. Peggy demurred. Being isolated in a rural economy was out of the question. She had social ambitions for her children and liked to associate with the upper crust. She added that she and Sophia would both be lonely away from London.

Kate Gannett Wells, writing a century after the revolution but imbued with local history, averred that Peggy felt isolated and for this reason the Arnolds left the island. So might anyone feel isolated when dark fell early in the winter, and Wells is a trustworthy source. However, there were people and society. A sea captain had built a cottage where he passed winters and visited his friends the Butlers (who disputed David Owen over the ownership of lots). Captains of the ships uploading the harbor would stop at the homes of merchants with their officers. Really any British officers of frigates with time to spare in the islands would make a point of calling at the Arnolds. What Wells' observation about Peggy's feeling of alienation on Campobello tells is that members of the Arnold family besides Benedict did come to the island with him.

A most striking bit of folklore—that Benedict was not only using Snug Cove, Campobello, as a depot but occupied a particular house on a rise over it—comes from several pieces of china quietly shelved in a glass cabinet of the chockfull one-room museum at the Campobello Library. This souvenir china is of Austrian make and of quality. The stamped decoration on each piece is "house of Benedict Arnold." These were curios for the wealthy of the Gilded Age, like Franklin D. Roosevelt's parents and their guests, to buy to take home. The label underneath each piece reads "Made in Austria for the Welshpool Market."

Insights
By Colin Windhorst

Early photographs from the mid–1880's depict the wharf and ware houses used by Arnold and his former aide de camp, Nathan Frink. They leased the property from Squire David Owen, the Island's contentious proprietor, who wrote his brother William, back in Wales, on September 25, 1791, about the burning of Arnold's effigy at St. John's, that Arnold "would have been killed by the mob, unless some officers from the 54th Regt. Had exerted themselves to save his life."

The letters from David Owen to William are cited in Paul Craven's excellent descriptive account *Petty Justice: Low Law and the Sessions System in Charlotte County New Brunswick 1785–1787*. They reside in the Glansevern estate papers in the National Library of Wales, Aberystwyth.

Neither was Arnold's defection forgotten by Revolutionary veterans on the American side of the boundary line. Colonel John Crane, whose military career commenced with the Boston Tea Party, and later settled at Orange River, in what is. Now the Town of Whiting, Maine, declined an invitation to dine with Arnold aboard his schooner, replying he had no intention of dining with a traitor.

The Campobello house occupied by Arnold burned in the 1890s, and now exists only as a black and white image made by Davis Loring, a professional photographer from Eastport, Maine, who sold albums of local scenes to supplement his income. His image shows the dwelling house perched on a slope, with cows and what appears to be a low stone wall.

In design and materials, the structure gives evidence of its late eighteenth-century Federal origins. An enclosed porch frames a doorway of simple but classical proportions. The windows of the façade are grouped to give balanced lighting to the interior rooms. A perpendicular ell shares the roofline and a large central chimney with the front portion of the house, while somnolent cattle—often allowed to run free on the island—recline lazily on the slopes around the dwelling. A low roofed shed, perhaps giving access to another entrance, is attached to the rear of the house, where a simple clothes pole, or the remains of a well sweep, complete the picture of decaying rustic gentility.

Arnold's presence on Campobello was noted by Kate Gannett Wells, one of the late nineteenth century rusticators who founded a small summer island colony. It attracted the likes of James and Sara Roosevelt of Hyde Park, New York, who arrived in 1883 with their young son, Franklin. In *An Historical Sketch of Campobello*, written in the 1890s to describe the island to prospective visitors, she noted the entry of "Benedick" Arnold's name in the account book of Allen's Store on nearby Treat's Island, also home to the local American customs inspector.

Arnold ... though in business in St. John, NB, was living for a short time on Campobello at Snug Cove.... In 1786, Arnold bought a new vessel, which he called "the Lord Sheffield," and made trading voyages in her along the coast and to the West Indies. Once, while crossing Passamaquoddy Bay, he invited Colonel Crane to dine with him aboard his vessel. But the Colonel, who was a revolutionary veteran, stamping his foot, wounded at the siege of Saratoga, replied, "Before I would dine with that traitor I run my sword through his body."

Wells observed the consequences of his commercial enterprise, his departure from Saint John, and the auction of his furnishings there. Impressed with his style, yet horrified by his infamy, in her conclusion she speaks to the tragedy of Arnold's career: "Yet whoever now owns them must be glad they are not family heirlooms. Auction sales are more honorable for some china."

Mrs. Wells' lively *Historical Sketch* was first published around 1895 and revised and reissued in 1902. She acknowledges the contribution of William Henry Kilby's *Eastport and Passamaquoddy* (1888), and the permission of William F. Ganong of Smith College to quote from several articles published in the Collections of the New Brunswick Historical Society. She adds that the Journal of David Owens and other family papers are in the possession of Samuel Wells, Esq., of Boston, Massachusetts, and President of the Campobello Land Company, her husband.

Benedict Arnold's residence on Campobello Island casts long shadows.

The early photographs from the studio of Davis Loring of Eastport, Connecticut are part of a collection given to the Campobello Museum, which is housed at the Campobello Library in Welshpool, N.B.

15

Breaking Point and Departure

And if at some point you go for a walk in the woods
and someone takes a photo of you, then for the next
80 years you're aways walking in the woods. There's
nothing you can do about it.—Thomas Bernhard

We have seen that Arnold was a frequent litigant in the courts.
Between July 1789 and May 1791, he filed 19 lawsuits against alleged debtors. He did not spare the more powerful Loyalists, who on first coming to New Brunswick may have overestimated their prospects. An officer declared that they were still eating partridge when they arrived but were soon as poor as others.

A pivotal moment in the economy of the province was when the British troops were withdrawn and sent to fight Napoleon and his allies. Barry K. Wilson elaborates the significance of the removal of soldiers from their active duty at Fort Howe:

> This took hundreds of thousands of pounds out of the Canadian economy. Just as had happened in the American colonies after the Seven Years War, a severe depression descended upon Canada. A lawyer who had just seen one of his clients hauled off to jail for a debt lamented the terrible economic situation in Saint John. Ward Chipman replied, "Really, everybody is so poor. There is no such thing as money to be had."[1]

The economic downturn was causation for the series of lawsuits that Arnold initiated. Among those who bought on credit and could not pay their accounts were residents of high status: Wilson notes that Arnold took to court three legislators and a county sheriff while living in the province, and, after his departure, Edward Winslow, who was continuing to ascend to prestigious administrative appointments in the province. Another of Arnold's lawsuits was against Daniel Murray, a former major in the King's American Dragoons, from Massachusetts, Harvard-educated, and from 1785 a representative in the New Brunswick legislative assembly (later he would return to America and live in Portland).

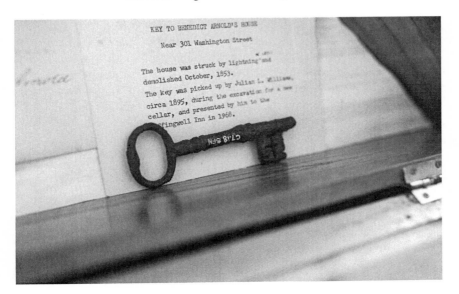

KEY TO BENEDICT ARNOLD'S HOUSE

Near 301 Washington Street

The house was struck by lightning and demolished October, 1853.

The key was picked up by Julian L. Williams, circa 1895, during the excavation for a new cellar, and presented by him to the ...ingwell Inn in 1968.

Miniature (courtesy Chateau Ramezay, Old Montreal, Quebec).

On the other side of the boundary, his old comrade Major General Benjamin Lincoln was on a similar trajectory of buying land and trading. He too conducted circular trade, had a more sanguine reputation than Arnold, being known as "consistent, businesslike and thoughtful," to quote Colin Windhorst. He mortgaged his farm in Hingham and came up with other settlers from Hingham and founded Dennysville, Maine, in 1786, from which his lumber went to the West Indies and grain came up from the middle States.

Besides the trip to England to bring his family, Benedict made another trip for trading. At this time, on the advice of friends, he insured his Lower Cove warehouse in Lower Cove, store and stock at Main and Charlotte's Streets. Saint John had been beset by several fires and another loomed as ever-present danger. Benedict contributed the maximum sum (ten pounds) to a subscription to procure two fire engines from London. He was the largest contributor (of 45 persons and firms who subscribed) to a second fund to sink several wells in town. It was a year after the townspeople raised by subscription a sum for procuring the fire engines, during his absence in England, on July 11, 1788, that Benedict's insured property burned down, and Munson Hayt perpetrated the gossip that Arnold had committed arson.

Munson Hayt was a former comrade of Arnold's in New York in the military too, having been a lieutenant with the duty of quartermaster in the Prince of Wales' American volunteers. He had an appointment as a justice of the peace for York County, New Brunswick. He quickly became Arnold's business partner, which allowed Arnold to resume his pattern of making a voyage while someone else minded the store. But they quarreled over who owed whom. Hayt said Arnold had robbed him and vice versa. While judgments were made in Arnold's favor amounting to several thousand pounds he insisted on issuing another action for a few pounds, shillings and three pence.

A partnership was a sensible arrangement for a restless seaman who didn't incline to mind the store all the time any more than when he had the apothecary–general store in New Haven. Munson Hayt was associated with the Upper Covers and had Loyalist credentials. He had known Arnold when a quartermaster in British provincial forces in America. Arnold owned four ships, a warehouse in Saint John, and trading stations in Fredericton and Campobello, a store by the docks and a bigger store in town. Cash was a problem from the start. Arnold had brought with him as much as £6,000 when he settled in Saint John but many there were buying on credit.

He made the business "Arnold, Hayt and Arnold," setting Richard up in business and having Henry work in the warehouse.

Arnold had gone to England to fetch Peggy and their children. Then when Arnold was in England a friend advised him to get insurance on these properties—an innovation for Saint John. He insured the warehouse and its stock for £5,000 and his other store for £1,000. He also contributed a sum to a subscription to procure two fire engines from London and sink several wells in town. There were 45 subscribers, of which he gave the most.

The warehouse caught fire and burned to the ground in July 1788, the same summer that Peggy visited her family in Philadelphia. Henry was sleeping in the building. He was burned but escaped. St. John had been beset by several fires, and this was a year after the townspeople raised by subscription a sum for procuring the fire engines.

After the gossip of arson, Arnold, states Willard Wallace, rented out his Saint John house in 1789 for £50 and took his family to Fredericton. Wallace also states he saw the rent statement of the Saint John house.[2] But if he did not settle in Fredericton, and only purchased lots there from Peter Clements, born in Cortland Manor near Yorktown, New York, and a captain in the King's American Regiment. Clements received his lot in Saint John but did not settle there; he took his family of seven children to Fredericton. (Later, Clements went to York County where he served as a magistrate.)

The dissolution of the partnership devolved into Arnold's biggest legal tussle, the province's first slander case. The insurance company would not pay the claim of £5,000 until the suspicion was laid to rest. Hayt hired a politician and lawyer and Arnold retained two lawyers—the solicitor general, Ward Chipman, and Jonathan Bliss, a former member of the General Court of Massachusetts. The Blisses and Chipmans were personal friends of the Arnolds. By hiring them in tandem Arnold was determined to discredit Hayt.

The trial took place in the parlor of Colonel Isaac Allen's house in Fredericton. At the trial, Hayt taunted Arnold by stating, "I will convince the Court that you are the greatest rascal that ever was, that you burnt your own store, and I will prove it." There were 29 witnesses, including Richard and Henry, who appeared for Arnold and a dozen for Hayt.

Chipman presented the facts. Arnold purchased the insurance a year before the fire and he was not even in the province when it occurred. He said Arnold during his years in Saint John had been a person "reported of good character" who "has kept and fulfilled his faithful contracts and promises as a merchant." He brought forth Arnold's reputation as a family man, which is interesting in that family closeness was so crucial to the Loyalist society.

> Had the plaintiff [Arnold] in this instance been guilty [of setting the fire], he must have been an infernal spirit indeed. The tide was out, one other house was actually burnt. Had the wind sprang up at southeast, at which point it blows fresh, the whole city might have been in danger. His son too he must have risqued sacrificing. His most inveterate enemies will not accuse him of a lack of paternal tenderness.[3]

Chipman waxed eloquent: If the man was willing to let the entire city burn to satisfy his greed for the insurance money, "Hell itself would not produce so great a monster."

About a month before the trial, Arnold and Chipman went up the St. John River in search of two black men who had been working that night in the warehouse, now in different locations. They gave matching versions of the night of the fire. Sewell wrote:

> One of them went up with Harry [Henry Arnold] to the top of the store that night that it was burnt with a candle after some oak to make a boat. There was such an appearance of veracity, and fear withal of what might be the consequences, their story so direct which they told without leading questions, the declaration that they had not seen any of the General's family, that no one ever said a word to them respecting the fire, their strong appearance of truth, candor and simplicity, which is always visible particularly in black men, altogether is sufficiently presumptive evidence against anything that Hayt can allege that the store was burnt otherwise than by accident.[4]

Sewell can be thought of as a dispassionate observer. He wrote his father in London, "Mr. Chipman takes a great deal of pain in the business and he has told me that it is one of the most hellish plots that ever was laid for the destruction of a man."[5]

Colonel Isaac Allen was one of the judges that awarded Arnold a pittance yet found him in the right. The parlor of his Georgian house, still standing in Fredericton, had high ceilings and this is where Allen held court for the case. Moreover, Hayt and Arnold were already at sword's points over money. Hayt said that Arnold had robbed him of £700 pounds while Arnold produced promissory notes proving Hayt's indebtedness to him of £2,000.

The trial in September 1790 lasted two days and there were, as Jean Sereisky puts it, "writs, charges, and counter-charges of theft, arson, robbery and slander flew."[6] Then Arnold sued for libel and as plaintiff won. Instead of the £5,000 that Arnold claimed, he was given 20 shillings sixpence. This legal case a year before Arnold's departure from New Brunswick dealt him a blow. Chipman stated to the court that the slander had damaged Arnold's business.

Barry Wilson astutely calls the verdict bittersweet and a rebuke against his harsh business approach. An opinion of New Brunswick attorney Eric Teed is cited by Wilson for what the outcome meant:

> a politically inspired loss ... driven in good part by the enemies he had made through his revolutionary past or his recent business dealings, which more often than not ended in court, with a new enemy for Arnold.'[7]

Oft recounted is an event where a mob gathered in front of the house on King Street, shouting of tar and feathering, and burned an effigy that wore a placard reading "Traitor." Quigley, steeped in local history, for example, writes that a magistrate dispelled the crowd which returned later to make an even greater disturbance. "The street was filled with blazing tar barrels. Finally, the militia were called in."[8] It seems too neat for there to have been an effigy with the word "Traitor" fastened to its chest. In any event, soldiers were summoned from the fort to the town to maintain peace.

Was Arnold a pariah? Was he mortally offended by the accusation he was an arsonist, to the extent he gave up on being a merchant in the Maritimes? Certainly this event galled him. It must have anguished Peggy and made her fear for her children's safety. She recalled the burning effigy wheeled through Philadelphia after her husband's treason, and this may have been repeated in Saint John. Randall credits the story while Wilson does not. David Owen's correspondence to his brother is a primary source. According to McNutt, "During the conflagration there were voices in the crowd calling upon Arnold to tell them if the fire resembled that of New London—a reminder of one of his bold but ill-judged actions during the war."[9]

Naturally, trading in New Brunswick and on voyages along the seaways of northern New England was not forgotten. While Arnold was cruising for supplies in the Passamaquoddy Bay he invited a Colonel John Crane to dine with him on board the Lord Sheffield.

Crane had been a faux Indian in the Boston Tea Party who got hit on the head by a tea chest, fell to the deck, and was almost left for dead. Crane became the original proprietor of the town of Whiting (now Maine), and had the clout to sputter publicly he would never shake the hand of Benedict Arnold. Colonel Crane was part of the attack on Breymann's Redoubt where Arnold led the charge in 1777, and in 1780 took part in an unsuccessful pursuit for the re-capture of Arnold, fleeing through Maine to the Canadian line.

Crane was incensed: "Before I would dine with that traitor I would run my sword through his body." Contrarily, the prominent Patriot John Allan, traded with Arnold without evident conflict. Comments Windhorst, "The man deeply wanted to be recognized. No one wanted to shake hands and be friends and that was the one thing he wanted." When Peggy, with baby George, went to Philadelphia in the fall of 1789 (she remained until spring), she regretted leaving Benedict in difficult times "alone and much perplexed with business."[10]

When Arnold folded up his tent, he had a great deal to dispense. Even just in Saint John there were 21 lots of land and belongings that made no sense to ship. The *Royal Gazette* of Saint John on September 6 advertised a public auction on September 22 of household effects at the Arnolds' home on King Street. The auction was outdoors as it was announced as taking place at 11 o'clock, "if fair weather if not the first fine day." The ad ran as follows and was signed by an auctioneer named John Chaloner:

A QUANTITY OF HOUSEHOLD FURNITURE comprising excellent feather beds, mahogany four post bedsteads, with furniture; a set of excellent Cabriole chairs, covered with blue damask, sofas and curtains to match; Card, tea and other tables, looking glasses, a Secretary desk and bookcase, fire screens, girandoles, lustres, an easy and sedan chair, with a great variety of other furniture.

Likewise: An elegant set of Wedgewood Gilt ware, two tea table sets of Nankeen China, a variety quantity of kitchen furniture. Also a Lady's elegant Saddle and Bridle.

There were also for sale a terrestrial globe, a jack for raising a wagon or carriage, and a quantity of kitchen utensils.

A Moving Sale
By Stephen Davidson[11]

At eleven o'clock on the morning of Thursday, September 22, 1791, the bargain hunters of Saint John, New Brunswick, gathered at the corner of King and Canterbury streets. One of the city's most prosperous merchants, a former loyalist officer, had hired John Chaloner to auction off most his family's worldly goods. The family would be moving to England in three months' time and needed to liquidate some of their assets. Did readers of the Royal Gazette raise their eyebrows when they realized that the auction was at the home of none other than Benedict Arnold and his wife Peggy?

The ad that Arnold placed in the city's newspaper did more than list the "quantity of household furniture" that was for sale, it also demonstrated the level of success that this Connecticut loyalist had attained in New Brunswick. The items to be auctioned off ranged from a chandelier to a coalscuttle and from card tables to fire screens.

Contemporaries described the Arnold house as "quite a pretentious home." It was situated in a neighborhood favored by the rich and powerful in the heart of the "Upper Cove," Saint John's business district. The house was just a block away from the site at which so many loyalist refugees disembarked from the ships of the first evacuation fleet out of New York in May 1783. But where the first arrivals lived in surplus army tents, Arnold and his family lived in a two and a half story oak house that was well finished, had large rooms, and was warmed by several fireplaces. Three dormer windows looked out onto King Street from the gambrel roof.

In the aftermath of the revolution, Arnold had put aside his British army uniform to trade in goods from the West Indies. By 1791, he had ships, a warehouse, wharves and an office on Saint John's harbor front. When his ships took West Indies goods to England, he was able to buy fine furnishings in the latest fashions, turning his house into a showplace for his wealth as well as a comfortable home for his wife, seven children, and their servants.

Arnold and his family certainly slept well. The master bedroom contained a four-poster bed made of mahogany, a wood found in the West Indies. There were also several "excellent" feather beds on the auction list.

As the auctioneer's hammer signaled the end of individual purchases on that Thursday morning, shoppers walked out of Arnold's house with fire screens, small tables, and mirrors. A globe of the world would no longer sit near the secretary desk (worth five to eight thousand dollars in 2022). "A great quantity of kitchen furniture" would be scattered over a number of Saint John homes, but only the richest shoppers could have purchased the girandoles—luxurious candelabras of French design, and lustres—chandeliers made of cut prismatic glass pendants.

Some of Arnold's possessions had been seen outside his home on a regular basis. The auctioneer sold Peggy's sidesaddle and bridle, gear that she would have used while riding her horse through the city streets. There was also a sedan chair, a clue that the family had employed a number of servants. This device was an enclosed chair that two porters carried between horizontal poles. Given the steep slope of the streets of Saint John, it must have been strenuous work to transport Peggy Arnold on her errands about the city.

Soon the auction was over. The bargain hunters and those who had just come to gawk returned to their homes. Over the next three months, Arnold sold his home in Saint John and a prime property in Fredericton, the latter for £325. After the family arrived in England, Arnold wrote back to a friend in Saint John with bitter words expressing his relief at having "escaped" that city.

Peggy Arnold was a little more nostalgic. "I hear much of the gaiety of your little city, but find party spirit, especially among the ladies, still rages with violence. I shall always regret my separation from many valuable friends."

It is often the children who have the greatest difficulty leaving the only place they have known to be their home. The fifth of Benedict's sons, James Arnold, had been just eight years old when his family moved to England. In the early 1820s, decades after he had last been in Saint John, James went back to the house at the corner of King and Canterbury. Witnesses recalled how he "wept like a child at the sight."

As for James Arnold's parents, history has not always been kind in remembering them. In fact, most people are unaware that Benedict Arnold and his wife ever lived in Saint John, New Brunswick—or had a most memorable moving sale in the fall of 1791.

Wedgwood and fine china were, to cite a label in the Wetmore Parlor of the Wadsworth Atheneum (Hartford, Connecticut), "exercises in stagecraft, calculated to embellish the image of its owner." A clock case said to have belonged to Arnold is displayed at the Morehouse at King's Landing Historical Settlement in Prince William, New Brunswick. It may be that the Arnolds took the clock and sold the case as furnishing, joiners being more readily available to replace the woodwork than clockmakers to construct a replacement of the clockworks. A clock was a more valuable item than its case. According to the same text related to the Wetmore Parlor, alluding to a slightly earlier period (Judge Seth Wetmore died in 1778), fewer than one family in 50 owned a tall clock in colonial Connecticut, while "An explosive demand for timepieces swept through New England after the Revolution." A new clock was put in the case later by the new owners (the family of a Dr. Skinner).

One of a dozen dining room chairs that the Chipmans acquired is in the New Brunswick Museum in Saint John—the others having burned in the Saint John fire of 1877. Ward Chipman bought it and then it went to the Gilbert family for generations until three Gilbert women gave it to the museum in 1946. The museum description states that the Gilbert family said that this "traitor's chair" was acquired September 22, 1791, by Ward Chipman and that it belonged to a set of 12 cabriolet chairs. Five years after the auction, Benedict was trying to get payment from Chipman. Another advertisement "on very easy terms" was for September 11 of two wharves, a house, 16½ lots in Saint John, a thousand acres of land, and the seasoned frame of a 300-ton ship. These were not sold like hotcakes. The farm had a tenant for some years and the ship frame was sold later.

Arnold with Peggy and their children returned to London in the new year. Arnold gave Jonathan Bliss and Ebenezer Putnam power of attorney, and wrote Bliss from England:

> Our reception has been very pleasant. The little property that we have saved from the hands of a lawless ruffian mob and more unprincipled judges in New Brunswick is perfectly safe here, as well as our persons from insult, and though we feel and regret the absence of the friends we had there, we find London full as pleasant! And I cannot help viewing your great city as a shipwreck from which I have escaped.[12]

He is understood to mean his life broadly. That would mean his business, his relations with some of the gentry, and the dissatisfaction of his wife with frontier living. He had choice words particularly for the "great heads" in Fredericton, except for "the few Righteous" who were his friends he had "no regard for Sodom and G-." When he sent Chipman flannel hose, socks, and a pair of gloves in 1792, he quipped he would have liked to transfer gout to "some of my *good friends* at St. John."[13]

The only known surviving object that belonged to Peggy is a sewing box. It had been lent to the American Museum in Bath, England, but has been removed by the original owner. The owner believed the box was given to Peggy by a member of the Mi'kmaq Tribe when the Arnolds left New Brunswick. Nasa Alvi of the museum explained to me the documented provenance and the box:

> The work box is inlaid birdseye maple with birch bark and satin embroidering fittings. The contents consist of nine small boxes of birch bark: oval, crescent shape, and triangular. Each is edged with green satin and tied with satin bows.

> The box was put on "long term" loan with the Museum by Frank G. Whittuck in 1962. It had belonged to his wife who had recently passed away. According to his original letter the work box was 'owned to [*sic*] Mrs. Benedict Arnold, according to repute made for her by the Mic Mac people in 1791. The work box was left to her daughter Sophia Arnold, who married Col. Pownoll Phipps and eventually came into the possession of my wife, who was her great-granddaughter.

Inside the box a paper, which, Ms. Alvi states, has since been removed by a family member, had on it a poem:

> *When more pleasing scenes engage,*
> *And you in polished circles shine*
> *Then let this wild this savage page,*
> *Declare that gratitude is mine.*
> *Elasaba of the Mic-mac Tribe October 1791*

The box maker and poet could be a friend of the elite—since Elasaba is the Miq-mac equivalent of Elizabeth, who perhaps had her lessons in embroidery on muslin, silk and bark from Mrs. Cottnam. Peggy's close friend and riding companion Elizabeth Chipman, six years younger than Peggy and also in a May–December marriage comes to mind. It was Elizabeth's husband who said he had never known real happiness until he was married. Somehow that is a hint that Peggy also felt very important to her husband, and, while Elizabeth Chipman was from a prosperous family, her father was not a heroic officer but a practical businessman; nor was her family Anglican, the faith of the status quo.

However, women of the Passamaquoddy tribe fashioned tourist items of beauty and intricacy for generations after the European invasion. Whoever did the embroidery using moose hair and birch bark for sections had learned these skills from the indigenous people.

Reticules were designed after what Napoleon's wife Josephine carried, and workbaskets were intended for ladies' needlework, sometimes with a handle to hang them on a chair. A man could buy this for his wife, but such a basket would also have been an ideal presentation gift. The interior might be by a woman of the indigenous culture and the bird's eye maple box of English cabinetry by an English Canadian. The Nowetah's Indian Store & Museum in New Portland, Maine, has an example of sweet grass on a base of ash splints which, satin lined, was clearly for a lady. Like the one given to Peggy Arnold it has "extras"—a scissor guard, pin cushion, and tiny thimble basket, laid out just like a formal French eighteenth-century garden.

The sewing box is a mystery. Indigenous people engaged with the Loyalists as guides for salmon fishing and bear hunting, and providing fish and foraged herbs, as well as making baskets. "A lot of things were made for sale," says Gretchen Faulkner, curator of the Hudson Museum of the University of Maine. "Native American objects were collected by British officers of the time. Baskets pop up in England, Wales and Scotland."

Professor Ruth B. Phillips, an authority on Canadian crafts, believes that the person who gave Peggy the sewing box playfully took on the identity of an indigenous person to reference her being exiled in a "savage" land. Phillips notes that "A popular plot in contemporary novels allowed lost or captured English ladies and gentlemen to experience the idyllic life of the noble savage for a period before returning to civilization."[14] A needlework encyclopedia gave Victorian ladies instructions in porcupine-quill and moose hair embroidery.[15]

It does seem incredible that the pincushion is made of birch bark in additional to silk; and ornamented with floral motifs done in a combination of silk embroidery and moose hair. The fragile birch bark insets lasted from then to now—the only known material object remaining from Peggy Shippen Arnold.

At Mrs. Cottman's boarding school in Saint John from 1786 she gave lessons in fancy work of course but that her advertisement in a Halifax newspaper included moose hair embroidery likewise takes one aback. The settlers had little budget for the stuff of needlecraft but their using indigenous materials must have also been an emotional connection to place.

From England, Arnold kept in touch with his lawyers as his goods and real estate continued to be sold. Richard, age 21, and Henry, 19, had stayed in Saint John to look after the remaining property while Benedict VI was serving in the British military. States David Goss:

> Some reports say that the offspring, John Sage, lived in the Spruce Lake area. He was about 14 when Arnold died in 1801, and his inheritance of 1200 acres and an annual sum until he was 21 was paid. He could have lived to the 1860s, not in Saint John, however, for records show he moved to Ontario with two of Arnold's other sons. As for Hoyt, or Hayt, he lived on, and to this day has relatives in Saint John, and they are proud of the Hoyt name, and with good reason.

16

Challenging a Duke

> It is astonishing that the murderous practice of dueling
> should continue so long in vogue.—Benjamin Franklin,
> Letter to Thomas Percival, Passy, July 17, 1784

By the late eighteenth century, duels were already an old-fashioned recourse for settling a dispute among men. Still, a man provoked might feel that to keep his reputation he had no choice. It has been suggested that Arnold challenged someone to a duel by whatever weapons they wished, including bow and arrow. In his two known duels Arnold was the challenger and the weapons were pistols. Like other historians, Nathaniel Philbrick interprets that Arnold was "honor-obsessed" and "hypersensitive to any slight."[1] He had to "free himself from the ignominy of his childhood," principally his father's drunkenness. In a debate in the House of Lords on May 31, 1792, after the King had proclaimed against seditious meetings, Lord Lauderdale opposed the proclamation as "a most malignant and impotent measure." In the debate, arguing against an appointment for Charles Lennox, the 3rd Duke of Richmond, he disparaged him for switching from being a liberal, known as "the radical duke," who introduced a parliamentary bill to remove the British from the American colonies, to a Tory who stifled reform: "If apostasy could justify promotion," the noble duke "was the most fit person for that command, General Arnold alone excepted."[2]

This was only weeks after the Arnolds returned from Canada to London. According to Sparks, Arnold was standing near the throne of King George when the petition for the bill was presented, "apparently in high favor with the sovereign."[3]

The Duke of Richmond rose up and denounced Lauderdale (mildly) as one of "these impertinent personalities." When the altercation was published, Lauderdale challenged Richmond to a duel, and Arnold challenged Lauderdale to a different duel. Friends interposed to prevent the first duel and word was sent from Lauderdale to Richmond with brandy and a bouquet of flowers, that "the expressions ... applied solely to the Duke of

James Maitland, 8th Earl of Lauderdale, oil painting by Colvin Smith (courtesy Thirlestane Castle Trust).

Richmond's public conduct, and that he meant nothing in any respect personal to his Grace's private character."[4]

But as in a Buster Keaton movie, further reversals of fortune were to come. Lauderdale said he was sorry but as one might brush off a fly and Arnold was not satisfied. A rumor circulated that Arnold was already shot dead, which Peggy had to deny to her family in Philadelphia lest they saw the falsehood in a newspaper.

A duel was set for seven o'clock Sunday morning, July 7, 1792, two miles beyond Oxford Street in a park near Kilburn Well, where people went for medicinal water. Peggy had found out but remained silent—her exemplary behavior as an eighteenth-century wife raising the point that she may well have remained outside her husband's decision to defect from the American revolutionary cause a decade before. She pretended that she was asleep when Benedict kissed her and departed at that early hour.

The exchange was as follows.[5] Arnold fired intentionally wide. Lauderdale lowered his pistol and said, "I have no enmity towards General Arnold, and did not intend to wound his feelings."

"That is not a sufficient apology," said Arnold.

"Very well, if the General is not satisfied, he is welcome to shoot again."

Lauderdale put down his weapon, conferred with his seconds, and made a better apology. "General, I hereby retract in full. I did not mean to asperse your character and I am sorry for what I said." Everyone shook hands and the general opinion of the duel was that Arnold showed courage for telling Lauderdale to shoot.

When the duel was over a messenger approached from Mrs. Arnold. She was sick with worry. "The earl expressed his regrets and begged Arnold's permission to wait upon her to make his apology." Peggy was supposed to have been confined to bed for several days afterwards. It was for her a siege given that for a week or two before the duel occurred, a London newspaper reported that Arnold had already fought Lauderdale and was dead.

Lauderdale's courtliness regarding what might have been a fatal event was fortunate. Regarding Arnold, the outcome was politically very good. He had been the subject of disagreeable anonymous newsprint, but now other gentlemen could see his dignity.

This was 38 years after a young George Washington deflected a duel over local politics with William Payne, by inviting him to his residence the next morning and having a decanter and two glasses on the table instead of pistols. It was twelve years before the tragic Aaron Burr–Alexander Hamilton duel.

17

Guadeloupe

The sea has never been friendly to man. At most it has been
the accomplice of human restlessness.—Joseph Conrad

When the French Republic had declared war on Britain, during the
Terror, Arnold was sending ships to the West Indies on privateering ventures. He had got a clear message that he would have to go on self-generated
ventures because of the way the director of the East India Company
turned him down for a post: First the director asked for an explanation
of Arnold's past and then said it would not do. He had been trading there
over a period of 35 years and the West Indies is where he had profited since
before the American Revolution. The West Indies market was dominated
by New England and the economies of the sugar-producing islands were
"indispensable to the development of the mainland colonies. Their economies so tightly intertwined that full understanding of developments in
one is impossible without an appreciation of developments in the other."[1]

In his West Indian trading, Arnold went to multiple islands, often on
a single voyage. Even if he had established customers, he did not restrict
his trade to just one island. This was broadly familiar territory. In Martinique before the Revolution, in the 1760s, he had traded cattle, horses, and
lumber, and he had traveled to the Caribbean while in Canada.

In his inveterate push-pull between living handsomely and living
with meager means he decided to trade once more in the region where
he had made his wealth. His family had been living for about two years
on Hollis Street, off Oxford Street, where nearby lived their friends from
America, the Fitch family. Before leaving for Guadeloupe, he moved his
family to a house in Saint Ann Street, London, as he was low on funds
and unsure when he could reap a profit from the trade goods he may have
bought on credit.

For a century, sugar was the key export from the English Caribbean.
"The English produced sugar the way the Spanish mined gold and silver,"
writes Susan Dwyer Amussen; "this was an extraction economy."[2]

The enslaved labor force had to be fed, and provisions had to be brought to this most profitable part of the British colonial empire. First from Connecticut as a young man, and later from New Brunswick in his 40s, Arnold was one of many traders who loaded their ships with staples, meat, grain, dried fish, and lumber and sailed back with semi-refined sugar to England and British Canada. They were not slave carriers but suppliers of the system of the slave labor force.

Slave uprisings began in the French and Spanish possessions. Raising sugar cane was backbreaking and during the harvest, work was organized in shifts so that production continued around the clock. Fighting for freedom was inevitable as the slaves vastly outnumbered the planters. Professor Amussen shows how the protection of property and wealth was at the heart of the legal system on all the colonial islands. Moreover, she states, before slavery was abolished, the social evils exacerbated: "The eighteenth-century Caribbean consolidated the behaviors of the seventeenth century and articulated them more systematically."[3] Thus, a 1755 English guide to planting and growing sugar gave advice on how to keep plantation slaves working non-stop so as to prevent idleness (which Amussen compares to the demands on industrial workers during the early capitalist industrial society).

In *Sugar: A Bittersweet History*, Elizabeth Abbott observes that different islands produced different grades for different grocers and needs. Distillers could use molasses, but tea drinkers needed white sugar. Moreover, supply was seasonal and there were political, banking and insurance factors to sugar commerce. One planter of the Pinneys dynasty lamented in a time of low sugar prices: "We sadly want the report of a war, a hurricane, or a something to give it a lift!"[4] Writes Abbott:

> Shipping was an intrinsically precarious business. Shippers faced competition from each other, from "seekers"—unscheduled ships hoping to attract business—and from foreign ships that illegally serviced the islands. Shipping was vulnerable to war, piracy, and, until the West India Docks were built, forced idling at anchor in ports and insufficient warehouse space to take their sugar.[5]

As to what Arnold was shipping, the items that Abbott enumerates are approximately what his vessels carried during his trading years: planters supplies "including cheap hoes for the slaves," riding gear, brass and copper fittings for the mills and boilers, iron shackles to stop runaways, and draft animals including horses, oxen and mules, and all the fashionable personal items, hats and clothing, musical instruments, books and magazines, pies and Madeira wine, toiletries, medicines, salted and cured meat, and "sugar refined in England and re-exported."

He made his last trading voyage to the Caribbean in the spring of

1794. There had been delays due to bad weather, but he was cheered to be on his way. He intended to stay four or five months and stop at Barbados, Granada, and Dominico (now the Dominican Republic). Peggy persuaded her husband to go overland to Falmouth and wait for his ship rather than risk encountering French privateers in the English Channel. Indeed, his own vessel was captured by the French a few days after it left Falmouth.

Charles-Maurice de Talleyrand-Périgord, known as Talleyrand, the greatest European diplomat of all time, makes a cunning appearance in Benedict's later life, in 1793. Talleyrand was a political refugee who had escaped to England from the Republicans in France. He stayed with Alexander Hamilton's brother-in-law, John B. Church, in London until being ordered by William Pitt to leave the country. Church paid Talleyrand's way to the United States and set up a meeting with Hamilton. However, the ship Talleyrand had sailed in from Greenwich was damaged in a powerful storm, and it docked at Falmouth for repairs. Talleyrand told this story in his memoirs:

> Happily, our danger was noticed fro m shore, and induced a party of seamen from Falmouth to brave the fury of the sea and come to our aid. We managed to reach the harbor. While our ship—all the riggings of which were much damaged—was being repaired, a remarkable incident occurred and added an impression of a new type to all those I was experiencing during this voyage.
>
> The innkeeper at whose lodging I took my meals, told me that an American general was staying at his inn. Thereupon, I attempted to find him. After the usual exchange of greetings, I posed several questions to him concerning his country, which, from the first, seemed to me to trouble him. After several useless attempts to revive a conversation that he continually allowed to drop, I ventured to ask if he would give me letters of introduction to America. "No," he said, and after a few moments of silence, seeing my astonishment, added, "I am perhaps the only American who cannot give you letters for the country ... all the relations I had are broken.... I must never return there."
>
> He dared not tell me his name. It was General Arnold! I must confess that I felt much pity for him, for which political puritans will perhaps blame me, but for which I do not reproach myself, because I witnessed his agony.[6]

In one account, Benedict pushed back his chair, rose to his feet and before he strode from the room handed Talleyrand a card that read "General Benedict Arnold."[7]

The two men of the same generation, and both notorious for self-interest, had in common their apartness from others. Talleyrand is likely to have felt a shudder at someone else who got caught in the machinations of politics and war. He had a sixth sense this stranger was a person with ties to influential Americans and for such contacts Talleyrand would go all out. We know this because after George Washington refused to meet Talleyrand, he made a trip to the remote District of Maine to visit Henry

Falmouth, England, **engraving by J. Farington, published as part of** *Britannia Depicted* **by William Byrne, 1806–1813 (courtesy the Cornish Studies Library of Falmouth).**

Knox, the former Secretary of War, and query him about American leaders over wine and billiards.

Arnold traded in St. Kitts and sailed on to Pointe à Pitre, on the Guadeloupe island of Grand-Terry, with 5,000 pounds to buy sugar.[8] He supposed it to be a friendly port but there had been some legerdemain. Earlier that year the French planters had sought British protection against a slave revolt and then the French slipped through the British blockade and regained Pointe à Pitre. According to Robin Blackburn, several thousand more people of color

The Port of Pointe-à-Pitre, 19th-century illustration from *Le Magasin pittor-esque* (courtesy Archives departmentales de la Guadeloupe).

including former slaves joined with the 1500 troops brought by the French revolutionary government and ejected the British—among them Arnold who had joined the British expedition as a war contractor. Victor Hugues, who won the soubriquet of "the colonial Robespierre" used Guadeloupe as a privateering base for the slave revolts he encouraged in neighboring islands.[9]

When Arnold thought the British had recently taken control, it was in fact the reverse and it was the French revolutionary forces under Victor Hugues who had control. Confusion of this sort was not unusual. The European powers vied for the colonies and the smaller possessions not easily defended went back and forth. Castine, Maine, familiar to Arnold from smuggling in the Passamaquoddy, changed flags eleven times—between British, Dutch, French, and finally American. According to Barbara Tuchman, the busy little St. Eustatius had 22 changes of sovereignty in little more than a century and a half. As if a coin were flipped, a different colonial power would take possession of an island. Except for Jamaica, it seems few were heavily defended.

After Arnold sailed into the Point à Pitre harbor he tried to bluff his way out but was taken prisoner and put in jail. He masqueraded under the name of John Anderson—the cover name John André had used. This is quite bizarre: why choose the alias that Major John André gave to the militia in New York? The jailors assessed that they had a special catch and put him on an outgoing French prison ship. Under threat of execution, Arnold bribed sailors for the information that British vessels were nearby serving

FRANCE MARITIME

The Port of Pointe-à-Pitre, drawing by L. Garneray, engraving by Traversier from *La France maritime*, 19th century (courtesy Archives departmentales de la Guadeloupe).

as a blockade. The sailors provided him with a raft as well and he stashed his valuables into a cask with a letter explaining whose they were, which he tossed into the sea. He lowered himself from a cabin window by a rope to the makeshift raft, which he propelled through the water.

By his daring escape, combined with the good luck of reaching a small craft that was moored at a distance between his French captors and the British flagship that had arrived to blockade the port, he managed to row on, guiding by its lights. Some say he wrapped the oars to pass silently in the night; by other accounts he rowed with one oar, or there were no oars and he used his hands. At some point he abandoned the boat and swam. He managed to reach the HMS *Boyne* with the French in hot pursuit (the ship was soon burned in action). The cask floated into a section of Guadeloupe occupied by a British landing force, so he recovered his valuables as well. According to Sparks, "Although hailed by a French guard-boat, he escaped under the cover of darkness, and at four o'clock in the morning was safe on the deck of a British vessel."[10]

Arnold's smuggling of the likes of rum and sugar, boards and staves had been benign, but now in the West Indies in 1794–1795 he allied to the planters in putting down the slave rebellions. Whether directly involved in the merchandising of people or not he was a reprehensible bystander. This

Sugar-cane plantation, 1876 (courtesy New York Public Library).

smuggling bears comparison to Joseph Conrad's smuggling guns from coves near Marseilles to Spain.

Arnold's decision to make a bright business future for himself by returning to his well-trodden path of Caribbean trade was retrograde. That is, the apologia for his changing sides in the American Revolution made sense but his participation in the ugly war against the enslaved people of Guadeloupe did not. People were questioning slavery publicly in Britain. The planters felt the pinch of that and also the alternate sources for sugar competing with them. That Arnold locked his activities in the hub of the slave system cannot but offend. He saw the wretchedness of that society. In *The Slave Trade*, James Walvin clarifies several points that add to the outrageousness of what Arnold must have observed (as we know he didn't stay shipboard), including how the enslaved people were kept willfully ill and underfed by the planters, and that some of the refining was done in situ under terrible conditions. At the height of the Jamaican slave plantations, the local slave labor force was 200 per plantation, and the small island of Barbados had about 1000 plantations. In the factories and distilleries, the complex production of sugar was managed by skilled slaves.[11] Slaves also worked on the coastal vessels throughout the Caribbean and up the North Atlantic, and at great peril some used that as a route to escape.

The backdrop is that in 1794, the National Convention in Paris abolished slavery throughout the French colonies. Hugues executed Royalist planters and, until Napoleon brought slavery back, the people on the island were free. Arnold became not only someone with heavy mercantile investment in slavery but also a combatant for slave societies. When he was an up and coming merchant in New Haven, he did not penetrate the planters' society beyond the periphery. He can be partially excused for a glib acceptance of its evils. But the late eighteenth century saw a public debate in Britain on slavery to which Arnold turned a deaf ear. Susan D. Amussen affirmed this to me, speaking of an era after her major study, *Caribbean Exchanges: Slavery and the Transformation of English Society, 1640–1700*:

> There was an emergent abolitionist movement in Britain, as well as defensiveness among planters in the islands. There are defenses of slavery to counter the criticism: scientific ideas of race emerge. Olaudah Equiano's autobiography was published in the 1780s. So there's no reason that Arnold would not know that there was a controversy about slavery. He took a side. Of course the planters praised him.

Benedict's callousness must have come from his status as one of the masters but also self-willed ignorance. How differently the cooper John Nicol, an ordinary seaman from Scotland, 14 years younger than Arnold, processed what he saw in St. Kitts and other West Indian islands at the same time. As a raconteur, Nicol told incidents of cruel abuse yet recalled also the humanity and brio of the slaves he got to know when they extended hospitality to guests like himself. (He told all this in a memoir published when he was old in 1822.)[12]

For a few months Arnold was now an unofficial aide to Sir Charles "Flint" Grey with the role of quartermaster. It was said by one officer on the ship that Arnold wanted a promotion to senior brigadier. This is unverified but mentioned by Randall. Grey was André's former commander during the war in the West Indies. Benedict was in his fifties and he really did the work. At the New York Public Library is a letter about paying him for the beef he had delivered. This aligns with another instance of Arnold's being "victualer," with certain contracts for supplying troops in New Brunswick when he moved there.[13]

Peggy was distraught when she had no letter from her husband for a year. She knew the flags had changed at his destination before he did and supposed him in prison. She gave birth to her last child, William Fitch, on June 25, and in August was beside herself from a report that Benedict had been imprisoned by the French.

The year after he was quartermaster was when Arnold organized a planters' militia. The planters feared slaves in Guadeloupe would gain

Colonel William Fitch and his Sisters Sarah and Ann Fitch by John Singleton Copley, 1800/1801 (courtesy National Gallery of Art).

the strength of the revolt in Haiti of 1791. In fact, the planters benefited from uprisings on other islands but wanted the slave system in Guadeloupe to go on undisturbed. Though the planters were mostly French, they appealed to the British for protection. Both sides were grisly. The British were still in the slave trade and the Jacobin general Victor Hugues governed (1794–1798). The son of a Marseille baker and of French and African descent, Hugues proclaimed freedom for the slaves, a liberty lasting until Napoleon enslaved them again.

During this time, besides managing army provisions under Sir Charles Grey, Arnold acted as an agent for the planters of Guadeloupe and Martinique affected by the British withdrawal of troops. This was familiar territory. In Martinique Arnold had traded cattle, horses and lumbering in the 1760s. Arnold wrote Bliss from St. Pierre in Martinique. After mentioning his approval of a debt that Mr. Putnam had settled for him in Saint John, he went on to Bliss, to whom he expressed himself in a leisurely personal fashion more than to anyone else:

> As you say nothing of Mrs. Bliss and your little or great little, or great little family, I suppose by this time, I conclude that you, and they enjoy health, and I hope happiness, you are doubtless free from the dangers of War, which is a

great happiness at this time, when it is carried on with a brutality unknown to former times, and very little to the honor of humanity or cause of freedom.

My situation has often been dangerous and critical, my affairs sometimes have prospered, and sometimes not. I have made and lost a great deal of money here, but I hope to return to England in April a gainer upon the whole.[14]

He also wrote Chipman of his "distress of burying two-thirds of my acquaintances in these islands since I came out."[15]

He did not get along with the commander Sir Charles Grey, however, which was another of the odd repeats in the life of Arnold, if it is true that he was denied a promotion to senior brigadier he felt he deserved. A doctor named John Park from New Hampshire spent a year at Martinique working at a hospital in St. Pierre and wrote a snatch of his memoir about Arnold's activities purveying for the English troops at that time and place. According to Dr. Park,

> Here, as in America, he was selfish, avaricious, and in his commercial dealings required looking after…. Whatever he might have been in early life, he was now soured in temper, and generally quarreled with every person with whom he had any business transaction.
>
> Arnold had bought a quantity of flour from a Captain Art from Philadelphia. Arnold rode up to a store (mid. 1796) and shouting disputed the price. At length the General shook his gold-headed cane at Captain Art, and with an oath called him a rascal. Art quietly replied, "General, you may call me by any name you please, except Traitor!" Arnold instantly wheeled his horse and rode off, while the bystanders, English as well as American, burst into a loud laugh.[16]

The picture of Arnold shaking his cane, and that he had learned to leave those who goaded him rather than get embroiled, are what comes across in Dr. Park's anecdote. Arnold wrote Bliss one letter where he had not had news of his friend, in which he explained,

> I expected ere this to have been on my way to England, but have been detained by the insurrection in some of the Islands, which I am sorry to say is not in a fair way to be quelled, I expect now to embark in the Fleet bound to England/ which is fixed to sail on the 12th Inst./ where I shall be glad to hear from you.[17]

When he departed for England, a standing committee of merchants and planters wrote the government in London wanting him back, saying he had covered a retreat of the troops and they needed him to carry out a relief expedition.

Forty thousand of the British were lost through battling the French, insurrection of the slaves and yellow fever. Arnold's eldest son Benedict volunteered to fight the French in the West Indies just after a brief return to England from being imprisoned in France, and against his father's wishes. In the hills of Jamaica, Benedict VI was wounded in the leg and—another repetition—like his father refused to let his leg be amputated—only Benedict the son perished there in 1795. Arnold wrote Bliss again in August 1795 from England:

> In this age of revolutions and the consequent horrors and devastations of war, you are certainly fortunate to be placed in a snug corner, in a great measure out of reach of them, a happiness which thousands of the great ones of the earth sigh for in vain. If we are disposed to philosophize, there is great consolation to be drawn from our situations, which are comfortable but not sufficiently elevated to be objects of envy and distinction. We therefore ought to be content, which is the greatest happiness to be expected in this world.[18]

The planters' association saw slave uprisings as brushfire and wanted the man who had acted as agent for them during his time in the Caribbean, Benedict Arnold back and heading special forces. Arnold was amenable but the government in London did not want him to command such an expedition. Neither that nor his offer to captain a privateer to fight Napoleon was granted by the War Office. But Arnold gave the planters a formal address in London in August 1795, which was applauded. The hall where he spoke is extant, now the Manor House, at 21 Soho Square (formerly Wright's House). One can almost hear the applause.

On his return, Arnold took his family on a long vacation to Chigwell, a village in Essex. He was now about 57. Peggy wrote Edward in India about his father's travails:

> the disappointment of all his pecuniary expectations, with the numerous vexations and mortifications he had endured, had so broken his spirits and destroyed his nerves that he had for some time before his death "been incapable of the smallest enjoyment."[19]

The father was weighed down by debts.

And yet, Benedict was well rewarded for serving in the West Indies. Based on his actions, the government gave him 13,400 acres in Canada—"in consequence of his late gallant and meritorious service in Guadeloupe." Initially he petitioned the Executive Council of Upper Canada for the grant, not that he ever intended to live in the "Inhospitable Wilderness" but for his sons and Arnold this time managed to finesse politics. As the petition, originally (1797) for 50,000 acres, progressed, the Canadian Home Department conferred with John Graves Simcoe, the former lieutenant governor of Upper Canada, back in England but still influential in Canadian affairs.

In a letter of 26 March 1798, Simcoe warned the Home Secretary, the Duke of Portland, that "General Arnold is a character extremely obnoxious to the original Loyalists of America." Nevertheless, Simcoe observed that there was no legal impediment to granting the petition—provided his demand were scaled down considerably.[20] Upon reflection he recommended that the petition be granted at the behest of the Crown rather than by the colonial authorities alone.

The Duke took up Simcoe's idea and Simcoe, who had much resented the death of Major André, at least got his jab in. On June 12, 1798, 13,400 acres were granted Arnold.[21] Furthermore, the King dispensed with the condition of residence in Canada. The grant (situated in the townships of Gwillimbury East and North in Ontario present-day) was so large that Arnold protested the usual fee, a tax per acre charged grantees. The Duke of Portland, the Home Secretary, agreed to waive the fee as well as to having Richard and Henry locate lands for their father.

Benedict's prestige rose. At a time when most Loyalists only were granted a shred of what they asked for, he had vast lands (even if they were known as wastelands) in North America. Before leaving for Guadeloupe, Arnold moved his family to a modest house in Saint Ann Street. In the fall of 1796, the Arnolds moved up to a townhouse in Gloucester Place.

Arnold still had dreams of great military action in his mind, again setting his sights where he had a brilliant record of success. In December 1796 he created a plan for an expedition against the Spanish West Indies, to capture Chile, Peru and New Mexico. Lord Cornwallis, who had been in touch ever since he and Arnold sailed from New York on the same ship in the British evacuation, presented Arnold's proposal to William Pitt. Isaac Arnold cites a draft of the letter to Earl Spencer of the British cabinet. If the government gave him a fleet and 5,000 men he would "raise so formidable an army of the natives, creoles, and people of color, that no force that Spain has there, or can send to that country will be able to resist or prevent their freeing the country form the Spanish government."[22] It was rejected and Arnold was frustrated in his other attempt as an old soldier to prove his valor, as well, to command a small fleet of fireships in the English Channel.

Peggy thought she could be contented in a very humble retired situation but to see her children's "rising prospects blasted" would fill her with agony.[23]

The next year he was granted 13,400 more acres in the "Wastelands of Upper Canada," now Ontario, for his "very gallant and meritorious service at Guadeloupe": 5,000 for himself, the remainder for his wife and five younger children, and for Hannah, 1,200. To the most powerful lobbyist group in the empire, he was deemed a hero. However, he was unable to return to the West Indies because of ill health. Instead he invested, indeed, over-invested, in others' privateering ventures during the last five years of his life.

18

Correspondents

it is necessary to write a letter to a friend,
—and, forthwith, troops of gentle thoughts invest themselves, on every hand, with chosen words.
—Ralph Waldo Emerson, Essay VI

One of my daughters, when teenaged, suggested I cultivate friends I could see more often than my closest friends, who live at a distance. The means to accomplish this would be to change my footwear from sandals to shoes with toes and a little heel. "But I have enough friends," I said, thinking of shoes and social occasions that pinch. She shook her head. "Those are pen pals."

In the late eighteenth century, friendship by correspondence had style. Once the Arnolds moved back to England, they had a coterie of Loyalist friends, but Arnold's friend of the heart was Jonathan Bliss, though they must have suspected they would never see each other again. Once (May 23, 1792), he went so far as epistolary demonstrativeness, telling Bliss that he and Peggy regretted the absence of friends in Saint John and wished they could be reunited for the winter in London.

Sometimes a second letter was written before a first was received, and sometimes a letter went on a ship to another destination before wending its way to London. Letter writing was of course the means of communication at long distances. However, for Arnold, back in London writing to Bliss in New Brunswick, their correspondence had more utility than that: When he wrote to Bliss, he could express feelings. When Sophia's health concerned him, or a son was taking prizes at school, Arnold wanted Bliss to know. The correspondence dates from Arnold's fifties but the friendship from a decade before. The two men must have been persuasive when they talked up Campobello to the universitarian, David Owen—giving him the idea he could master a Welsh kingdom at the edge of North America, along the lines of how Thomas Hardy would invent Wessex. Arnold wasn't prone to write, and his rhetoric was unembellished. He picked up pen and paper to calculate and carry out his enterprises.

Polished prose was something that he did not attempt outside of a few early love letters. Nevertheless, he made his discontent crystal clear in letters to George Washington during the Revolution, and in middle age, when this present work catches up with him, he had a perfect medium of unburdening thought while conducting his business affairs, in his correspondence with his attorney. In the potpourri of a letter he could tuck in a philosophical thought too.

The friendship of the wry, cynical New Englanders continued despite slight rebukes, as when Bliss said it was uphill doing Arnold's business because he was unpopular in the province, and Arnold's prodding once for a small debt from Bliss himself. Nevertheless, the contrast is marked between the tenacious way that Arnold pursued debts and the relaxed way he gave business instructions to his friend. The writer of a personal letter now may wish to show special consideration, or avoid communicating face to face, for whatever reason, including the polite gesture, but in the eighteenth century a friendship at long distance was frequently deemed emotionally strong. The Arnolds wrote from London to their acquaintances in New Brunswick, after their departure, bragging about their children and apprising friends of ups and downs, as though they were neighbors, and of course Benedict had some business there; Louis Quigley states that the last property in the Arnold family name was sold in 1839.

Arnold wrote numerous letters to Jonathan Bliss that are preserved and have particular interest, which vary from personal to business. Combining the two was typical of the period, and thus rather than quote entire letters, it is more revealing to look at selected passages from a few of them.

One testimony of friendship was Arnold via Bliss offering fleecy hosiery to Ward Chipman and Judge Upham, thinking of them in the fall of 1792. He sent a gift of hosiery, gloves and under-hose to each, together with a packet for Mrs. Chipman.[1] As a seaman Arnold was accustomed to bone-chilling cold and was thinking of what had made his gouty legs less tired. He was of course not being randomly generous as these were men of influence in the Maritimes and he had quite a bit of unfinished business regarding his properties in the province.

In 1795, Arnold conveyed to Bliss the news that Arnold's son Benedict had died in Jamaica. Bliss would have heard by other means. It is painful for a good friend to suppose all is well when one's family has suffered such a loss; sharing somber news is connecting with a friend who cares.

And when Bliss's wife died, Arnold wrote a letter of sympathy that while conventional has the coin of sincerity: "It is vain to offer you consolation, time only with the hope of meeting again in happier regions can reconcile you to so heavy and distressing a loss."[2] Such a letter writes itself, and this one begins with a disclaimer of not being able to console, and yet there is more weight to the expression, and the sentence is drawn out with seeming regret. Arnold too had lost a wife and had worries over Peggy's health.

The topics discussed in the letters vary from personal to business to abstract observations. Combining the intimate and the mundane was typical of the period. It is revealing to look at a few of them simply as letters rather than bring all into the story chronologically.

In her correspondence Peggy displayed a pretty warmth to the old friends in the province. The Blisses had moved into the Arnolds' former home on King Street by 1795. Peggy wrote in a tone that was pleasant without nostalgia that she was glad "that you are so comfortably settled in our old habitation and that you enjoy so much domestic happiness."[3] It was about four years later she wrote the Chipmans, "I hear much of the gaiety of your little city.... I shall always regret my separation from many valuable friends among the first of whom I shall reckon Mrs. Chipman."[4] By then, another best friend, Mary Worthington Bliss, had passed away (delivering their fifth child after ten years of marriage).

Yet Bliss for Peggy too was the faraway friend she wrote. Bliss was still looking after Arnold's affairs in New Brunswick and was a lifeline for Peggy. She wrote him directly and honestly as she struggled to clear debts from Benedict's estate and keep a good outlook. Pride overarched her emotional and economic hardship.

A dozen of the letters that are part of the correspondence between Arnold and Bliss are included here for their insight into General Arnold ten and fifteen years after betraying his comrades in arms in 1780.

Sharing with a nonjudgmental equal is the importance of Arnold's letters to Bliss during the fraught years when his health and finances, and Peggy's health, were in decline. Arnold might have said of them that they were like instruments whose lives and views wove into a single song. Both had lost a previous identity, devoted themselves to their families, had gout, loved their wives and worried about their health, worked hard and often were frustrated. They were a remnant of another society, carrying on. They were also quite discreet and had to read between the lines of what each heard from the other.

Gout is a treatable form of arthritis. It has been understood since the nineteenth century to be caused by urate crystals in the joints. The body produces uric acid which is secreted naturally, keeping a balance in the blood, but in this condition, urate crystals form in the joints and cause inflammation and needles of pain. That it was in the past called "The King's Disease" correlates with why people put up with it longer and more than they had to. King Charlemagne dragged a leg but refused to follow his doctors' advice to switch from roast meat to boiled.[5] The affliction of gout became a literary cliché so when an author like Herman Melville describes a man as having gout, a picture arises of a heavyset older man moving creakily.

Age-Old Gout
By Dr. Martina Scholtens[6]

Historical literary references give insight into the popular perceptions of and fantasies about gout. An early example is the fable involving Monsieur Gout and his traveling companion, a spider, first recorded in a medical handbook by Richard Hawes, a Puritan minister, in 1634. Monsieur Gout lodged with a poor man and the spider with a rich one. They both had complaints which they exchanged the next day.

"Mine," said Gout, "was the worst as I ever had, for I had no sooner touched the poor man's legs, thinking there to take my rest, but up he gets, and to thrashing he goes, so that I had not rest the whole night."

"And I," said the spider, "had no sooner begun to build my house in the rich man's chamber, but the maid came with a broom, and tore down all my work."

It occurred to them to switch places, and when each was gratified by his new abode, they decided to put up permanent residence. Henceforth the spider's webs were not disturbed by the poor man, and "the Gout he was entertained with a soft cushion, with down pillows, with dainty caudles, and delicate broths. In brief, he did like it so well, that ever since he takes up his lodging with rich men."[7]

The fable professes to account for why gout was more common among the upper class. It was dubbed *morbus dominorum et dominus morborum*, "the disease of lords and the lord of diseases." Its name even had the status of a deity—Podagra being the daughter of Dionysus, the god of wine, and the goddess of love, Aphrodite, in Greek mythology. The ancient Roman writings hypothesized that gout resulted from service to these gods and afflicted those who overindulged in sex, food, and wine, a hypothesis carried over into medicine of the Middle Ages and Renaissance.[8]

A sufferer could also pin hope in 16th to 18th century Europe on a belief that gout was a remedy. Jonathan Swift articulated this concept in a birthday poem for an acquaintance ("Bec's Birthday," 1726).

> As, if the gout should seize the head,
> Doctors pronounce the patient dead;
> But, if they can, by all their arts,
> Eject it to th'extreamest parts,
> They give the sick man joy, and praise
> The gout that will prolong his days:
> Rebecca thus I gladly greet,
> Who drives her cares to hands and feet.

In keeping with a pre-modern idea that diseases were mutually exclusive, better gout than a worse affliction. Gout was understood to be a sort of insurance policy preventing other illnesses and prolonging life. By the late 18th century the English writer Horace Walpole said he was serious when espousing this view to a friend, yet sounds a little facetious when after advising the friend to keep his limbs warm in all seasons, declares he himself is perfectly recovered from my last fit; and am persuaded you will be so too, if you let the gout take its full career. It comes exactly to offer you health; and, as your feet swell, I presume upon easy terms. I have as good an opinion of the gout, that, when I am told of an infallible cure, I laugh the proposal to scorn, and declare I do not desire to be cured ... no wonder there is no medicine for it, nor do I desire to be fully cured of a remedy.[9]

A 16th century Italian physician and mathematician, Hieronymys Cardanus, penned a witty encomium to gout that underlines its connection with voluptuousness, how "those who are restrained by her are compelled to lead lives that, except for the pain itself are happy. For she does not render them sterile but restores them to Venus with increased Prowess."[10]

There are several reasons why gout was associated with sexual prowess. First, as Michel de Montaigne wrote in an essay "Of Cripples" ("Des Boyteux") in the 1580s, when the legs did not receive nourishment it was available to make the genitals more vigorous. Secondly energy was not dissipated in walking. Thirdly, bedrest of the person suffering gout meant that sperm wended easily through channels from the kidneys to the loins (a concept suggested by Gerhardus Feltmann, a Dutch jurist in 1693).

On the other hand, it is now understood that steak, organ meats, and beer, so integral to the diet of amply fed 18th century English gentlemen, contributed to the prevalence of the disease, increasing the frequency and severity of attacks over time.

Benedict Arnold suffered gout for weeks at a time. He lived during a period of more modern medicine, yet aphrodisiacs were still very popular. He must have been aware of the lore around the disease. It would have reassured him that the condition conveyed increased social status and, for men, increased potency. Dr. Scholtens notes that the modern treatments for gout were not available until the 19th and 20th centuries, and that the fleecy stockings he wore may have been to cushion his joints against his boots. "Any footwear, especially if tight, restrictive or ill-fitting, would apply pressure to inflamed joints and cause pain. Untreated flares typically last days to weeks. Some sufferers have more than one joint involved and can be disabled for longer periods."

This affliction that must have upset the self-image of these distinguished men. Benedict's children's welfare, his honor, and his gout were on his mind more than anything else in his last two decades. It was best to tread lightly when mentioning one's gout. In his letter from New Brunswick to Halifax, Mather Byles, Jr., was careful in his wording to keep things light:

Major Upham has had a return of his disorder and is now very low.
Mr. Brittian tells me that your gout is still hanging about you. I hope it does

not carry on the attack so violently as to prevent your amusing yourself with your sleigh, or sporting at the Annapolis Assemblies.[11]

Arnold and Bliss wrote often in the years after 1791 until Benedict's death. The following letters, transcriptions in whole or in part from the collection of the New Brunswick Museum, constitute a sampling. From Saint John to Hollis Street, London, Bliss wrote almost jocularly about a debt paid:

> *Sir*
>
> *You have herewith a copy of my last of 23d of Oct. I have just returned from Frederic-ton in time to forward by Robinson on the Paymaster General, value One Hundred and Fifty Pounds Sterling payable to myself or order and indorsed over to you. This is the first Bill I have been able to procure, without giving a Premium, since the last payment received on Hayt and other Bond; and I would not omit so good an opportunity of mak-ing you a Remittance of a larger sum that is due to you.*
> *I am your most obed. Servant.*
>
> Jon. Bliss[12]

From Saint John to London, July 2, 1793, Bliss's run-on account of all the debts/actions he was following up on had him remarking as though at the end of his tether:

> I observe what you say respecting Munson Hayt's Bond of Indemnity for the Costs in the action against Murray. I don't find that Bond among your papers in my hands, but presume it is in the Trunk, which still remains in in Mr. Put-nam's warehouse. I shall look it up if occasion require. I have before written to you that I had communication with Mr. James Hayt upon this business, and of Mr. James Hayt for his Brother's answer, but none has yet been received. Mr. James Hayt says he expects soon to hear from him; but I confess I have great doubts whether it will be to your satisfaction.[13]

He promised to settle with the sheriff about Lyman's farm in Fredericton (which Arnold was trying to sell). "But I shall not know what to do with the Land if we get it. Here all are sellers and none buyers."[14] Then, Bliss on the upswing says he encloses a bill of exchange for one hundred pounds and "I hope to be able in a few days to procure and send you another bill." He addressed his correspondent formally as General Arnold in this letter but in the postscript told him,

> I have the great happiness to acquaint you and Mrs. Arnold that Mrs. Bliss was this morning safely delivered of a fine Boy. And they are both, God be praised! as well as can be expected. Accept Mrs. Bliss's and my best respects for you all.

An unusually long letter Arnold wrote Bliss discussed the baker, Jabez Cables, who didn't pay for flour, had a key to the storeroom and claimed he was due pay for watching over it. This is of interest because it demonstrates how Bliss fell in with Arnold's punctiliousness, that indeed some in Saint John might have wanted to gull the rich merchant Arnold, and also that a barrel of flour was a valuable commodity. Then again, this was on Benedict's mind when he had not been away from Saint John for a year yet. Barry Wilson explicates the trouble the account with Cables the baker caused. On the back of the letter (October 4, 5, 1791) Arnold wrote that the matter had been settled by arbitration.

Returned to London, Arnold was relying for practical matters on his friend. Much of what he had was still in Canada and he wanted to show gratitude to Bliss for being such a good support: The "shipwreck" letter is here reproduced in entirety:

Dear Sir

A severe fit of the gout on my voyage from St. John, and since my arrival in London (until within a few days that I am tolerably well) has prevented my writing to my Friends at St. John, from whom we have not heard since the arrival of Mr. Thompsons ship.

We had a very rough and disagreeable voyage home, but our reception has been very pleasant, and our Friends been, more than well attentive to us since our arrival. The little property that we have saved from the hands of a Lawless Ruffian Mob, and more unprincipled judges in New Brunswick, is perfectly safe here, as well as our Persons from Insult, and tho we feel and regret the absence of the Friends we had there, we find London full as pleasant! And I cannot help viewing your great City as a ship wreck from which I have escaped.

I have not heard from, or of my Son Richard since he left the States bound to the West Indies, and am very apprehensive for his safety—should an accident have happened to him. I suppose Henry will be in St. John on receipt of this letter, I have wrote to him respecting the Frame of the Ship, and other matters, and have requested Mr. Putnam to open his letters (in case of his absence) for your government, respecting the same. I hope you will be successful in collecting the debts left in your hands.

I have taken the liberty to Inclose a patern of a New Manufactory, called Flury Hosiery, much wore in this Country, and I think much better calculated for yours, especially Gouty People, and those who are Old, or travel in winter, the prices are fixed to the Card, I beg you will be so good as to show it to Judge Upham, and Mr. Chipman & present my compt. To them, should they, or you wish for any of it I will send it with pleasure. My Bankers, Messrs Donet & Co inform me that they sent you out a small bill £10.18.4 under protest, which I recd from Thos. Chandler Esqr. I hope you have recd it. I must refer you to the Public Papers for news.

Mrs. Arnold writes with me in best Respects to Mrs. Bliss, and yourself, in Sincere wishes for your health & Happiness, and a tender of our services in this Country:— with much esteem

> *I am*
> *Dear Sir*
> *Yours Sincerely*
> *B. Arnold*[15]

Thanks came back to Arnold from Bliss for the patterns of the fleecy hosiery.

Bliss's communications abound in who owed whom and whose debt was hopeless to collect, who might pay and sometimes who Arnold was owing (a small amount). Judge Upham held a note to pay, and Mr. Botsford communicated with Jonathan Bliss about a debt. Mr. Putnam, who handled some of Arnold's affairs, was out of the province but was expected in the spring and would proceed in the affair of someone named Joseph Ward. Bliss was given by Mr. Wetmore a copy of an account by which Arnold owed him, but he stated later that he had received money from "Executive Agent Thos. Fowler, which will make the Ball. A little in your favor. I shall examine this matter more exactly, expecting soon to see Mr. Wetmore." (Thomas Wetmore, an attorney, originally of Rye, New York, had studied law in the office of Ward Chipman.) Bliss continued:

> I have not received a single offer, or Proposal for the Purchase of any part of your Property in this Province.
>
> As I go constantly to Church by Day and to Bed by Night your present of fleecy hosiery Cap & Stockings would have been very acceptable—[unreadable] the French citizen Bonapart for detaining them! I lost some Books too....[16]

From "Chigwell near London" on August 15, 1795, Arnold opened all stops and wrote to Bliss a ruminating letter about war and his family. It was the Napoleonic War, and one can imagine Benedict melancholy at a desk writing his friend while Peggy was ill. This is one of half a dozen letters that mention the bonnet for Mrs. Bliss, as though the Arnolds suspected she was poorly and wanted to betoken their affection for her.

Dear Sir

My last letter to you was dated the 4th of May from Martinique.... I arrived safe here in the ... Frigate, when I had the pleasure to observe by your letters to Mrs. Arnold, that yourself & Mrs. Bliss & your little Boys enjoyed health & happiness, even as you say at New Brunswick; In this age of revolutions, and the consequent honors and devastations of War, you are certainly fortunate to be placed in a snug corner, in a great measure out of the reach of them, a happiness which thousands of the great Ones of the Earth Sigh for in Vain. And if we are disposed to Philosophize there is great consolation to be drawn from our Situations, which are comfortable but not sufficiently Elevated to be the objects of envy and distinction—we therefore ought to be Content which is the greatest happiness to be expected in this world. Mrs. Arnold has been here about six weeks, with her little family, for the benefit of the Country Air. She is not in a good state of health but I hope the Country Air and Exercise will restore her. Our three Boys and little Girl are placed at exceeding good schools where they improve very much. Edward the oldest will soon have the start of me in height & is a remarkable forward & fine boy. We propose to go to Town soon when Mrs. Arnold bids me say, that she will certainly procure & send the Bonnet. She then proposes writing to Mrs. Bliss. Interim joins me in best respects to her & yourself and in sincere wishes for the health and happiness of you & your little Boys. I beg my Compl. To all Friends and am with great regard and Esteem

> *Dear Sir*
> *Sincerely Yours*
> *B. Arnold*[17]

The postscript of Benedict's last letter to Jonathan Bliss: "Pray be so good as to inform me of our lots on the Road to the French Village of which I have 1000 acres/are now, or likely hereafter to be worth any thing" (courtesy New Brunswick Museum).

Bliss's notation of the intervals between when the above was sent, received and answered suggests how long news of one's friend had to last: "Genl. Arnold Aug. 15 '95. Recd. Decr. 8th '95. Ansd. Jany 22d '96."

The Arnolds' spell at Cheltenham coincided with an improvement in Peggy's health which Benedict did not attribute to the spa. Doctors brought out his irony and when a doctor who had tended Peggy died, Benedict noted he was rich from his patients but not able to save himself. Regarding a recurring theme, Jonathan Bliss had asked Peggy Arnold for a favor back in October (1794). She answered the next June that it "never came to hand" until late May and she replied a fortnight later, apologizing:

> I am greatly mortified at, as it put it out of my power to execute the little commission you favored me with, in time for the first spring ships ... but be assured that I shall avail myself of the first opportunity of complying with your wishes.—and I beg It in my power to be useful to you, should you want any thing done in this Country, I beg you will command me.—I received your favor inclosing John Robinsons Bill for £60 stirling, which was duly paid. I fear I have been remiss in not sooner acknowledging it, but you Lords of the Creation will make all due allowances for the ignorance of our sex.[18]

Peggy self-deprecated and expressed warmth, even at the close telling "Mrs. B." "to kiss her darling boys for me." In a lower register, the man to man letter also folded in emotional content. The minuet of happy and sad news, and what is of moment for oneself, the condition of one's family, and a pinch of levity is especially evident in this next purely friendly letter from Benedict to Bliss (September 5, 1795). One senses how the General needed to tell Bliss he would be out of contact for a while, but was *en mission*, and that the situation of his children was thriving, so the time was right for him to leave:

> *Dear Sir*
>
> *I wrote to you the 15th Ult. And left my letter in Town to go by the Post with several others for St. John, the Servant (in my absence in the Country) omitted sending yours & Mrs. Putnam's which I intended should go by the Packet, & which you will receive by this opporty.*
>
> *Mrs. Arnold I am sorry to inform you is very much an invalid, but as her disorder is in great measure nervous, I hope she will soon get the better of it.*
>
> *I have been applied to, to go out to the Wt. Indies in a Military Character, & have agreed, if my terms are complied with, in which case, I shall soon leave England for the Wt. Indies, a few days will determine the matter.*
>
> *Mrs. A has wrote to Mrs. Bliss & by Capt Mall sends her a Bonnet, which I hope will please her, as I am told it is very fashionable, a thing of great importance;—I think it pretty.*
>
> *I have the pleasure to say that my little family are all well & improved very much since our arrival here, Edward is nearly as tall as myself, & bids fair to be very tall. They are both Excellent Scholars & have lately carried most of the prises in the Academy, where*

Cheltenham Spa (courtesy Cheltenham Trust and Collections).

they are near one hundred Boys—They all speak French as well as English, and the Master of the School assures me that George (who is Master of his Grammar) will make a Figure—he has great ambition. If you was not a fond Father yourself I should apologize for troubling you, with the history of my little family.
I beg my best Respects to Mrs. Bliss & to be remembered to all friends in particular Mr. Park & Mr. Chipman.

> *I am with great regard*
> *Dear Sir*
> *Very Sincerely Yours*
> *B. Arnold[19]*

A further letter referencing the bonnet epitomizes how the friendship of the two persons dovetailed with their business:

Dear Sir,

You will with this receive copies of my Letters of the 9th and 10th of November inst. With a copy of Mr. Chipman's Letter to me on the Business of the Demand of the Corporation for Rents &c—Have now to thank Mrs. Arnold for a very elegant Bonnett, received a few Days ago, in the Brig Hope, from London. The amount of the Milliner's Bill, viz 29.6 Sterlg I have carried to your Credit in my Books, and notwithstanding the Receipt of this Bonnett I still beg the Favour of Mrs. Arnold's ordering one in the Spring, as requested in my letter of the 9th. But wish it to be an undress Bonnett and less costly Mrs. B. will write to Mrs. Arnold by the present Opportunity

> *I am with great Regard &x &c &c*
> *Jon. Bliss[20]*

Abbreviating one's first name showed economy of time, writing and paper. Arnold sometimes wrote the addressee as "Jona." The whole form of a letter from salutation to signature allowed for much variation. Spelling too could be expressive, like Frenchifying the hat with an extra "T." An entire letter, from Benedict to Bliss in March 1796 and received close to two months later, dealt with bonnets:

> *Dear Sir*
>
> *The foregoing is Copy of my last, since which I have not had the pleasure of hearing from St. John.-*
> *Mrs. Arnold has procured the Gown & Bonnet for Mrs. Bliss according to your directions. I hope that they will arrive safe & please her. Mrs. A. will write to Mrs. Bliss and send her the part; Acct. which is abt £8.14. I have advised her to send them to Harrison Ansley & Co. or to Messr Holms & Co to go out with Mr. Putnams goods—as they will probably go safe than in loose packages.*
> *I am with best Comps to Mrs. Bliss*
>
> > *Dear Sir yours Sincerely*
> > *B. Arnold*
> > *The gown & Bonnet go by the ship Catharine, C— Master pack'd at by Holms & Co. among Mr. Putnams goods.*
> > *B.A.*[21]

A favor such as buying a bonnet for the wife of a friend in a remote part of the empire was a nice frill. Two other exchanges and another bonnet were topics addressed to Bliss by Benedict in 1799 from Gloucester Place. Such a topic is tucked in rather than dominating a letter. He begins one thanking Bliss "for your exertions in recovering my debts, which I have experienced to do business in your Country attended with much trouble." Next the bonnet, cheek to jowl with the war with Napoleon and Arnold's over-imbibing:

> Mrs. Arnold has with pleasure executed Mrs. Bliss's Commission for a Bonnet, which will be pack'd up tomorrow and sent to Messrs. Banbridge Ansley & Co, as directed to go by the Oriana—Cpt Patterson, who is to sail for St. John in a few days, by which ship she intends to write to Mrs. Bliss.
>
> The War on the Continent has lately taken a favorable turn, and we have reason to hope & believe that the Career of the French is nearly at an End, and that in the Course of this Campaign they may be beaten into a just & hon'ble peace for Europe.-
>
> From your Silence respecting your Family we hope that you all enjoy perfect health—which unfortunately has not been the case with us the last winter:—for more than three months I have had a sever fit of the Gout, and it is only within a few days since the beginning of Feby that I have excaped from the Confinement of my room;—I am now thank God able to move about and attend to business. I believe the fit was owing to my having lately Indulged too

freely in drinking Cyder which I had for many years before given up, but having had very little of the Gout for six or seven years past I had flattered myself that it would never return. This fit will however make me Cautious for the future.—Mrs. Arnold & the rest of the family are as well as usual & request that you & Mrs. Bliss will accept our best Compliments and Sincere wishes for your health and happiness.[22]

A final exchange cannot be omitted. In June 1799, Bliss informed the Arnolds of the death of Mrs. Bliss. A half-year later (December 20, 1799) the news is received, and Arnold writes back:

My Dear Sir

We were greatly shocked & distressed on the receipt of your letter of the 14th of June informing us of the death of our very valuable and beloved Friend Mrs. Bliss, and most sincerely do we condole and grieve with you upon the irreparable loss you have sustained; both Mrs. Arnold and myself had a very great regard and Friendship for her, as one of the best of women, and I do assure you that we feel most sensibly for you, and more than we can express:—Having been in a similar situation, I am sensible that it is in vain to offer you consolation, time only with the hope of meeting again in happier regions can reconcile you to so heavy and distressing a loss,—I am glad to hear that your little ones are well, and so well disposed of.—that health, may attend you and them and happiness restored to you is the sincere prayer of my Dear Friend
P.S. Mrs. Arnold has not been able to write to you until within a few days, but being now better will soon embrace an opporty–& I have many apologies to make for so long neglecting it, indeed the subject was so melancholy a one that I have wished to avoid it.

B.A.[23]

With a heavy heart, Arnold grappled with writing his condolences. In fact, he waited weeks before accomplishing the task. He offered the most intimate expressions of grief, praising the deceased with an awkwardness that bespeaks of sincerity and casting back to when he too had lost and grieved. One might hope for the afterlife, meeting again in happier regions, He also joked to Chipman that a gift of clothing items to protect from the gout would warm Chipman's feet at Church, as he was "so fond of going there." If Arnold had religious faith it would seem not to well up in words.

That Bliss was fine with stirring personal matters into business, or vice versa, must have comforted Arnold, as if he and his friend were musical instruments who could play the same score (although of course Bliss wasn't a risky entrepreneur but an attorney). About two months before Benedict's death (1801), Bliss received a letter penned the previous fall. He appreciates his friend's work on behalf of small moneys for him, Peggy is so unwell she cannot write a letter, they both are at a low ebb because Edward has departed for India (never to be seen by his parents again), and a postscript about lots to sell—he was in financial chaos till the end.

Arnold had lost his old arrogance. The following September he launched into accounts, but with a two-fold apology, that "indisposition" has gotten in the way of his keeping up with business and that he was "extremely sorry that I have given you so much trouble in my trifling councerns." The rest of a long letter (his last to his friend Bliss) was a *plainte* about Peggy's health and their emotional distress:

> Mrs. Arnold and myself felt much indebted to you for your good wishes and expressions of Friendships to us:—I am sorry to say that her health at times is indifferent occasioned by a fullness of habit which frequently affects her head more or less with a giddiness that renders it not only painful, but dangerous to her to write, which must apologize to her friends for her not being a punctual correspondent. Indeed her Physicions have frequently forbid her writing at all when her head is afflicted—and she has lately been much distressed in parting with her eldest Son, Edward, who left us the latter end of June for India, where he goes to Bengal in the Engineer department under the Patronage of Lord Cornwallis, we have just heard from him at Madeira where he was very well and going on pleasantly,—It is a great trial to both of us to part with him, but it is necessary, and we have no doubt of his doing well. If he retains his health—He is much beloved & respected by all his acquaintance, to good abilities he has acquired great knowledge is of pleasing manner & strict principles of honor.—James our second son is in the same line, he has been at Gibraltar near two years, where the officers speak very highly of him. He has lately been selected from all the young officers there to go to Malta, where he has been about four months, as second Engineer in Conducting the Siege. Genl. Brinfield [unreadable] lately returned from Gibraltar has brought over a drawing of that Place & one of Malta taken by James, so remarkably well done that he has promoted the former to the Duke of York.—Sophia is grown very tall, but very delicate, we hope when she has done growing that her health will be better established—George & William are fine Boys & coming on well, you who know the feelings of a Parent will indulge one in saying so much of my young Family....[24]

Edward is often described in biographies as Arnold's favorite son and Sophia too is described as her parents' pet. Looking interiorly and at friends and family, I don't think it is human nature to have a favorite child. We can only imagine the drawing of Gibraltar that singled James out, and how proud it made Benedict to have a general show this to him, calling on the "old lion," knowing he was ailing. As for Sophia's place in her parents' hearts, that she was delicate made her of special concern, like Beth in *Little Women*.

This last letter has a postscript. Arnold's mind went back and forth between concerns for his family and for his business the whole last third of life—this was his sphere. Having relayed how Peggy is so ill she is instructed sometimes not even to write a letter, and how successful his children are, he reverts to his "trifling concerns," querying Bliss if a certain parcel of 1000 acres is "now, or likely hearafter to be worth any thing."

19

Last Years in London

I am always a stranger, ever alone, always
a little in love with death.—Eugene O'Neill,
A Long Day's Journey into Night

The *Pennsylvania Law Review* of June 1975 carried a humorous note, "The Common Origins of the Infield Fly Rule," that became one of the most celebrated analyses in legal history. Its author, William S. Stevens, said that no matter what else he did in his life, he knew he was going to get a *New York Times* obituary based on that one short piece of writing from his days at law school, and he did. From the trillions of moments in a life, one act can define a person in the public view; for Benedict Arnold his life went on after his attempt to turn West Point over to the British. He continued as a soldier, merchant, husband, brother and father. Whether that decision lengthened or shortened the war, and cost or saved lives is unknown, but certainly he wasn't a tragic figure to himself and he continued to be very involved in business and his family during his last years. He was in fact ailing from his war injuries, but engrossed in a panoply of enterprises and, often, basking in his children's successes. As for the cloud of infamy his treason brought, it lifted enough outside the United States for him to conduct a normal life.

Something will turn up on his part, and I will never desert you on hers, is the picture of them in late years. He would no longer have an accessory mistress (as he probably did in his forties), and Peggy did not go see her family in Philadelphia again.

But returning from the Caribbean, Arnold found Peggy in poor health. He wrote Bliss in September 1794 that she was "very much an invalid." He moved the family to a more upscale address again, a townhouse on Gloucester Place, and took Peggy to Cheltenham Spa for the waters in 1794 or 1795. Known for its alkaline water since the early 1700s, Cheltenham became very popular following King George III's visit in 1788. Edward was still at boarding school and excelling at games, and Sophia was at home.

Friendships with people in New Brunswick continued and friendships in general became tremendously important to the Arnolds. In this chapter, reference is made to the Blisses, the Fitches, and the Vassals, much of the information borrowed from J.G. Taylor's detailed 1931 study, *Some New Light on the Later Life and Last Resting Place of Benedict Arnold and of His Wife Margaret Shippen.*

In her correspondence Peggy displays affection to old friends in New Brunswick. A few letters have survived. In her pleasant missive to the Blisses, wishing them well now that that family lived in the Arnolds' old house (1795), Peggy comes across as a Good Fairy and as if the years in Canada were a long time ago.

It was four years after that that Peggy wrote the Chipmans, "*I hear much of the gaiety of your little city.... I shall always regret my separation from many valuable friends among the first of whom I shall reckon Mrs. Chipman.*"[1] Her tone seems nostalgic now, perhaps for that period when her children were small and at home, and she and her husband were in better health. Or it may be that living in England created stress—keeping up with her social obligations and managing the household budget.

There are records of Benedict's entering into privateering ventures—"a last frenzied attempt to make money quickly," what Peggy termed "unfortunate speculation."[2] Peggy, now 36, told her father that she was sick of the struggle "and I think I could be contented in a very humble retired situation, but to see my Children's rising prospects blasted would fill me with the keenest anguish."[3] The next year she found she was pregnant again. She named the child William Fitch Arnold after the brother of her friends the Fitches.

The Arnolds also went to a spa in Margate in the spring of 1799. Like most of the visitors they must have arrived from London by sea in a single-mast ship. This had been a holiday resort for Londoners since the early eighteenth century. There they met John Collins Warren, a young man who was the nephew of Dr. Joseph Warren, who died at Bunker Hill and whose children Arnold sent money to help. Isaac N. Arnold has his account of the meeting:

> In the diary of the eminent surgeon, John C. Warren, who was a near relative of Joseph Warren, dated 1799, at "Margate, England" is written: "I met General Arnold, the 'traitor,' so called he was there with his family, I recollect a son, very handsome, and a daughter. Arnold was rather a stout man, broad shouldered, large black eyes. He walked lame from a wound received at the attack on Quebec, I think."[4]

Warren was a small child when Arnold turned coat. The quotation marks around the word traitor evidence Warren's sophistication at about 21. He became a prominent surgeon who did the first public demonstration of surgical anesthesia. He was a founder of the *New England Journal of Medicine*, the first dean of Harvard Medical School, and the third president of the American Medical Association.

The Arnolds may have been strolling on the beach or in town, or in the popular and spacious library-bookstore where people went to be seen. The resort had two theaters, converted from a barn and a stable, assembly rooms in an inn for dancing, and a brand-new Georgian-style mall called Cecil Square. Sights included a 2,000 square-foot shell-encrusted grotto of mysterious origins and a building called India House, the home of a tea planter from India which was a replica of his house in Calcutta. Peggy could go to a little bathing establishment on High Street where one stepped down into a canal of sea water, or Arnold could hire a bathing wagon with a canvas modesty hood to take her to the water's edge, from which she could step down under a canvas umbrella.

In 1800 Arnold left London for a trip to Warwick and Bath for his health. Being out of doors in the fine spring weather did him good. On May 23, the Arnolds had gone to Gallywood (later Galleywood, 9 miles from Chelmsford) and he was better. After eight days, business drew him back to the city. Soon he was to return to the country but after three days unable to swallow or speak he died on Sunday, June 14. "Without a groan," Peggy added in the letter to her father, as if she were susceptible to Benedict's very breath, confessing that Benedict's death had reduced her to a "despairing state."[5]

As to Peggy, however, as Milton Lomask writes, "her nerves lay close to the surface."[6] She kept up appearances. It had been advised when Benedict was still alive that it was dangerous for her to write when she was poorly, but her correspondence was an outlet. To her brother-in-law Edward Burd she expressed an unreadable and longer type of grief, that "my sufferings are not of the present moment only,—Years of unhappiness have past, I had cast my lot, complaints were unavailing, and you and my other friends, are ignorant of the many causes of uneasiness I have had."[7]

Ann Fitch wrote to Judge Shippen:

> My sister & myself were with Mrs. Arnold when her husband expired. She evinces upon this occasion—as you know she has done upon many trying ones before—that fortitude & resignation, which a superior & well regulated mind only is capable of exerting.[8]

Peggy showed her high caliber of forbearance upon the reading of the General's will. The executor was Peggy and the joint trustees of his estate were Ann and Sarah Fitch. The Arnolds made Samuel's soldier son the godson of their William Fitch Arnold and the sisters (Peggy's age) were recognized women of integrity and business sense. The astonishing bequest of the will was to John Sage. Sage's identity has been sleuthed by Barry Wilson. The bequest was laid out firmly:

> Item. I give, devise and bequeath to John Sage, now in Canada, living with my Sons there (being about 14 years of age) Twelve hundred Acres of Land made to me as an Half Pay Officer for myself and Family by Order of the Duke of Portland, by his Letter directed to Peter Russell Esqr. President of the Council in Upper Canada, dated the 12th of June 1798, which said 1200 Acres of Land I give to him to be located altogether in one place out of the before mentioned Grant as my Executors may judge equal and fair.[9]

Peggy seemed not to brood. She wrote her father praise of her children in late 1801, her love and enthusiasm focusing on the next generation. The boys became men

> ...without having by any misconduct, given me an hour's uneasiness; and that my third Son is exactly treading in their steps, you will not think it a vain boast when I do justice to their worth. And my dear girl is in point of disposition, temper, rectitude of conduct, & goodness all that a fond Mother can wish her, with a pleasing person, and cultivated and well regulated mind.[10]

In January 1804, Peggy wrote to her eldest son Edward of Sophia's education and marital prospects. She was 18. She was progressing in Drawing and Painting and "she reads a great deal and turns her attention greatly to religious subjects. She will make a most excellent Wife, to any man who is so fortunate as to get her." The mother adds, however, there is "little chance of her marrying, having but a moderate share of beauty, and no money." In fact, ever since Sophia had what was identified as a stroke in May 1800, the family must have feared for her. The family was close. It was natural when she said to Edward that "I trust my dear sons ... will be able to assist their Sister, should my death, or any other event, render their aid necessary."[11]

J.B. Taylor recounted at length who the Arnolds' friends were in his last days and why he was buried in Battersea (as friends were associated with that place). For the circle of friends which the Arnolds had in London we turn to Taylor. He apprises the reader:

When the Arnolds moved back to England from Canada in 1792, they first settled on Hollis Street off Oxford Street. Nearby, on Gloucester Place in Cavendish Square, lived their friends from America, the Fitch family. The Fitch daughters, Ann and Sarah, were especially close to Peggy, whose last child was named after one of the Fitch brothers.

Samuel Fitch had died in 1799. He had been a resident of Cavendish Square in St. Marylebone. He was the father of Col. William Fitch, who in turn died in Jamaica and his heirs were Ann and Sarah Fitch, "spinsters," the only next of kin to their father and brother, therefore an adequate estate. As if extending Arnold's last cheerful days, Peggy returned to the "dear Miss Fitches" at Gallywood after her husband's funeral, Ann and Sarah being joint trustees of his estate. Colonel William Fitch (circa 1756–95) had bequeathed £500 to her youngest son, William Fitch Arnold, born in 1794, while his godson William was in London. The Colonel had fought in Ireland and then Jamaica, where Governor Balcarres sent him to force the "Maroons" (descendants of former African slaves), who were demanding more land, to surrender. Colonel Fitch was slain, shot in the head, and 800 Maroons were sent to Sierra Leone. Sir Thomas Lawrence painted a full portrait of the gallant Colonel Fitch in uniform, leaning on a country gate with sword in hand. Copley painted the Colonel after his death, with his sisters Sarah (in white) and Ann (in mourning dress), as if he were leaving for battle.

The Arnolds' closeness to the Fitch family went back to Connecticut roots. Ann was the elder sister (1759–1839) and Sarah was the younger (1763–1851), a British subject born in Boston. Samuel and his wife were from Lebanon and New Haven, Connecticut, respectively. Samuel was the grandson of the Rev. James Fitch who came to New England in 1638 and lived in Norwich. Samuel was born in Lebanon, Connecticut, in 1724; educated at Yale, he married and became a barrister in Boston. He was listed in Sabine's *The American Loyalists* (1847) as an American Loyalist who left Boston for Halifax in 1776. In Samuel Fitch's correspondence with the Commissioners was a letter from Benedict Arnold, dated 1787, saying he was "long and intimately acquainted" with the late Colonel Whiting of New Haven, Connecticut, and his family—of which Samuel Fitch's mother Anne Whiting was a member. Samuel Fitch's uncle, Nathan Whiting, had presented Arnold for membership in the Masonic Lodge.

Samuel Fitch's clearest connection with Arnold related to Samuel's properties in Norwich when Arnold was a young merchant there. Samuel Fitch's memorial noted he had been "stript of his Fortune and Income with a family bred up in Ease and Affluence.... He will ever remember with bitterness the loss he sustained as his immediate consequences of the hardships to which they were subjects."[12]

The year of 1788 found Samuel unable to write well his latest demands due to gout in his right hand. He entertained and was hospitable—and it was said "perpetually involved in a Cloud of Tobacco Smoak."[13]

Elizabeth Lloyd Fitch, Samuel's wife, was also from a Loyalist family; notably her brother was James Lloyd, a physician in Boston. According to Taylor's research, the Arnolds when they settled in London in 1791 "were living hard" by and the revival of the earlier acquaintance tween the two families originated in Benedict's pre-war intimacy with Samuel Fitch's uncle, Colonel Nathan Whiting of New Haven and his family. The Fitches and Arnolds had common claims for recompense from the British government; their association "now ripened into a firm friendship."[14]

Anne and Sarah were Peggy's age. They were, states Taylor, recognized as women of integrity and business sense. The Fitch sisters left the Cavendish Square house when their parents and brother died.

Second to the Fitches, Benedict and Peggy's other good friends after the return from New Brunswick were the Vassals. Peggy's close friend Sarah Fitch married William Vassall's son Leonard. William Vassall (1715–1800) was a Harvard graduate (1733) who inherited a large estate of sugar plantations at Hanover in Jamaica. William Vassall was High Sheriff for Middlesex County (Massachusetts) when the War of Independence broke out. He was an avowed Loyalist and "excessively garrulous."[15] In 1778 he fled to England with his family. He had an easier time than Samuel Fitch. William Vassall's plantation in Jamaica gave him a large income and he was able to sell some of his Boston property by proxy through the help of Fitch's brother-in-law, Dr. James Lloyd, for £4000. In Samuel's memorial to the British government, he said his problem was not merely putting bread on the table but with "a family bred up in Ease and Affluence."[16]

William Wilberforce was William Vassall's neighbor in a country house that became known as "Maisonette." A biography of J.S. Copley suggests that William Vassell was harsh in public dealings and good to his family.[17] In Vassall's will, he directed that the slaves on his Green River Plantation in Jamaica be kindly treated, and "that they have everything that is necessary for their comfort and well-being."

In the group of Loyalist friends were also Nathaniel and Anne Middleton, who lived in Cavendish. Nathaniel Middleton had East India interests. In very last letter to her son Edward, Peggy said "Mrs. Middleton is still near Windsor."[18]

The other friends Taylor mentions are Daniel and Sarah Coxe. He was a member of the governor's council in New Jersey and an official of George Germain's Board of Directors of Associated Loyalists in New York City when monies for a deposit for Benedict's treason were passed through him. He helped Peggy regarding her finances after Benedict died, as noted by his advising her father to put the children specifically in his will.

All these people shared animosity to the War of Independence. All would have members buried in Benedict Arnold's final resting place, in the crypt of Saint Mary's of Battersea Church, now in South London.

The Arnolds were very partial to visiting their friends the Fitches in the country. Since January (1801) he had suffered acutely from gout in both legs and a cough. In spring Arnold's health rallied and the aging lion astonished his friends by driving as much as ten miles in a day in a chaise cart without springs. After Benedict's death, bills were coming from every quarter "among which were some to the amount of 800 pounds from your brother in Canada," Peggy wrote Edward. Benedict "was under the necessity a week before his death of disposing the Lease of the House."[19]

Gout, dropsy and a disease of the lungs conspired to kill Arnold when just 60. It was also thought that a "nervous disorder" hastened his end. Ann Fitch took on the responsibility of informing Edward Shippen:

> Gen'l Arnold died on the 14th instant at half past six in the morning—you probably will have heard before this reaches you—that his health had been in a declining state for several months ... but the physician saw no cause for alarm.... His complaints (supposed to be occasioned by repeated Gout) were a tendency to a general Dropsy, and a disease of the Lung.[20]

Six weeks after Benedict Arnold's death, Peggy wrote to her son Edward, "I intended copying the Will but am not at present well enough." She said she had been "deprived of an excellent husband," echoing other statements over the years, e.g., to her father (March 1786) that Benedict was "the best of husbands." His financial setbacks, she told Edward, "had broken his spirit."[21]

Wallace's valuable biography speculates that Benedict confessed an extramarital affair to Peggy, and her subterranean hurt comes out in some letters where she claims misery. The Arnold family must have suffered continual tension from Benedict's treason, and uneasiness about his pie in the sky privateering ventures. These plus dislocation—being unwelcome socially even when she did go back to Philadelphia—made her miserable. The picture is of Count Almaviva kneeling and asking his wife for pardon, but the way that Benedict was the best of husbands may have had more to do with keeping her in her socioeconomic caste, which he succeeded in doing. Her children went to the best possible schools and he provided a status house for her. When he died and left her with debts, she suffered from having no carriage, not, as she explicitly said, because this hindered her movements (comfort) but because of lost status/respectability. Prosperous men kept mistresses. It was considered good for their health and a sign of prosperity. A man kept the affair private and it caused no grief.

Loyalist families with whom the Arnolds were on terms of close intimacy and friendship—Fitch, Vassall and Middleton—all now had members lying in the vaults at Battersea Church—the parents of the Miss Fitches interred in 1799 and 1800, and William Vassall, the father of Sarah Finch's fiancé in 1800.

It is recounted that on his deathbed Benedict called for his old uniform and the French epaulettes that George Washington had given him. It is suggested in a number of books that he was awash with contrition at his ignominious treason. It could well be otherwise. He could have been recollecting his old battles better than the present scene, gaining a sense of his lifeline, or looking at his old image to understand the shifts of self and the enigma of selfhood. He might have regretted his personal betrayal but believed he had acted right. The sources that quote his last words seem too dramatic to be true. For example, this version by Roger Kemper Rogan:

> On the morning of 14 July 1801, realizing the end was but a few hours distant, he asked for his old Continental uniform. He put it on with his epaulets and his decorations, and even pulled on his boots. Exhausted, he threw himself on the bed and called for his sword which had been presented to him by Congress. He placed it across his breast and took the golden sword knots that had been presented to him by Washington. His last words: "Let me die in this old uniform in which I have fought many battles, and may God forgive me for having put on any other."[22]

It seems Lord Cornwallis rode in one of the mourning coaches in the cortege. That discounts the idea that Benedict was a pretend Loyalist. Many years later a private donor paid for a stained-glass church window at St. Mary's Church in Battersea in Arnold's honor. His picture is surrounded by the U.S. and British flags.

After Benedict Arnold's death, Jonathan Bliss looked after the Arnold affairs in New Brunswick and so was a lifeline for Peggy in clearing up

Plaque of place of death (courtesy Charles C. Ripley III).

debts. She wrote to him of the most urgent matter, her promise to resolve the debts of Arnold's estate. In the family it was to her son Edward that she confided the "embarassed state in which he left his affairs," and how she was "afraid the property would be inadequate to pay their debts." She confided to him her determination "while it is in my power to prevent it, that the fortunes of my Children shall not be marred by the change in our situation."[23]

For years Peggy had stood by and seen Benedict make faulty investment choices. Now she recovered from "the wreck" (using the same ship metaphor that Arnold used looking back at New Brunswick to his friend Bliss).[24] She paid off £5,000 of debts in a year and a half, and continued to support her two youngest boys, George and William, in their schools. According to N.R. Stuart, she had her father invest her royal pension in an American annuity for the support of her five children. Her pride did not prevent her admitting hard times to her father, son, and brother-in-law, but she was unflinching in having cast her lot.

She didn't succumb to helplessness or connive, she rose to the occasion. Benedict had been a good husband and she was attached to him. She was now on her own and came out from the shadows as a widow. Paying off the debts sparked her to action, to clear his name and leave their children something. She performed a duty and seemed to soar. The impression is, from her remarks about her husband's finances, as with the Lauderdale duel, that she deferred to her husband while he lived. As poor as her health was, she performed staunchly and emerged strong.

After selling the Gloucester Place house and furnishings, Peggy moved into a "small, but very neat house" at 32 Bryanston Street. Most touching personal economies are described in correspondence to family. Furnishings from the old house were sold but she bought back a few personal items from the estate (including, from "a little family pride," the family silver). She described to Richard and Henry, off in North America, how to furnish the house she resorted to buying items from her servant "who is now a more independent woman than her mistress."[25] She wrote the next year how the claims against the estate were so great she had to part with "my furniture, wine, and many other comforts provided for me by the indulgent hand of affection."[26] But, balancing this astonishing situation for a high-born woman, she wrote them proudly, two months before she died, "I have not a teaspoon, a towel, or a bottle of wine that I have not paid for."[27] She had her children and it wasn't so terrible to live within her means. She applied and received a royal pension for three-year-old William, corresponded with Jonathan Bliss over the properties still remaining in New Brunswick. She maintained cheer and diligence settling accounts. The kind of brief, darting references to how difficult it was to manage her life, and deeper regrets, come across in a letter to Richard and Henry:

"Although I have suffered, in my choice of evils, almost beyond human endurance, I now repent not at having made it."[28]

By the spring of 1804 Peggy was mostly confined. Her only prospect of a cure was an operation to remove a tumor that was too dangerous in her poor health. Yet it brought Peggy great comfort that each of the children was doing well. Edward in India was paying for little William's education from his pay, and James was also living on his pay and assigning his full pension to his family. "My dear girl is all that is amiable and excellent, and George and William promise fair to emulate the example of their elder brothers. Such children compensate for a thousand ills."[29]

George had departed Nova Scotia and, the summer of 1803, was at the New Royal Military College through the influence of Lord Cornwallis. The India Company was paying half his education in exchange for which he would enter their service. By August 1803 George was soon to leave for India, Edward was serving under General Lake, and had been wounded in the arm but recovered, and James was "Stationary Commanding Engineer" at Barbados, and Adjutant, with quarters overlooking the sea.

Peggy had settled the debts by 1803. The descent she perceived for herself on the social scale was not without grief. If she left London and friends, "Among strangers, I should be rated according to my present means of appearance, which would place me in a very inferior rank in society, which my pride could but ill brook."[30] Sarah Burd, Peggy's sister, must have loved her. She left in her will "four diamond rings for the four daughters of Sophia, from the love and esteem she had for Sophia's mother."

Peggy had considered moving back to America, writing Edward on January 17, 1804, "Should George go to India, I have a resource in America, where I should probably be under the necessity of taking Sophia and William; political reasons would render me very averse to taking a Son at a more advanced age."[31] This was a backhanded way to acknowledge that she felt Benedict's treason was a memory in the United States that could injure his son.

On July 5, 1804, Daniel Coxe, a friend of the Arnolds, added to the picture of the children, writing to Edward Shippen as Peggy was too weak to write. He recounted that James was commended "in the late capture of Surinam" and that Sophia, who copied the letter of commendation, might need and deserved looking after by her grandfather:

> She is a dear Girl, more worthy of your notice and attentions than any other of the family, tho all the most meritorious—she is the most amiable and correct of her sex I ever saw, leave her not, no dear Sir, in distress … the boys are provided for & can & ought to shift for themselves—a Girl cannot.[32]

The tone of the instructions Peggy left at her death is extraordinary. She requested in her will that her funeral be as plain as was "consistent with the situation" of her family, "avoiding all superfluous expense," and that her just debts be paid. All household goods to Sophia, 500 pounds to George to outfit him for India, 100 pounds each to her sons Edward and James after paying her debts, and all the rest of her personal property be divided equally into three shares to Sophia, and two to William Fitch Arnold. And the remainder of her property in Great Britain and its Dominions, Canada, New Brunswick, etc., was to be equally divided among sons Edward, James, George and William and Sophia.

Sophia wrote to her aunt from Gloucester Place on Christmas day, 1804. She must have been visiting the Fitch sisters. She was responding to her grandfather's invitation to reside in Philadelphia. Despite its appeal, she wrote, her children would be too far, and "especially William, so young, so destitute, as he is left, looking now solely up to me."[33] She said she would like to come for a year after James returned to England from his engineering posts, as James too would need a sister's sympathy, to bear seeing his close family come to pieces. In correspondence she revealed her searing thoughts, how worry over bad speculations had darkened her husband's life, and that only for her children's sake did she cling to life.

Benedict sought glory and attention and gained neither.

Sitting on the deck overlooking Snug Cove, or along the St. John River lunching at a sophisticated café near the 1812 Blockhouse in St. Andrews, I have interviewed scholars and professors about my subject. Of numerous riveting discussions one remark of Colin Windhorst of Dennysville, Maine, stays in my mind. "As I have come to know him, Benedict Arnold is a tragic figure inopportunely changing sides, and committing his treason, when staying the course would have brought him the glory and attention he sought. Dante placed the most perfidious traitors in the lowest circle of hell, and while our national story has linked Arnold to these supremely disloyal men I wonder if that is really the place he belongs. In a real sense, I think he deserves the title of the man without a country. A sad fate in itself."

Appendix:
The Children and Hannah

La fortune fait paraltre nos vertus et nos vices comme la
lumière fait paraltre les objets.—René de Chateaubriand

Works by J.B. Taylor, Isaac Arnold, and Willard Wallace (see bibliography) were the author's main guides through stories of the next generation on the family tree.

When Benedict Arnold left the cause of American independence in 1780, he was 39 and Peggy was 21. He had three sons by his first wife, Margaret Mansfield, whom he married in 1767 and who died at 34 in 1775: Benedict, 12, Richard, 11, and Henry, 8. He had an infant child, Edward, by his second wife. Benedict had often been away on long commercial voyages and Margaret did not write as often as he wished, but it is clear the children were born of a loving marriage. He wrote from a trip (not dating the letter) that he had written her "almost every post" but hadn't heard back: "My dearest life, you cannot imagine the troubled fatigue I have gone through since here.... I shall be very unhappy if I have not the pleasure of hearing you and our dear ones are well.... My heart is anxious and aching."[1] His second family, with Peggy, grew up loved as well and by both parents.

The conduct of the Arnold sons and daughter gave their parents (with the exception of Henry) not an hour's uneasiness; the younger tread in the virtuous steps of the older. There is no indication of rancorous rivalry between the first family and the second. When their mother died, the oldest three boys, ages seven, six, and four, were cared for Hannah as by a mother but they needed their father more than they had access to him, so Hannah would say gently to her brother that her nephews were eager for any news related to him.

In line with the large size of Loyalist families, not only did Benedict have eight sons and a daughter, but the next generation continued with the high fertility: Richard had nine children, Henry eleven (only a daughter survived), Sophia, five. John Sage had seven.

It is said that he was giving blessings to his children on his deathbed. The boys were ambitious and staunch, and Benedict was proud of their taking prizes at school, their fluency, good manners and judgment. His whole effort to accrue money was on behalf of these children, who would be punctiliously fair to one another about their inheritance, and always wrote one another in terms of lively affection. Peggy was equally devoted to her children. She wrote the Blisses to congratulate them on the birth of another child that "For my own part, I am determined to have no more little plagues, as it is difficult to provide for them, and I shall never again try a new country for the benefit of posterity." (She looped back at the letter's end to her little joke, remarking that "After all, no happiness equals that of a domestic kind.")[2]

Benedict and Peggy's baby, Edward Shippen, was born in New York City after Benedict's defection. Three more sons and a daughter followed—James, George, William, and Sophia. Due to the difference in their ages, the older sons were often away at school and not at home, and Sophia had a delicate constitution and was home-schooled from some point in her teens.

The salient practical feature of the Arnold family is that the father instilled in the children a military tradition. All his seven sons who lived to adulthood served in the British army. Benedict died of a wound in his leg in Jamaica, two served in the cavalry in India. Edward died in combat, and William became a general. Isaac Arnold notes that a grandson, William Traill Arnold, was killed at Sebastopol in 1855, and that a great-grandson, Theodore Stephenson Arnold, was a major-general in World War I. The military lineage was more characteristic of Great Britain than America of that time, when colonial soldiers were mostly militia. During the period of Empire, the tradition remained very strong among the British. Accordingly, in the province of New Brunswick, home to most of the disbanded British soldiers of the Revolutionary War, a strong military tradition continued through the world wars.

My maternal grandfather was an army engineer who died of influenza contracted in World War I. A remaining photograph is of Will in uniform on a horse, riding next to General Pershing. My widowed grandmother, a country schoolteacher, married up, a banker we called Bampa. Bampa tried to bribe my mother with a yellow Buick roadster to attend Cornell as he, his sons, and his aunts (among the first female graduates) had. My mother turned down the attractive offer, became a model, and married a naval officer. Her brother and my father served in the U.S. Navy in World War II and the Korean War.

Being raised in a family with a military tradition 150 years after the Arnold children I recognize shared traits. You bond closely with your siblings because in moving around a lot these are your best friends. You follow orders. You take chances. You can summon up bravura. You rebel.

The British class structure interplayed with and reinforced the prestige of military rank. My parents were godparents to a child of a British officer. The officer had lost a leg climbing Mount Kilimanjaro, shot by one of his own men in error. My mother said the Major was a superb dancer, she didn't know what the squeak was when they danced until she learned it was his prosthetic. When we attended a Christmas church service in Nottingham England, Major Pexton and his fellow officers wore their uniforms, while my father dressed in civilian clothes except on duty and for parades. When my father and uncle retired they were never addressed by their rank, but the major was, like Captain Hastings in the Agatha Christie "Hercule Poirot" novels. The Major gave the regimental Christmas cards he received from all over the globe to my brother Tom. The beautiful cards had the regimental colors tied into their borders as a multicolored ribbon. Once I said how pretty they were, and the major lectured me on the serious meaning and lineage of regimental colors.

It was important to Benedict and Peggy to have their sons placed advantageously for advancement, under commanders who either knew the Arnolds or were alerted by the Arnolds' friends to take note of the young officers. One can imagine they were not always on the front lines. Peggy wanted one son to join a regiment where she thought he'd be out of danger. Another son thanked his family for recommending he go into engineering instead of artillery. *En bref*, the Arnold sons dealt with the negative view some people outside the family had about their father by distinguishing themselves in the army. They were good brothers, and lived in far-flung places most of their lives.

Coming from a military family, I am guessing that Arnold never spoke of his treason to his sons. To join the army was not only following in the father's footsteps, it was preordained as the best alternative. They had access to this career and were prepared for it. What one did in the service stayed in the service. Moreover, Arnold did not converse much with the boys, admitting to the headmaster whose school he sent them to in 1779 that his "situation has prevented my paying that attention to them I otherwise should have done."[3]

Benedict was concerned that his tailor had not completed their clothes and gave the Reverend headmaster a large pocket for these and other expenses. He said to correct any bad habits the boys might have picked up in the city—"a bad school," which sounds so much like my father, who when my parents brought me a mattress for my baby's crib, my father refused to get out of the car on East 10th because he held the morals of New York City in low opinion.

Besides the bounty for his treachery, Benedict received from the British annual pensions for Peggy and their children, and army commissions for Benedict, Richard and Henry.

And what of the children regarding the military child's rebelling? Benedict was a powerful model and there was powerful motivation to show distinction for his sons. But one son (see the entry below on the third son) below did rebel. There was such an expectation of staying in the military and rising in the ranks that (in an April 2, 1832, letter) James critiqued William, well set up as a public official in Buckinghamshire, for having shortened his military career. William "is a half-pay captain (if he'd stuck to service might have been Lt. Col.)."[4]

The great bequest of Arnold to his sons consisted of portions of the 1799 grant of 13,400 acres in Upper Canada, now Ontario. It was located in Gwillimbury East and North, today in Georgina, Ontario, north of Toronto. However, their father did not expect his sons to be farmers. The Arnold family never lived in this area and the land was later sold. Of the sons, Richard and John Sage were the ones who stayed in farming. Henry was for some years a farmer as well but then left to go into business in New York State.

Benedict Arnold (first son by first wife)

Benedict VI served as an artillery officer. His father had been proud of his eldest as a rising star. There was war with France and this son was imprisoned for two years there, returned to England in 1795 and, to his parents' dismay, went at once to serve in the West Indies. Fighting on the northern coast of Jamaica in Iron Shore (now an upscale part of Montego Bay) in October 1795, the son suffered a severe leg wound, refused to have the leg amputated, and died of gangrene. He must have thought of his father sustaining a wound at Saratoga, only the son did not recover.

When the father heard in February 1796 that Benedict had died in Jamaica of fever, he was devastated. This was six years before he himself died. He wrote Bliss that "His death ... is a heavy stroke on me as his conduct of late years had been irreproachable and I had flattered myself with seeing him rise to eminence in his profession."[5] Poignantly Arnold reminded himself of his son's having such valor and competency that Lord Balcarres had promised him a promotion. This point must have been very meaningful to the grieving father as Balcarres had once refused Arnold's proffered hand in the drawing room of the king.

Richard Arnold (second son by first wife)

Eleven-year-old Richard was commissioned as lieutenant of cavalry in the American Legion, raised by his father in 1780. This later gave him half-pay as a retired officer, from the British government. Richard's name was on his father's erstwhile partnership (established 1786) with Munson Hayt and Richard suffered burns during the fire of the store.

By the late 1790s Richard and Henry had taken up lands in Wolford and Augusta Townships. Richard married Margaret Weatherhead, of Augusta, Maine, when she was 15, in 1804, became an elected magistrate and farmer, and left a family of nine sons and daughters. Richard was the only Arnold son who brought some embarrassment to his family. Whatever this was, a Dr. Jas. Adair who in the summer of 1791 put up security for the debt incurred, assured Benedict it was no worse than his own son's youthful indiscretions.

One of Richard's daughters, Margaret, became a heroine. Margaret married John McEwan, who was in the lumber and warehouse business, first in Sarnia then Windsor, Ontario, and they had six children. The Great Western Railroad was built through the lumberyard whereupon John McEwan closed the business; he was made the first station agent at Windsor in 1853. He founded the Windsor Herald and was Essex County sheriff from 1856 until his death in 1886. On July 15, 1854, a train derailed near Windsor. It was hot and the passengers, a group of immigrants traveling to the Midwest of the United States, had no food and water. The train was overcrowded and the cars in which they rode had no windows.

The town of Windsor was only a few hundred people and had no doctor. Many passengers became sick and died. Margaret and John exhibited courage and charity at the scene of crisis. According to James McEwan's *Commemorative Biographical Record of the County of Essex Ontario,*

> Leaving her own little ones in the care of a colored woman who had escaped from slavery in the States, Mrs. McEwan joined her husband with the assistance of a Mr. Blackadder went among the poor, suffering foreigners and tenderly ministered to their wants, endangering their own lives by doing so.[6]

This account said the immigrants had cholera from having drunk water from a frog pond as they passed and that they were German. A news report in the *Detroit Free Press*, July 4, 1854, under the heading "Mortality among Emigrants" said they were Norwegian and that the sickness was "ship fever" or typhus.

Researching the story for the *Walkerville Times*, Elaine Weeks added two facts to the aftermath of the railway tragedy. The surviving children of one couple who died in the tragedy were raised by the McEwans. Also, the railway presented

Margaret with a gold watch. The home the McEwans had built in 1871 is of yellow brick and Italianate style, and still stands at 131 McEwan Avenue in Windsor. The *Commemorative Biographical Record* noted that one of the McEwans' children, James, had many old documents "many of these having been the property of his great-grandfather Benedict Arnold," proclaiming they would someday be the nucleus of a historical collection, but these have not surfaced.

When Richard died, James wrote from Southampton to his niece Margaret condolences for her father's death.

> As you know, I have not seen your dear Father since I was a child; But he was often in my recollection and I most sincerely lament him, though I had little or no hope of ever seeing him again. I am, now, the only one left of the older branches of the family and God, only, knows how long it may be ere I am called to join those who have gone before me, which I humbly hope to do, in a better world such is happiness eternal.[7]

Henry Arnold (third son by first wife)

Henry was in the American Loyalists regiment, riding a cavalry horse at the age of eight. Therefore he was awarded half-pay for life like his big brother. After the Revolution he and Richard lived in Troy, New York, with Aunt Hannah. Henry was the son who was injured when the warehouse of his father caught fire one night in Saint John.

When Henry was a youth, he was offered by Sir Charles Grey to be an officer in the West Indies and his father blocked it. Sir Charles, father of Earl Grey, the prime minister after whom the perfumed tea was named, was called "No-flint Grey" after ordering his troops to take the flints from their rifles and fight with their bayonets during a night conflict in the American Revolution. In the spring of 1794, Sir Charles' troops took Martinique and Guadeloupe before losing them back to the French in the summer. Benedict told his friend James Adair that Henry had neither the sense nor the prudence. He sent him back to New Haven to live with Hannah and Richard. He was having to cover some folly, sexual or financial, and believed his son was not mature enough. Indeed, Benedict Arnold seemed entirely out of patience, though for what cause is unknown. He refunded Henry's friend owed "for some indiscretion, and expressed his dissatisfaction to Josiah Blakesley, from St. Pierre, wishing Henry would improve his conduct. Henry eventually came to the West Indies and father and son 'made peace.'"[8] Arnold may also have been protecting his son, given the high casualty rate of British military in the Caribbean campaign, from gory battles and yellow fever.

Henry married Hannah Ten Eyck of New York in 1806. For some time, they lived as farmers in Grenville County, Canada, where Loyalists had settled on land grants. They tragically lost ten of their eleven children when they were young.

For a few years Henry and his wife lived in the lakeside town of Skaneateles, New York. Hannah had a relative here, John Ten Eyck, the town postmaster from 1813 to 1817. Hannah bought a small frame house opposite the residence of the Ten Eycks, now the site of the St. James Episcopal Church. According to a November 8, 1957, article in the Skaneateles Press, they soon moved to Canada and then to

New York City. Hannah lived two years longer than Henry. Of their eleven children, only their daughter survived, named Sophia, like Henry's stepsister.

In 1819, James wrote Richard one of numerous letters merging real estate and family. At this time William was captain of a troop in India while George had a staff appointment at Agra. But Henry was, as it were, not with the program. James asked after Richard and his fifth child, and fretted about their Henry:

> I wish poor Henry had followed your good example, and worked earnestly at his land, instead of running about the country as he has been doing for some time past—He is now, or was, on the 21st November last, at a place called Gonanees [possibly Gowanes, bordering Park Slope] near Brooklyn, opposite New York to which latter place he talks of moving in May—I have no idea of his motives for these frequent changes, for fear they cannot be beneficial either to himself, or his family.[9]

Writing Richard from Essex, England on March 6, 1827, James passed along that his half-brother Henry had died (the previous December). The indication is that Richard and Henry, raised together and only about three years apart in age, were not much in contact: "He had long been complaining, and I fear, poor fellow, that his illness was greatly caused by his want of prudence."[10] James said he was looking into a pension for the widow and thought she and the daughter would be able to live on the inheritance.

Edward Shippen Arnold (1780–1813, first son by second wife)

Both parents spoke of Edward, "Neddy," with affection. Indeed, Arnold told Bliss that Edward, then age 20, was beloved by all who knew him. Edward was born in Philadelphia while his father was commander there. At 20 (June 1800), he left England for military service in Bengal under the personal patronage of Lord Cornwallis, a good friend of the Arnolds, to become a cadet in the engineering corps. His parents would never see him again. He became paymaster for his regiment and died serving in Dimapoor in the 6th Bengal Cavalry in northeast India eight months after his sister Sophia's wedding, in 1813.

Letters by Benedict and Peggy to Edward in India, 1800 to 1804, demonstrate their great love for their firstborn child. A pressing issue in the minds of both parents early on was their concern that Edward needed to pay attention to the influence of people with political clout in the army. Benedict gave direct advice on the issue:

> I enclose you a letter that I yesterday recd. from Lord Cornwallis, which is very friendly indeed, & I make no doubt, but his letter to Genl. Lake will be of great service to you, and that he will, as he has promised me, do all in his power to promote your Interest.... I need not observe to you that great Civility, and attention to every body, will do more for you than most young Men are aware of, and tho' I should despise you for being a Sycophant, I would have you espouse the cause of any Man, who is spoken ill of, in his Absence, as far as you can do so with truth and propriety.[11]

To do his son Edward good he rejoiced to be paid compliments by General Lake, and not only told Edward to make himself "agreeable and useful" to Lake but "to form if you can an intimate acquaintanceship with his son."

Benedict and Peggy thought alike. Both were involved in their sons' careers, and after Benedict's death, Peggy stepped in to try to procure a cavalry cadetship to Bengal for George, the youngest child, while telling Edward "My heart bleeds at the idea of giving up another beloved Child; but I have no means of providing for him here,"[12] and to curry Edward's contacts in India. Peggy spoke of two parties, "Mrs. M" and General Lake, whose favor Edward would do well to curry:

> Much will depend upon yourself; nature has been bountiful to you as far as external appearance goes; a knowledge of life will convince you of the great utility of a conciliatory manner, and an apparent wish to please and oblige. Without adopting the Chesterfieldian system to its extent, there are many useful hints to be collected from it, without deviating from that honorable line of conduct which, with pride I boast it, you have uniformly pursued.[13]

On August 16, 1814, James wrote his brothers that Edward had died the previous December:

> He had suffered a long, painful and severe illness, from which Sophia and George fondly hoped he was recovering, and, to all appearances, he was so, but on his way to Calcutta, either to make a voyage to sea, or to come to England, as might be recommended, he was attacked, again, with a violent fever and ague, which proved too much for his exhausted constitution.
>
> While I live, I shall regret him, for, to me, his loss is irreparable.
>
> I cannot enter, just now, on indifferent subjects. My heart is too full of sorrow to permit it. God bless and prosper you, my dear Brothers, and may it be long, very long, before we have to deplore the loss of another dear object.[14]

By August 7, 1815, when James writes to his brothers as a lieutenant colonel, he says he has his parents and Edward to thank for coming into the Engineers and quitting Artillery. In this letter, James' lament for Edward and his parents includes a philosophy of duty imbibed from his early training:

> But all is for the best, and we have no right to doubt the goodness, and wisdom of that kind Providence, who grants, or withholds, as He knows to be right. If prosperity, and the completion of all our worldly desires, makes us happier, they do not always make us the better, or more deserving; adversity, and those disappointments which mankind call cruel, and which appear so, at the time, seldom fail to teach us that it is not here we are to look for happiness, that though we may enjoy it for a time, it cannot last, and that it is only by endeavoring to do our duty, that we can expect to obtain it in the state to which we are all hastening.[15]

The letter dates from a decade after his mother's death. When I read James's words about his brother, I see the look in the Major's eyes when he told me the cards of the British colonial regiments were more than "pretty."

James Robertson Arnold (1781–1854, second son by second wife)

James wrote expressive letters to his siblings so comes across most in relief, as confident and loyal—in the Arnold mold.

He was born in New York City while it was still in British hands. Unlike the case with other Arnold children, we know where he went to school, the King's College School, which boarded boys from 1788. Under the patronage of Lord Cornwallis, James went on to the Woolrich Academy in England in January 1796. He was short, and of the sons looked most like his father.

Benedict had "designed" his son for an engineer and James followed suit, joining the Royal Engineers at 18 and served in Gibraltar, Malta, Egypt, the West Indies, Bermuda, Surinam, and Nova Scotia. He became a brigadier general in the Corps of Royal Engineers. James, as a colonel, went to Bermuda in 1816 to design improvements to the fortifications of the naval dockyard at Ireland Island, consequent to an idea germinated by the Duke of Wellington on preparedness to launch a Royal Navy invasion of the United States. This dockyard had been building cedar-built vessels from wood that, unlike oak, did not need to be seasoned and was resistant to shipworm, but during his two years in Bermuda James completely revamped the dockyard. His achievement there led to his appointment to improve the Citadel in Halifax, Nova Scotia, two years later. He was knighted by King William IV, and before the accession of Victoria transferred from the engineer corps and made a full colonel and an aide de camp to the King. While explaining to his brother Richard that the distinction would not put him among the King's intimates, in fact at the King's death he wrote his brother:

> The death of an excellent King has cast much gloom over London. He will long be deeply and sincerely lamented, and I, for one, feel that, in him, I have lost an excellent friend. I had the honor of dining with him at Brighton last February and had an audience of him the next morning of nearly an hour.[16]

James' final rank was major general. He was very aware of remedying his father's reputation. He wanted to visit the United States but only if rancor against his father became obliterated. He endeavored to prove his valor in battle to redeem the family name. Isaac N. Arnold writes that he led the storming party against the redoubt of Fort Leyden. Before the attack, James said:

> I claim the privilege of leading this assault. No braver man than my father ever lived, but you know how bitterly he has been condemned for his conduct at West Point. Permit me, I beg you.[sic] To do what I can to redeem the name.[17]

James led gallantly and showed the impetuous courage which had so distinguished his father. The redoubt and fort were taken but James was wounded in the leg. The scions did not hold back in battle. The eldest son by Benedict's first wife and the second son by his second wife both took bullets in the leg, living up to their father's reputation for bravery. Part of the defensive complex (in Paramaribo, Suriname) that had the two fortifications is preserved and open as a museum.

It is wrong to think of the Arnold sons as rigid as lead just because they all had careers in the military. It is best to balance the fact they were trained soldiers with the powerful if slender fact, recounted, in for example, *Sabine's Loyalists*, that James wept upon seeing the Arnolds' old home at King and Canterbury streets when he returned there as an adult (1819).[18]

James told Richard the year before that he had left "the delight of the heat and mosquitoes of Bermuda," and was in Halifax with his wife Virginia (Godrich Arnold). He was overjoyed at the transfer except that Virginia had had sore throats and colds in the winter. There were references to Sophia's and Richard's children and to how much James wanted to visit Canada one day, before he returned to England.[19] Similarly when billeted to Ireland he told Richard he would wish it were Canada except that the climate of Canada was too severe for his wife.

John Sage (1786–1831, unknown mother, illegitimate)

Born in Saint John, New Brunswick, birthdate unknown, we hear of him first in the will of Benedict Arnold,[20] said to be about 14 and living with Richard and Henry on land grants in what was called Upper Canada (now Ontario). Sage was left 1,200 acres of the grant, and an annual sum for his expenses ("board") and education under Richard's and Henry's direction. There was a small annual stipend as well.

Some biographers think John Sage's existence was the cause of Peggy's bleakness when Benedict was absent from her and in New Brunswick. If Peggy, executor of her husband's will, knew about John Sage, an illegitimate child, she only alluded to him as "a young man" or (several times) "The Boy," and not by name: She wrote Edward that Benedict gave Richard and Henry £770 to pay their debts and to settle them on their farms, £40 a year to Sophia, and £20 per year to "a young man in Canada." He was "the Boy who is with you." More revealingly, she went beyond the simple mention of John Sage to advise on how her stepsons in Canada should treat him: "The Boy who is with you ought to be taught, by his own labor, to procure his own livelihood;—he ought never to have been brought up with any other ideas."[21]

Otherwise, John Sage is invisible in all Arnold communications that have come to light. Some think John Sage was the child of one of Benedict's sons but given the era, it was completely usual for a gentleman on a long absence from home to have a mistress. It was considered good for his health just as to

John Sage Arnold's grave, in Lehigh Cemetery, Lehighs Corners, Ontario. He and his wife Sarah Brunson, originally of Vermont, raised seven children in Kitley Township. Sarah and three of their children are also buried in the cemetery (courtesy Barry K. Wilson).

retain sperm was considered deleterious. Also, Benedict was an officer and it was acceptable for British officers then to take a mistress while stationed away from Britain in the empire. Sometimes an officer married his Indian mistress. For the sake of one's wife, to not acknowledge the kinship with one's illegitimate offering in life but to give the male child his due at one's death was common practice for a gentleman. Yet if John Sage was equal in all ways to his brothers, would the word "board" have been used by Benedict in his will.

The Mysterious Saga of John Sage
By Barry Wilson[22]

As a daring, creative soldier and aggressive, enterprising businessman, Benedict Arnold often wore his plans, goals and life on his sleeve.

Of course, like most people he also harbored secrets—none more explosive than his treacherous September 1780 plan to turn over both West Point and George Washington to the British.

Then there was his best-kept secret, the one he carried for the final 15 years of his life only to reveal it from the grave.

It was the existence of a hitherto unknown heir, John Sage, first made public in the summer of 1801 when his last will and testament was read in London after his death.

The assumption of historians has been that John Sage was born in Saint John, New Brunswick where Arnold lived for almost six years (1785–91) as a ship owner, merchant and trader. There are no official documents to confirm the "Loyalist City" as the site of his birth.

He became a successful farmer and died 45 years later in Upper Canada, now Ontario. His gravestone records his name as "John Arnold," his date of birth as April 14, 1786, and his date of death as October 22, 1831.

However, more than two centuries since that birth, the full nature of the Sage secret and his origins remains swathed in mystery and speculation.

Since census, birth and death documents for the then–British colony of New Brunswick do not exist in historic official files maintained by the provincial government or the Maritime United Church archives prior to the early decades of the 19th century, there is no paper trail to document Sage's beginning years.

Arnold's will, written August 30, 1800, and read after his 1801 death in London, first publicly revealed his existence (although his name had been included in a private 1798 petition to the government for a land grant to his descendants). "I give, devise and bequeath to John Sage, now in Canada living with my sons there (being about 14 years of age) twelve hundred acres of land," his will directed. … "I also do hereby give and bequeath to the said John Sage twenty pounds per annum to be paid by my sons Richard and Henry for his use for Board, Cloathing and Education until he shall be of the age of twenty-one years."

The money would be paid out of Arnold's estate and an additional £50 was to be paid when he turned 21.

Initially, the wording of the will was all that history had to work with, although the boy soon made it into official records. Two years after Arnold's death, a census for Upper Canada identified Sage as a 16-year-old living with Richard and Henry along with Richard's wife Hannah.

In August 1804, a land grant document for the bequeathed 1,200 acres of Upper Canadian farmland was filed identifying him as "John Arnold of the City of London, gentleman, son of the late General Benedict Arnold." The claim that he was from London, England, only added to the mystery and historical confusion.

The vacuum created by the paucity of facts has been filled with speculative assertions and conclusions, most of which do not reflect well on Benedict Arnold. The most common explanation, gleefully advanced by American writers of the "Arnold the Villain" storyline, is that Sage was his son, born of a mistress.

The *Encyclopedia of the American Revolution* saw it as a straightforward story: "He produced an illegitimate son, John Sage, who was born about 1786 to an unknown woman he probably found in Saint John." A 1960 biography declared, without citing sources: "He fathered a half-breed Indian son." In a 1994 biography, Clare Brandt accepted that the mother was in Saint John, claiming that Arnold left the port city for a 1786 business trip "turning his back … on his pregnant mistress."

However, the chronology of Arnold's arrival in Saint John makes impossible the scenario that John Sage was conceived by Arnold and a mistress he found in Saint John after leaving his wife in London. When he arrived in New Brunswick December 2, 1785, John Sage's mother would have been more than four months pregnant. He could not have met her there.

Was she his London mistress who accompanied him across the Atlantic? Did records of John Arnold's death and burial in 1831 get his birthdate wrong? Or perhaps he was not born in Saint John. And perhaps Benedict Arnold was not his father.

In 1960, Indianapolis researcher James Speers was planning to write a book about Benedict Arnold and trying to pin down John Sage's origins. Based on the fact that Sage was first mentioned in a 1798 petition from Benedict to the government of Upper Canada requesting a land grant for his heirs, Speers speculated in a letter to the Ontario chief archivist that Sage was a child of Benedict's first son, Benedict VI, who in 1785, he would have been 16 and probably living with his aunt Hannah and brothers in New Haven, Conn. In 1787, she and her nephews moved to Saint John to be near Benedict and his wife Peggy.

Could John Sage actually be Benedict Arnold's grandson, treated as a son in the 1800 will to ensure him financial stability? Benedict VI had died from an infected wound at age 27 in 1795 while serving with the British army in Jamaica, unmarried and officially childless. His fatherhood was Speers' speculation but there is no record that he ever got to the bottom of the riddle nor wrote his book about Benedict Arnold.

What is left for certain is an August 13, 1804, land grant document referencing the family story that he was General Arnold's son and an eroded and moss-covered tombstone in a pioneer graveyard in eastern Ontario marking his existence, date of birth and death. As a teenager, he lived with Arnold sons Richard and Henry in Upper Canada.

In a letter (now in the Penrose Library, University of Denver) to her stepsons after Benedict Arnold's death, Peggy Arnold (Shippen) did not add clarity to the relationship. She asked them to choose suitable land for themselves in Upper Canada in accordance with Benedict's will and wishes.

Then she turned to John Sage, although not by name. He was 'The Boy.' She asked that they chose land for him and hold it in trust until he turned 21 in 1807 as the will specified.

John Arnold's lasting legacy, whatever the circumstances of his conception, is the many generations of Canadian descendants who spread across the country from their eastern Ontario roots. They can trace their origin back to the spot where John (Sage) Arnold is buried among the trees. The grave also holds the mystery of his family lineage.

The hidden story of John Sage was similar to how Ambrosio O'Higgins, who died the same year as Arnold, handled his by-blow. Higgins was a Spanish officer of Irish origin who rose to be governor of Chile and viceroy of Peru. O'Higgins had very limited contact with his son Bernardo. Bernardo's letters to his father from Spain went unanswered, and when Bernardo was sent to England to complete his education, he was so impoverished he nearly starved to death. Ambrosio died and left his son a large hacienda, and the son, rather than be crushed by the same aristocratic pretensions as his father, led a revolutionary movement under Ambrosio's name.

In the same time period, William Wordsworth took but a mild interest in Caroline Vallon, the child of the woman he had an affair with in France on his tour. This "phantom of delight" was indeed "a moment's ornament."

John's mother is unknown which is a puzzlement since one would have expected information to have been passed down. A rumor was that she was an Indian princess. This is a bit complicated since she is supposed to have been 19-year-old Aaron Burr's lover on the March to Quebec—Jacataqua, sachem of Swan Island. While there is clearly a mix-up there, the idea that Benedict had a child by an indigenous woman is plausible. He would have not had to deal with gossip if he had a mistress outside the British society. And the Native American fantasy girl titillated men of this era. René de Chateaubriand visited America just before the French Revolution and wrote a volume on his travels. He claimed to have been infatuated by a pretty young Native American who sang to him where he spent the night with a tribe.

When he was alone, without a wife, for the first time in many years, and working hard for his family, it seems reasonable he would have felt deserving of a mistress. She would take care of his sexual needs and give him the comfort of a woman he was used to, his whole adult life. But Arnold was calculating and standoffish; one cannot see him having a backstairs affair with someone in the community where he lived. One can speculate as more likely he had a mistress who was a stranger to the people in his community, whether she belonged to one of the tribes of the Passamaquoddy, or was of noble British rank, or was a concubine who came over with him.

Yet the descendants of John Sage have the story in the family that Benedict had an affair in England, and when the woman became pregnant, he thought it wise to leave the country, that the secret liaison propelled him to relocate in New Brunswick.

During Arnold's lifetime, not only was having frequent sex the means to a man's robust health but, additionally, many men had only the merest discomfort for spawning a child they left helpless in the world. Once there was and was not.... A version of this begins many fairy tales and another of an illegitimate at the same era whether it is fact or fiction supports that John Sage was Arnold's son.

Before 1800, a young boy appeared in Canada who seemed to come from nowhere.[23] A family took him in and he was posted by the customs authorities with a menial job as searcher and waiter of tidal waters in St. Andrews. It was remarked in that town that this person, as Barry Murray relates, named Charles Briscoe (1778–1842) "always had money in his pocket—considerable funds that seemed to come from thin air." Mr. Briscoe married and had children, and was known as autocratic, imperious, aloof and mysteriously well-off. He liked to ride around town in a scarlet hunting coat on a white horse. His wife had been at the British court before coming to Canada. Her sister was the wife of the painter Sir Thomas Lawrence.

Many wondered about the identity of Mr. Briscoe. He was reputed to be a son of King George IV, and his mother said to be a lady of the court (a rumor he did not dispel). When Charles Briscoe died he was buried in the Loyalist cemetery, having left a request that his grave be opened after the demise of his last child, when papers proving his royal birth would be found buried with him. He gave minute details about this ceremony and who should be in attendance. When his grave was opened the papers had crumbled to dust but in the coffin was found an ivory miniature of George IV, set with pearls with a lock of hair at the back.

George, Prince of Wales and the future George IV, cast off one mistress after the other. When a mistress had notoriety, more is of course known. Mary "Perdita" Robinson, a married actress and mother, was 21 when she became mistress of George, 16. Briscoe could have been her child, or of any other casual affair of randy George, regarding whom were over a dozen claims of children out of wedlock. Mr. Briscoe was more discreet about his identity than he would have been in the present day. One can conjecture that John Sage was discreet about his identity as well, and that someone cared for him to have a successful life.

John lived with Henry and Richard (and some say their Aunt Hannah) and then as a farmer on his one inherited lands in Canada. Richard's letters do not mention John but then the overriding topic of the correspondence of the brothers was their Canadian land holdings, and John's was settled; he would receive no more income from whatever sales were made of Benedict Arnold's land after his death. It is notable that the will specified money for education, suggesting John was not seen by Arnold as working class.

John Sage left an indication he felt a relatedness to Benedict and his half-brothers in how he named his four sons: William, Henry Edward, John and Richard.

Benedict Arnold, however one casts his actions, was an alpha-male. He would have been considerate to the feelings of his wife, but this would not have stopped him from giving an illegitimate child his due in his will. Arnold was not puritanical and his comportment in another earlier situation regarding his good friend Dr. Joseph Warren speaks for a tolerance to out of wedlock births. Arnold had approached Warren with his strategic scheme to take Fort Ticonderoga.

Warren championed the project with the Massachusetts militia officers and shepherded acceptance of and funding for the foray through the Massachusetts Provincial Congress. Warren was a widower and when he was killed, his children were orphans. Discord ensued between Mercy Scollay, the governess and mistress of Warren, who was caring for several of the children, and Warren's two brothers and the woman at whose house the eldest, a girl, was staying. Displaying utter indifference to what exactly Mercy's role had been in Warren's life, Arnold donated 500 silver dollars to the children. Mercy taught in a church school in Medfield, Massachusetts, and remained unwed. The man was dead and any propriety regarding the doctor and his household was irrelevant—the children counted. Similarly, Arnold made his own decisions and was very individualistic: John Sage's destiny counted not whatever were the circumstances of his birth.

Sage lived until age 45. He and his wife Sarah had seven children, three of whom had the same given names as General Arnold's legitimate children. His descendants farmed an area between Smiths Falls and Brockville, Ontario, and multiplied. They placed a marker where he is buried in Leeds, Ontario.

Taking a magnifying glass to Benedict Arnold's will (July 18, 1801), one finds Sage mentioned three times:

> John Sage, now in Canada, living with my Sons there (being about 14 years of age) 1200 acres of land being part of a grant of 13,400 acres of land made to me as a Half Pay Officer for myself and Family by Order of the Duke of Portland by his letter directed to Peter Russell Esquire President of the Council in Upper Canada dated the 12th of June 1798 which said 1200 Acres of Land I give to him to be located altogether in one place out of the before mentioned Grant as my Executors may judge equal and fair. I also do hereby give and bequeath to the said John Sage 20 pounds per annum to be paid to my Sons Richard and Henry for his use for Board Cloathing and Education until he shall be of the Age of Twenty one Years to be paid out of the Estate I may die possessed of. I also give and bequeath to the said John Sage fifty pounds to be paid to him when he shall attain the age of twenty one years.[24]

Why only fifty pounds?—this may have been in the order of a typical birthday present. The will's very next line starts "I do hereby Constitute and Appoint my Beloved Wife Sole Executrix to this my last Will and Testament." When, telling Edward about the details of his father's will, Peggy alluded interstitially to a bequest to "a young man in Canada," she does seem to be condescending. Politeness and distance were her refuge from discomfort. Peggy wanted to show that John Sage was nothing noteworthy—by not naming him to make him seem like a nobody.

Sophia Matilda Arnold (1785–1828, second wife, only daughter)

Sophia was 15 when her father died. Her mother was proud of her skill at needlework, and her manners and appearance, her writing and French. She was homeschooled from about nine years of age. Her parents were always worried about her health especially after she had a seizure; if this repeated it was mentioned in letters only as a single fit. In his last year Arnold wrote Bliss on that "Mrs. A. and my Family are as well as usual except Sophia, who tho' not sick is very delicate and we have had to take her from School for the Country Air."[25]

This would strike many mothers and daughters as familiar. I was out of the nest at 20 but returned at 40 with a child in whose life the father was uninvolved. My parents were warm to the baby and accepting of me. Meanwhile my mother was evaluating our future. Only once, but memorably, she espoused her view that "You would make a man a good wife if you weren't a writer."

Sophia was a girl who lost her mother. Her brothers Edward and George took charge of her spinsterish situation by inviting her to the British marriage mart in India. She fell in love with her brother Edward's friend Pownoll Phipps, a young widower and officer in the Bengal Cavalry, in 1813, and they wed in India.

Captain Phipps had become engaged while recovering from an injury on duty in France. The young lady, Henriette, was the daughter of Count Beaurepaire, but unacceptable to the Phipps. When he told his parents, they dispatched him to Calcutta in the Bengal army of the East India Company. He served in Egypt and when he returned to Calcutta in 1802, he found Henriette waiting for him and they wed. When she died in 1812, he was eligible again, and Sophia fell in love with him. She was violently ill, so the wedding was hastened, but she recovered, lived until age 44 and had four or five children before dying of consumption. Pownoll rose to the rank of lieutenant colonel.

The Phipps were well suited, both had an evangelical faith, and the marriage was happy. Taylor states that Sophia and Pownoll settled at Mount Pleasant, Sunbury, which is where the Arnolds had lived for a time, but Benedict sold on one of the times he downsized. Both Phipps were devout and "played an active part in the local evangelical circle."[26]

The evangelism may have engendered rebellion in the next generation as James wrote from Dover on April 2, 1832: "Phipps chiefly in London—oldest girl 'a sadly distressing object' other three nice children, second girl 16 or 17."[27] A year later (1833), after writing Richard how he and his wife Virginia both liked the seaside, "where there is always something to amuse," he struck a more sober tone, that Phipps and his brood of six children were also well.[28]

George Arnold (1787–1828, third son by second wife)

George, born at Saint John in September 1787, did not have a middle name, presumably as he was named after the King. Benedict saw great ambition in the boy when he was only eight. In December 1799, Benedict Arnold asked Lord Cornwallis for aid for his son George, then twelve, to prepare for an army vocation. Of George's future, after his father's death, Peggy wrote her sons that George was at the Royal Military Academy, "and if I live, will go to the East Indies next year."[29] Benedict had signaled out that George had ambition. Like his four brothers George went into the army. He married Anne Martinex Brown and they had a boy and a girl. A year before he died, James wrote Richard that George was going up the Ganges to join his regiment and was the senior major of all the Bengal Cavalry, "and must soon get a Lt. Colonelcy—in about four years he will, if spared, retire on his rank and pay for life ... feather his nest tolerable well."[30]

George left a bequest of 200 pounds to Richard and the same to each of Richard's children. He left his "'Canada lands' to William, James and Sophia."

William Fitch Arnold (1794–1846, fourth son by second wife)

William's father was openly affectionate about his youngest child in correspondence. In September 1800, Benedict wrote Edward of William as a child of six that the child's first missive was done without any assistance, and observed that "the Dear little Fellow is coming on very well." Peggy wrote of William in 1804 that "little William gives a fair prospect of turning out well."[31] William was the proverbial youngest whom parents and older siblings feel free to cherish openly; to Sophia he felt like her eldest child.

William's namesake was the brother of the Fitch sisters, the Loyalist friends of the Arnolds who lived close by after the Arnolds returned to London. (Charles Ripley says they first settled on Hollis Street, just off Oxford Street. The Fitch family are said to have lived in Portland or Cavendish Square.)

William confessed he had an aversion to writing letters; consequently there seem to be few of them in archives. He started a military career like his brothers and became a captain in the 19th Lancers but became an administrator in England, rising to the high position of Justice of the Peace for Buckinghamshire. That he wasn't cut out for the army comes through in a statement to his brother Richard that "The uncertain movements of our little army for some time past, have prevented me from writing to you before—Nothing of the slightest consequence has taken place since we joined the Army; the utmost a trifling skirmish." The tongue in cheek continues when he concludes, "I must now apologize for the shortness of my letter and the bad hand in which it is written. About three weeks ago my horse fell under me and nearly broke my wrist."[32] He complained that the British army in India was in "a state of vegetation."

When Peggy warned William once against speculation, she was thinking of his father, as William would not have financial troubles. He was serving in Canada in the 19th Light Dragoons when Sophia wrote him of her marriage in December 1814. "I will consider you my eldest child," Sophia wrote him, advising him that "a soldier may be as pious and excellent in every way as any other man, as I hope my darling William will prove."[33]

While at Fort Chambly, an historic fort in Quebec, William responded to Richard that he would visit him in the winter. He would drive a "tandum" and take two saddles, one for himself and one for his servant, in case the roads were poor and they had to mount the horses.[34] It is unknown whether William was able to make the trip. He went from being captain in the 19th Royal Lancers to justice of the peace, and a magistrate, for the county of Buckinghamshire, England. He had six children. He remained close to his former brother-in-law after William retired and Sophia had died.

William's name comes up in an unexpected source. President Pierce appointed his old college friend Nathaniel Hawthorne to be consul to Liverpool in 1853. Hawthorne held the post for four years and enjoyed outings; at the beginning of the second he was off exploring in the early spring and noted in his journal the picturesque landscape, halls and cottages of the English countryside. After a passage describing the nesting pattern of rooks at a gentleman's home, he brought a gossipy sensibility to his mention of the estate of General Arnold's youngest son, seen on his tour:

Little Missenden Abbey was built with some parts of the old abbey that Nathaniel Hawthorne gazed on during an excursion. This photograph is of Little Missenden Abbey, circa early 20th century (courtesy Buckingham County Museum Trust).

A son of General Arnold, named William Fitch Arnold and born in 1794, now possesses the estate of Little Messenden [sic] Abbey, Bucks County, and is a magistrate for that county. He was formerly Captain of the 19th Lancers. He has now two sons and four daughters. The other three sons of General Arnold, all older than this one and all military men, do not appear to have left children; but a daughter married to Colonel Phipps, of the Mulgave family, has a son and two daughters. I question whether any of our true-hearted Revolutionary heroes have left a more prosperous progeny than this arch-traitor. I should like to know their feelings with respect to their ancestor.[35]

It's no wonder Hawthorne did not attempt to be introduced. The Phipps family had gained by marriage in the eighteenth century the royal Mulgrave titles, and their country house was Mulgrave Castle in Yorkshire.

Nikolaus Pevsner's *Buildings of England* states that there were two buildings on the grounds of the Chiltern Hospital, both known as Little Missenden Abbey, the early nineteenth century one having been William Arnold's home. According to Paul Evans, an officer of the Centre for Buckinghamshire Studies, "it would appear the only item relating to Benedict Arnold and his descendants is a notebook containing a sermon and a biographical sketch of Reverend (Edward?) Arnold" (personal communication).

Hannah Arnold, Benedict's Younger Sister

Hannah's life was circumscribed first by taking care of Arnold's shop in New Haven during his absences and then, it is believed, taking care of his three older sons. Beyond her friendship with the Frenchman which Arnold nixed in her youth, she is not known to have been courted. She was devoted to her brother and must have endured scorn and suspicion after his defection. She wrote a friend after her brother's betrayal, "Let me ask the pity of all my friends; there never was a more proper object of it."[36]

It is said that Hannah came to Saint John in the late 1780s and also lived with Henry and Richard in Henry's house at Montague, Canada, but was sometimes back in Connecticut, attending, conjectures Wallace, to business for her brother. It is known that when Benedict died, Peggy wrote Henry and Richard one letter and Aunt Hannah another. Yet they—Henry, Richard, John Sage, and Hannah—may have been living together, as important letters would be addressed individually not to the household. The contents of the letter are known through a letter to Henry and Richard. Peggy states that she had written Hannah that she feared debt would swallow up all the property, but to draw 20 pounds and that Peggy would honor the 40 pounds per annum which had been left her by Benedict's will. Peggy had not heard back yet when she wrote the two sons. She added that she supposed they were supplying Hannah with what she needed.[37] Might Peggy have expressed warmth towards the maiden aunt who had helped her family at many terms? There is no indication in her letters of such feeling.

Hannah died in Ontario on August 31, 1803.

There is a single letter of unreserved sentiment for her family that has survived. Despite the frustrating fact that we don't know what part she played in raising her brother's children, her goodness and directness come through when she wrote Peggy four days after Peggy and baby Edward left Philadelphia in the wake of Benedict's treason. First Hannah jokes that she was abed, with a fever that "attacks all orders of people (old maids not exempted)." She continued:

> If you could conceive how we miss you and the dear little bantling, you would pity us. Harry was inconsolable the whole day you left us, and had, I believe, not less than 20 of the most violent bursts of grief; his little brother Edward seems to be the principal theme of the mournful song—not one day has escaped without his shedding tears at his absence; he laments that just as he began to know and love his brother, he must be removed so far from him that he cannot even hear how he does; this day with a falling tear, he obser'd to me that he thought it very hard when he had so few relations, that they should all be at such a distance from him.[38]

"Harry" (Henry Arnold) was Benedict's son who would suffer the traumas of being burned in the warehouse fire and losing many of his and his wife Hannah's babies.

* * *

The father was very concerned to leave patrimony to his children, what his father (Benedict IV), had failed to do. The brothers conferred by letter about the land in Canada that had been secured by their father (according to a grant of June 12, 1798). The grant of 13,400 acres made in 1799 was in Upper Canada (Ontario). The land was later sold.

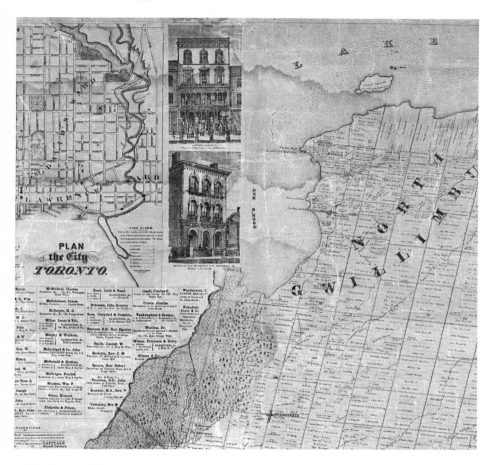

The "Arnold Estate" appears in various locations of *Tremain's Map of 1860 (York County)*. Part of Arnold's land fell within present-day Georgina, formerly North Guillembury; see for example under the "I." Guillembury took its name from the maiden name of Elizabeth Guillem Simcoe, wife of Sir John Simcoe, Ontario's first lieutenant governor. After taking up his command of Domingo, Sir John expressed his dislike of Benedict Arnold to the Duke of Portland, who nevertheless carried out the Canadian grants to Arnold and his family (courtesy Georgina Pioneer Village & Archives, Keswick, Ontario).

There was a 5,000-acre block northeast of present-day Toronto and south of Lake Simcoe; the rest was in Upper Canada, located in Gwillimbury East and North, today in Georgina, Ontario, north of Toronto. To meet the requirement of the grant, Richard, Henry and John Sage had to remain there for six months of the year for three years, which they did.

Peggy after Benedict's death was encouraging Richard and Henry to get "situated in the best terms possible." In August 1803 she wrote as matriarch to them, glad the difficulties over the Canadian lands were overcome and that they would certainly be of considerable value "if judiciously located."[39]

The family was spread remarkably in the empire. When Edward was billeted in his mid-twenties, his parents having died, he regretted not knowing his family in Pennsylvania, but he never went there.

James repeatedly told his brothers in Canada that he wanted to sell his Canadian land. He heard from William "that some vagabond had been cutting down a good deal of my best timber."[39] This indicates William had visited Ontario. He jested that it was too bad they couldn't tack the Canadian land onto England; and bring the brothers and their families over with it. In that letter, turning practical he continued:

> I am very sure that you and Henry will do everything needful about the land, for us, and act as we should for ourselves. I hope your farming concern is coming on much better than it was, and that the war, by increasing intercourse, has made your property more valuable.

By 1837, James was asking Richard what the prospects were to sell the Canadian land, while in the same letter saying, "I am not sure that when steam travelling comes more fully into play, I may not feel disposed to take another trip cross the Atlantic."[40]

Richard lived in Canada all his adult life, and Henry lived there until he moved to the United States. We know John Sage lived with them as a boy. Why he wasn't mentioned in the round of the brothers' epistolary "How are you's?" could be a function of randomly preserved letters or might suggest an attitude towards John's illegitimacy. The John Sage descendants multiplied and flourished in Ontario and Saskatchewan.

Chapter Notes

Preface

1. Quoted in Willard Sterne Randall, *Benedict Arnold: Patriot and Traitor* (NY: William Morrow, 1990), 572.

Chapter 1

1. The episode is told by Isaac Newton Arnold, *The Life of Benedict Arnold: His Patriotism and His Treason* (Chicago: Jansen, McClurg & Co., 1890, 27–28.
2. Curtis Fahey, "ARNOLD, BENEDICT," in *Dictionary of Canadian Biography* [DCB], vol. 5, University of Toronto/Universite Laval, 2003-. http.//www.biographi.ca/en/bio/arnold_benedict_5E.html
3. Peter Andreas, *Smuggler Nation: How Illicit Trade Made America* (New York: Oxford University Press, 2013), 18.
4. Thomas M. Truxes, *Defying Empire: Trading with the Enemy in Colonial New York* (New Haven: CT: Yale University Press, 2008), 6.
5. Cathy Matson, *Merchants and Empires: Trading in Colonial New York* (Baltimore, MD: Johns Hopkins University Press, 1998), 277.
6. *Ibid.*
7. Truxes, 2.
8. Truxes, 75.
9. Willard Sterne Randall, *Benedict Arnold: Patriot and Traitor* (New York: William Morrow & Co., 1990), 56.
10. George Canning Hill, *Benedict Arnold* (Boston: E.O. Libby, 1858), 25.
11. Andreas, 14.
12. Edgar W. Ames, "Benedict Arnold—Patriot," *The Quarterly Journal of the New York State Historical Association* (Cooperstown, NY: New York State Historical Association, 1919), vol.12, 143.
13. Charles Royster, *A Revolutionary People at War: The Continental Army and American Character, 1775–1783* (Chapel Hill, NC: Published for the Omohumdro Institute of Early American History and Culture, Williamsburg, VA by the University of North Carolina Press, 2005 c1979), 4.

Chapter 2

1. Joyce Lee Malcolm, *The Tragedy of Benedict Arnold: An American Life* (NY: Pegasus, 2018), 268.
2. Carl Van Doren, *Secret History of the American Revolution: An Account of the Conspiracies of Benedict Arnold and Numerous Others Drawn from the Secret Service Papers*, quoted in Malcolm, 358.
3. Benedict Arnold [BA] to George Washington [GW], Feb 1777 quoted in Nathaniel Philbrick, *Valiant Ambition: George Washington, Benedict Arnold and the Fate of the American Revolution* (New York: Penguin, 2017), 91.
4. Gene Procknow, "Personal Honor and Promotion among Revolutionary Generals and Congress," *Journal of the American Revolution*," Jan. 23, 2018. https://allthingsliberty.com/2018/01/personal-honor-promoiton-among-revolutionary-generals-congress/.
5. George Washington Green, *The Life of Nathanael Greene: Major General...* (New York: G.P. Putnam and Son, 1867), vol.1: 339.
6. Joseph J. Ellis, *American Creation: Triumphs and Tragedies at the Founding of the Republic* (New York: Random House, 2007), 70.

7. Procknow.

8. John Adams quoted in Edward Teitelman and Richard W. Longstreth, *Architecture in Philadelphia: A Guide* (Cambridge, MA: MIT Press, 1974), 121. Ironically the house was eventually sold to Jonathan Williams, the grandnephew of Benjamin Franklin and superintendent of West Point.

9. E. Pendleton to W. Woodford, November 1, 1779, quoted in Lori J. Ducharme and Gary Alan Fine, "The Construction of Nonpersonhood and Demonization: Commemorating the Traitorous Reputation of Benedict Arnold..." *Social Forces* 73, no. 4 (1995), 1315. https://www.jstor.org/stable/2580449.

10. Quoted in James Kirby Martin, *Benedict Arnold, Revolutionary Hero: An American Warrior Reconsidered* (NY: New York University Press, 2000), 324.

11. Benson Bobrick, *Angel in the Whirlwind: The Triumph of the American Revolution* (New York: Penguin, 1997), 407.

12. *George Washington Papers, General Orders*, April 6, 1780. Founders.archives.gov.

13. Barbara Tuchman, *The First Salute: A View of the American Republic* (NY: Knopf, 1988), 189.

14. BA to GW, Sept 25, 1780. https://founders/archives.gov/documents/Hamilton/ 01-02-0867-/0002.

15. BA, "Letter to the Inhabitants of America," *London Chronicle*, Nov. 14, 1780 in Oscar Sherwin, *Benedict Arnold* (New York: The Century Co., 1931), 331.

16. Margaret Shippen Arnold [MSA] to Edward Shippen [ES], June 26, 1792 in Lewis Burd Walker et al., "Life of Margaret Shippen, Wife of Benedict Arnold" *Pennsylvania Magazine of History and Biography* [PMHB], 25 (1900), 25: 170.

17. PMHB, vol. 25, 2, 164.

18. The inventory pages are at the New York Historical Society.

19. Nathaniel Philbrick, *Valiant Ambition: George Washington, Benedict Arnold, and the Fate of the American Revolution* (NY: Penguin, 2017), 35.

20. Philbrick, 377.

Chapter 3

1. Founders.archives.gov/documents/Washington/99-01-02-03636

2. Wilbur C. Hall, "Sergeant Champe's Adventures," *William & Mary Quarterly* 18,2, July 1939, 323–342 passim.

3. Mildred Holladay and Dean Burgess, *History of Portsmouth, Virginia* (Portsmouth, VA: The Portsmuoth History Commission in commemoration of the 400th anniversary of the landing of the first colony at Jamestown, 2007), 53

4. Heritage Frederick, Maryland has variegated information about the school. This inset on schoolmaster Booth is based on research compiled by their enthusiastic research service.

Chapter 4

1. This chapter is written by John Endicott. John has practiced law in New York and Connecticut. He lives in Litchfield, Connecticut.

2. Joyce Lee Malcolm, *The Tragedy of Benedict Arnold* (NY: Pegasus Books, 2018), 289.

3. Stephen Brumwell, *Turncoat* (New Haven: Yale University Press, 2018), 168.

4. Malcolm, 390.

5. Mark Jacob and Stephen H. Case, *Treacherous Beauty: Peggy Shippen, the woman behind Benedict Arnold's plot to betray America* (Guilford, CT: Lyons Press, 2012).

6. Jacob and Case, *Treacherous Beauty*, viii.

7. Mark Jacob and Stephen Case, book talk on "Treacherous Beauty" at Politics and Prose Bookstore in Washington, D.C., published August 27, 2012 by BookTV, found on YouTube

8. ITV, "The Jury," Season 1, Episode 5 (2002).

9. Wikipedia contributors. "Not proven." Wikipedia, 26 Jan. 2019. Web. 12 Feb. 2019.

10. Sylvia Prince, "History versus Historical Fiction." *Sylvia Prince Author,* blog post published September 19, 2016. http://www.sylviaprincebooks.com/blog/?offset=1475521951905.

11. Richard P. Feynman, *The Meaning of it All: Thoughts of a Citizen Scientist* (Reading, MA: Perseus Books, 1998), 76

12. "Richard Feynman on the likelihood of Flying Saucers," excerpted from Richard P. Feynman lecture on The

Character of Physical Law, Cornell University Messenger Lectures (1964), http://amiquote.tumblr.com/post/4463044318/richard-feynman-on-the-likelihood-of-flying.

13. Julia Courtwright, "Whom Can We Trust Now? The Portrayal of Benedict Arnold in American History." Fairmount Folio: Journal of History, 1998, Vol. 2, 1–16, 8.

14. Lori J. Ducharme and Gary Alan Fine, "The Construction of Nonpersonhood and Demonization: Commemorating the Traitorous Reputation of Benedict Arnold." Social Forces, 1995, Vol. 73, No. 4, 1309–1331, 1311–12.

15. E. Irvine Haines, "The Fatal Web Spun by Peggy Shippen." *New York Times* December 4, 1932.

16. A.O. Scott, "Vice." *New York Times* December 17, 2018.

17. Laurel Thatcher Ulrich, *Well-Behaved Women Seldom Make History* (NY: Vintage Books 2008).

18. Charlene Boyer Lewis, interview "Another Badly Behaving Woman" at The Washington Library, Mount Vernon, VA, June 7, 2018, audio at https://www.mountvernon.org/library/digitalhistory/podcast/another-badly-behaving-woman/

19. Allison Pataki, *The Traitor's Wife* (NY: Howard Books, 2014).

20. Pataki, *The Traitor's Wife,* fourth page of Reading Group Guide, at end of book.

21. Pataki, *The Traitor's Wife,* 462.

22. Wikipedia contributors. "Peggy Shippen." Wikipedia, 6 Jan. 2019. Web. 12 Feb. 2019.

23. Website: "Spy Letter of the American Revolution from the Collections of the Clements Library," found at http://clements.umich.edu/exhibits/online/spies/index-main2.html

24. Nancy Rubin Stuart, *Defiant Brides: the untold story of two revolutionary-era women and the radical men they married* (Boston: Beacon Press, 2013).

25. Stuart, *Defiant Brides,* 67.

26. Brumwell, *Turncoat,* 173.

27. Carl Van Doren, *The Secret History of the American Revolution* (New York: Viking Press, 1941), 209.

28. Ducharme and Fine, "The Construction of Nonpersonhood," 1327.

29. Brumwell, *Turncoat,* 280.

30. Quoted in Lewis Burd Walker, "Life of Margaret Shippen, Wife of Benedict Arnold." The Pennsylvania Magazine of History and Biography, 1901, vol. XXV, no. 2, 145–190, 148–149.

31. AMC, "Turn," Season 3, Episode 9 (2016).

32. Matthew L. Davis, *Memoirs of Aaron Burr* (New York, 1836), 162.

33. Lewis Burd Walker, "Life of Margaret Shippen," 152–156.

34. Jacob and Case, *Treacherous Beauty,* 127.

35. Jacob and Case, Treacherous Beauty, 111.

36. Opinion of Chief Justice Marshall (August 1807), https://www.famous-trials.com/burr/165-opinion

37. *Ibid.*

38. The Supreme Court Historical Society, 2006–The Aaron Burr Treason Trial–Eugene Scalia and Robert Fiske as advocates, Justice Scalia for the Court (National Heritage Lecture) https://supremecourthistory.org/events/archive/past-reenactment/index.html

39. See, "Catching Up: Treacherous Beauty at NEHGS," June 30, 2017, https://gabridge.com/catching-up-treacherous-beauty-at-nehgs/; and "'Traitor's Wife' Movie About American Revolutionary War in the Works at Radar," Variety online, September 14, 2016, https://variety.com/2016/film/news/traitors-wife-movie-benedict-arnold-radar-1201859855/

40. Jacob and Case, *Treacherous Beauty,* viii.

41. Lon L. Fuller, *Legal Fictions* (Stanford, CA: Stanford University Press, 1967), 1; 4.

42. *The Man Who Shot Liberty Valance,* Dir. John Ford. Perf. James Stewart, John Wayne, Lee Marvin, and Vera Miles. Paramount, 1962. Film

Chapter 5

1. www.encyclopediavirginia.org/Tobacco_in_Colonial_Virginia

2. The Rangers wore black and white feathers on their horses' bridles as a sign of mourning for Major André, a close friend of Colonel Simcoe. "During the dark days of André's captivity, Simcoe and his Rangers had volunteered to try to rescue him;

now, with enormous good grace, they agreed to serve under the command of the man who was widely blamed for his death." Clare Brandt, *The Man in the Mirror* (NY: Random House, 1994), 241.

3. Mark Edward Lender and James Kirby Martin, "A Traitor's Epiphany: Benedict Arnold in Virginia and His Quest for Reconciliation, *Virginia Magazine of History and Biography*, 2017, Issue 4, 314–357, 8.

4. Michael Kranish, *Flight from Monticello: Thomas Jefferson at War* (NY: Oxford University Press, 2011), 185.

5. Sara B. Bearss, www.encyclopedia virginis.org/Byrd_Mary_Willing_ 1740–1814.

6. Kranish,188.

7. Henry M. Ward, Invasion: Military Operations near Richmond, 1781. Sponsored by the Richmond Bicentennial Commission and Central Fidelity Bank. No date, 7.

8. Ward, 8.

9. "Proposal by Brigadier General Arnold to the Inhabitants of Richmond, Virginia." Virginia Historical Society ViHMss2Ar642a1.

10. Captain Johann Ewald, *Diary of the American War: A Hessian Journal* [May 17, 1781]. Translated and edited by Joseph P. Tustin (New Haven: Yale University Press, 1979), p276.

11. *Baron Von Steuben and the military forces in Virginia during the British invasions of 1780–81*. University of Richmond, April 1979, Repository, Master's Theses, Paper 431]. P26, note 27.

12. Francis Earle Lutz and Dorothy Fuller Silvers, Chesterfield: An Old Virginia County, vol. I, 1604–1954 (Chesterfield Historical Society, 2003 c1954), 117.

13. Holladay and Burgess, 55.

14. Writings of GW, ed. Jared Sparks (Boston: Russell Odiorne and Metcalf, 1835), 7:419 in Kranish, 228.

15. Lender and Martin, "A Traitor's Epiphany," 14.

16. Milton Lomask, The Aftermath of Treason, Oct. 1967, vol 18, issue 6).

17. Mark Edward Lender and James Kirby Martin, "Target of New London." *Journal of Military History*. January 2019.

18. Lender and Martin, "A Traitor's Epiphany," 12.

19. Arnold to Clinton, Jan. 21, 1781, in

Dacies, Documents of the American Revolution 21: 40–43. In Kranish, 195.

20. Ewald, Diary, 277.

21. Lender and Martin, "A Traitor's Epiphany," 16.

22. Lender and Martin, "A Traitor's Epiphany," 20.

23. Lender and Martin, "A Traitor's Epiphany," 17.

24. Wayne Lynch, "Mrs. Byrd's Affair at Westover," Journal of American Revolution. https://allthingsliberty.com/2013/06/mrs-birds-affair-at-Westover

25. Kranish, 197.

26. "An Unrecorded Bit of History. Benedict Arnold's Narrow Escape from Death at the Hands of a Woman," *New York Times*, Jan. 1879.

27. Harry Clinton Green and Mary Wolcott Green, *Pioneer Mothers of America* (NY: Putnam, 1912), vol. III, 353 etc.

Chapter 6

1. Isaac Newton Arnold, *Life of Benedict Arnold his Patriotism and his Treason* (Chicago: Jansen, McClurg, 1880), 359.

2. A.S. Barnes, *Magazine of American History* (A.S. Barnes, 1879) vol. 3, issue 2, July 1879, 675.

3. Drake's *Historic Fields and Mansions of Middlesex* quoted in Isaac Newton Arnold, 259.

4. Isaac Newton Arnold, 364.

5. Benjamin Franklin, *Letters from France: The Private Correspondence of Benjamin Franklin, 1776–1785*, ed. Brett F. Woods (NY: Agora, 2006), 67.

6. Jared Sparks, *Benedict Arnold* (New York, Harper, 1902), 332.

7. Mary Theobald, "What ever happened to Benedict Arnold?," Colonial Williamsburg Journal:summer01.foundation/journal/feature2.cfm

8. Ruma Chopra, *Unnatural Rebellion: Loyalists in New York City during the Revolution* (Charlottesville, VA: University of Virginia Press, 2013), 226.

9. Thomas B. Allen, *Tories: Fighting for the King in America's First Civil War* (NY: HarperCollins, 2010), 328. The last chapter has an excellent overview of the evacuation of Tories from the colonies.

10. Roger Kemper Rogan, Benedict Arnold, *Our First Marine: His*

Contemporaries and the Story of his Life (Cincinnati, OH: Jones Brothers, 1931; rep. Kessinger 2010), 206.

11. Henry Cruger Van Schaack, *Life of Peter Van Schaack* (NY: D. Appleton, 1842), 147 quoted in Willard M. Wallace, *Traitorous Hero: The Life and Fortunes of Benedict Arnold* (New York: Harper and Brothers, 1954) 288.

12. Brian Richard Boylan, *Benedict Arnold and the Dark Eagle* (New York: W.W. Norton, 1973), 242.

13. Jim Murphy, *The Real Benedict Arnold* (New York: Clarion, 2007), 228.

14. Noel Rae, *People's War: Original Voices of the American Revolution* (Guilford, CT: Lyons Press, 2012), 572.

15. Quoted in Henry Phelps Johnston, John Austin Stevens et al., *The Magazine of American History with Notes and Queries*, by Henry Phelps Johnston, John Austin Steven et al., vol. 10, 316.

16. Samuel Salter Blowers to Ward Chipman, Nov. 22, 1785, quoted in Louis Quigley http://new-brunswick.net/Saint_John/benedict/benedict.html, 44.

Chapter 7

1. An overarching source for this chapter is Esther Wright's pioneer research on the people who were compelled to go to the northern colonies during and after the Revolution, especially *The Loyalists of New Brunswick* (Moncton, New Brunswick [NB]: Moncton Publishing Co. 1955).

2. J. Upham to E. Winslow, Dec. 8, 1780, in *The Winslow Papers*, ed. W.O. Raymond (Saint John, NB: New Brunswick Historical Society, 1901), 64.

3. W. Chipman to E. Winslow, Nov. 29, 1783 in *The Winslow Papers*, 152. The letter was written on board the *Tryal* off Staten Island.

4. Robert L. Dallison, *Hope Restored: The American Revolution and the Founding of New Brunswick*, vol. 2 (Fredericton, NB: Goose Lane Editions and the New Brunswick Military Heritage Project, 2003), 49.

5. Beamish Murdoch, *A History of Nova-Scotia, or Acadie* (Halifax, Nova Scotia: James Barnes, 1867), vol. 3, 13–14.

6. W. Chipman to E. Winslow, Aug. 3, 1783. *The Winslow Papers*, 115.

7. D.G. Bell, *Early Loyalist Saint John: The Origins of New Brunswick Politics, 1783–1786* (Fredericton, NB: New Ireland Press, 1983), 150.

8. Kim Klein, "Paths to the Assembly in British North America: New Brunswick, 1786–1837," *Acadiensis, Journal of the History of the Atlantic Region*, vol.39, 2010. https:journals.lib.unb.ca/index.php/acadiensis/article/view/15387/16529. According to Kim Klein, men from the same families that gained preferential access to land grants and patronage appointments were two-fifths of the colony's first-generation assemblyman, while military rank and civic leadership among the refugees were also indicators of status.

9. Valerie H. McKito, *From Loyalists to Loyal Citizens: The DePeyster Family of New* York (Albany: State University of New York Press, 2015), 46.

10. E. Winslow to J. Wentworth in David Bell, *Loyalist Rebellion in New Brunswick: A Defining Conflict for Canada's Political Culture* (Halifax, Nova Scotia: Formac Publishing Co., 2013), 66.

11. Stephen Kimber, a professor of journalism and creative nonfiction at the University of King's College in Halifax, is the award-winning author of nine books, including *Loyalists & Layabouts: The Rapid Rise and Faster Fall of Shelburne, Nova Scotia, 1783–1792.*

12. Charlotte Gourley Robinson, *The Pioneer Profiles of New Brunswick Settlers* (Belleville, Ontario: Mika Publishing, 1980), 85.

13. Bell, 57.

14. John J. McCusker and Russell R. Menard, *The Economy of British America, 1607–1789* (Chapel Hill, NC: University of North Carolina Press, 1998), 113–114.

15. Randall, 598.

16. Ronald Rees, a former of historical geography at the University of Saskatchewan, has written the outstanding *New Brunswick: An Illustrated History* among other works including studies of the St. Croix River and his native Wales.

Chapter 8

1. H. McKay Gordon to E. Winslow, Nov. 20, 1783, *The Winslow Papers*, 321.

2. John Adams to John Jay, *The*

Diplomatic Correspondence of the United States of America, from the signing of the definitive treaty of peace, 10 Sept. 1783, to the adoption of the Constitution, March 4, 1789, vol. 2, 548.

3. William Stewart McNutt, *The Atlantic Provinces: The Emergence of Canadian Society, 1712–1857* (NY: Oxford University Press, 1965), 35.

4. Mrs. Cottnam, a widow, founded her school in 1786, boarding young girls. She was born in the garrison at Louisburg and, when that fell to the French, was sent to Boston. Her husband was a Salem merchant.

5. https://www.starclippers.co.uk/the-different-types-of-tall-sailing-ships.html and Charles A. Armour and Thomas Lackey, *Sailing Ships of the Maritimes: An Illustrated History of Shipping and Shipbuilding in the Maritime Provinces of Canada, 1750–1925* (Toronto: McGraw-Hill Ryerson, 1975), 10.

6. Barry K. Wilson, *Benedict Arnold: A Traitor in Our Midst* (Montreal: McGill, Queens University Press, 2001), xvi.

7. Wilson, 188.

8. Letter to Mrs. Weston from D.M., Feb. 1, 1796 (128), *John Porteous Papers: 1764–1862*, 128. The Loyalist Collection, University of New Brunswick, Fredericton, NB.

9. Louis Quigley, *The New Brunswick Reader*, Nov. 15, 1994 in new-brunswick. net/Saint_John/benedict 1. Html.

10. Adrian Leonard and David Pretel, *The Caribbean and the Atlantic World Economy: Circuits of Trade, Money and Knowledge, 1650–1914* (London: Palgrave Macmillan, 2015), 42–43.

11. Lilian M. Beckwith Maxwell, "The First Canadian Born Novelist," *The Dalhousie Review*, 59–60. http://dalspace.library.dal.ca/bitstream/handle/10222/63895/dalrev_vol31_iss1_pp59_64.pdf?sequence=1

12. Koral LaVorgna, in her capacity as a Research Consultant for the City of Fredericton, has been uncovering the "inside story" of local history properties for the past decade.

13. Maud Maxwell Vesey, *Manuscript Biography of Benedict Arnold* (Fredericton, New Brunswick University of New Brunswick Archives, n.d.), 21.

14. William Henry Kilby, *Eastport and Passamaquoddy: A Collection of Historical and Biographical Sketches* (Eastport, ME: Edward E. Shead & Co., 1888), 446.

15. Tom Standage, *A History of the World in 6 Glasses* (New York: Bloomsbury, 2005), 121–122.

Chapter 9

1. As a journalist, Barry K. Wilson has covered Canadian politics, agriculture, international food trade negotiations and world food issues for four decades. A Life Member of the Canadian Parliamentary Press Gallery, he is most recently the author of a biography of Prime Minister Sir Mackenzie Bowell.

2. Jean E. Sereisky, "Benedict Arnold in New Brunswick," *The Atlantic Advocate* 53, no. 7 (1963), 36.

3. Randall, 321.

4. Charlotte Gourlay Robinson, *Pioneer Profiles of New Brunswick Settlers* (Belleville, Ontario: Mika Publishing Company, 1980), 110.

5. Leonard and Pretel, 42–43.

6. Isaac Allen to Edward Winslow, May 31, 1783, *Winslow Papers*, 86. George Black was a freed slave described as a "brave fellow."

7. William Henry Kilby, "Benedict Arnold on the Eastern Frontier," The Maine Historical Magazine, vol. 2, 190.

Chapter 10

1. Lorenzo Sabine, ch. 4 quoted in Kilby, 142.

2. Georges Cerbelaud Salagnac, "Abbadie De Saint-Castin, Jean Vincent D,'" Baron de Saint-Castin, *DCB*, vol.2.

3. Jeffrey Meyers, *Joseph Conrad: A Biography* (New York: Cooper Square Press, 2001, c 1991), 37.

4. Quoted in Michael Lee Lanning, *American Revolution 100: The Battles People, and Events of the American War* (Napierville, IL: Sourcebooks, 2009), 175.

5. W. G. Godfrey, "CARLETON, GUY," *DCB*, vol. 5, p147.

6. Truxes, 42.

7. James McGregor, *History of Washington Lodge No. 37 Lubec* Maine (Portland, ME: E.W. Brown, 1892), 11.

8. Kate Gannett Wells, "Campobello An Historical Sketch," 35.

9. Roger F. Duncan and John P. Ware, *A Cruising Guide to the New England Coast including the Hudson River, Long Island Sound, and the Coast of New Brunswick* (New York: Dodd, Mead, 1983), 648–9.

10. William Pagan to Dr. William Paine, May 2, 1784. Winslow Papers, 201.

11. Joshua Smith, *The Rogues of 'Quoddy: Smuggling in the Maine New Brunswick Borderlands 1783–1820.* Dissertation University of Maine. Retrieved from Electronic theses and dissertations 189. https"/digital commonslibrary.umaine.edu/etc189, 2003.

12. Paul Craven, *Petty Justice: Low Law and the Sessions System in Charlotte County, New Brunswick, 1785–1867* (Toronto: Published by the Osgood Society for Canadian Legal History for the University of Toronto Press, 2014), 58.

13. Proceedings vol. 102,48. 1976 Naval Art and Science. U.S. Naval Institute. ejournal/em Magazine. Annapolis, MD: National Government Publication, 1976.

14. Joshua M. Smith, "Humbert's Paradox: The Global Context of Smuggling in the Bay of Fundy" chapter 8 in Stephen J. Hornby and John G. Reid, *New England and the Maritime Provinces: Connections and Comparisons* (Montreal & Kingston: McGill-Queen's University Press, 2006), 123.

15. Lorenzo Sabine in Smith, *The Rogues*, 34, note 58.

16. Thomas Jefferson to Albert Gallatin, May 20, 1808. *The Writings of Thomas Jefferson: Correspondence* (NY: Derby and Jackson, 1859), 292. "I hope you will spare no pains or expence to bring the rascals of Passamaquoddy to justice."

17. Joshua M. Smith ("Humbert's Paradox" in *New England and the Maritime Provinces*, 119–120) states that the smugglers in the Maritimes "came from all walks of life"—poor mariners, wealthy merchants, and British adventurers from afar who came the region to smuggle. Small-time fishermen could bring in from America items like tobacco, soap and candles, packed in their barrels of codfish. Some gained great wealth. like Samuel Cunard, founder of the famous Cunard shipping line, who engaged in smuggling in the Passamaquoddy region as a young

captain; or Christopher Scott, a trader "on the lines" who founded the Bank of New Brunswick.

18. Joshua Smith, *The Rogues of 'Quoddy: Smuggling in the Maine New Brunswick Borderlands 1783–1820.* Dissertation University of Maine. Retrieved from Electronic theses and dissertations 189. https"/digital commonslibrary.umaine.edu/etc189, 2003.

19. Thomas Carleton to Thomas Townshend, Baron Sydney, October 1787 in Craven, 59.

20. Smith, *The Rogues*, 145.

21. "Deposition of Colin Campbell, King v. Wine, Brandy and Tea," 1796 and Affadavit of Colin Campbell, King v. Thomas Ross et al., RS 42, "Supreme Court Original Jurisdiction Case Files," Provincial Archives of New Brunswick.

22. *Ibid.*

23. Quoted in Craven, 38.

24. Ronald Pesha, *Remembering Lubec: Stories from the Easternmost Point* (Charleston SC: History Press, 2009), 56–57.

25. David Owen to William Owen, Oct. 10, 1787 quoted in Craven, 47.

Chapter 11

1. Ronald Rees, *New Brunswick: An Illustrated History* (Halifax, Nova Scotia: Nimbus, 2014), 35.

2. John Coffin to E. Winslow, April 1784 in *The Winslow Papers*, ed. W.O. Raymond (Saint John, The Sun Printing Co., Printed under the auspices of the New Brunswick Historical Society,1901). 179.

3. W. Chipman to E. Winslow, March 7, 1784, *Winslow Papers*, 169. For the role Thompson played among the refugees, see Jane Merrill, *Sex and the Scientist; The Indecent Life of Benjamin Thompson* (Jefferson, NC: McFarland, 2018).

4. Louis Quigley, "My New Brunswick," https:/my newbrunswick.ca/bene dict-arnold.

5. Phillip Buckner, "BLISS, JONATHAN," *DCB*, vol. 6. University of Toronto/ Universite Laval, 2003. http:www.biographi.ca.

6. It was three or four years from making this statement before Bliss was wed.

7. Buckner, BLISS.

8. Phyllis R. Blakely, "BLOWERS, SAMPSON SALTER," in *DCB*, vol. 7.

9. W.G. Godfrey, "CARLETON, THOMAS" in *DCB*, vol. 5.

10. W. Chipman to E. Winslow, March 7, 1784. *Winslow Papers*, 170

11. Phyllis Bruckner, "CHIPMAN, WARD" *DCB*, vol. 5, University of Toronto/ Universite Laval, 2003.

12. Blakely, BLOWERS, 157.

13. Wilson, 200.

14. Jonathan Bliss [JB] to BA. July 12, 1796. New Brunswick Museum.

15. Traitor in Pomfret, CT. https:// caisct:wordpress.com/tag/Nathan-Frink.l

16. C.M. Wallace, "LUDLOW, GEORGE DUNCAN " *DCB*, vol. 5. http:// www.biographi.ca/en/bio/ludlow_george_duncan_5E.htm.

17. Chipman to Bowers quoted in D.G. Bell, "Slavery and the Judges of Loyalist New Brunswick." UNBLJ 1982.

18. Alfred C. Bailey, JONATHAN ODELL, *DCB*, vol. 5. http://www.biographi. ca/en/bio/odell_jonathan_5E.html. A Gregory was a rather long evening party, typically celebrated with card-playing, fiddling, and first cakes and then vituals on St. Gregory's Day, March 12.

19. Ed. Charles Francis Adams, ed. *The Works of John Adams* (Boston: Charles C. Little and James Brown), 1850, vol. 2, 35.

20. Sir Guy Carleton to Col. Beverley Robinson, June 17, 1783 for Sir George Yonge, Secretary of State in England, in Charles Walker Robinson, *Life of Sir John Beverley Robinson* (Edinburgh & London: William Blackwood and Sons, 1904), 11.

21. Jonathan Sewall to John Adams, Feb 13, 1760. John Adams, *Works of John Adams*, vol. 1, 51.

22. Quoted in Gordon S. Wood, *Friends Divided: John Adams and Thomas Jefferson* (New York: Penguin, 2017), 80.

23. John Adams to Abigail Adams, March 17, 1776. *Adams Family Correspondence*, vol.1, Adams Family Digital Edition 2018, Massachusetts Historical Society.

24. *Sewell Correspondence* vol. 3, Sept. 7, 1790 in Wilson p194–5.

25. *Winslow Papers*, July 7, 1783, 100.

26. June 25, 1783, *Winslow Papers, 92*.

27. W. Chipman to E. Winslow, 1783, *Winslow Papers, 92.*

28. E. Winslow to Benjamin Marston, March 16, 1786, quoted in Ann Gorman Condon, WINSLOW, Edward, DCB, 868.

29. E. Winslow to G. Townsend, Jan. 17, 1783, *Winslow Papers,* 399. tohttps:// archive.org/stream/winslowpapersad 100raym/winslowpapersad100raym_djvu. txt Winslow.

Chapter 12

1. Blowers to Chipman, Jan. 14, 1785 in J.W. Lawrence, *Foot-prints; Or, Incidents in Early History of New Brunswick* (St. John, NB: J. & A. McMillan, 1883), 13–14.

2. J. Russell Harper, *The Maritime Advocate and Busy East*, vol. 45, no.6, Feb. 1955, 5–10. The quotes related to the Loyalist gardens all come from this article.

3. The quotes without citation about relationships through the end of this chapter are from Ann Gorman Condon's article "The Family in Exile: Loyalist Social Values after the Revolution" in Margaret Conrad, ed., *Intimate Relations: Family and Community in Planter Nova Scotia, 1759–1800* (Fredericton: Acadiensis Press, 1995), 42–53: https:// lib.unb.ca/winslow/exile.html.

4. E. Winslow to His Wife, April 29, 1785 in *Winslow Papers*, 318.

5. Ann Condon. https://lib.unb.ca/ winslow/exile.html.

6. Condon: https://lib.unb.ca/winslow/ exile.html.

Chapter 13

1. William A.R. Chapin, *The Story of Campobello* (1960), 7.

2. Mary W. Gallagher, *The Outer Island: A History of Campobello Island* (copyright Campobello Library and Museum), manuscript, n.d.

3. www.loyalamericanregiment.org/ virginia/htm.

4. Machias Seal Island, a 20-acre island ten miles off the coast of Maine, is the only disputed territory between the U.S. and Canada.

Chapter 14

1. In "Bootleggers and Benedict Arnold," St. Croix Historical Society. Posted April 3, 2016 by Schsuser.

2. Craven, 20.

3. Craven, 41.

4. David Owen to William Owen, Oct. 23, 1787 quoted in Craven, 41n5.

5. David Owen to William Owen, enclosure in Oct. 23, 1783 letter quoted in Craven.

6. Alfred G. Bailey, "ODELL, JONA-THAN, DCB, vol.5.

7. Ralph Dennison is captain of the *Lorna Doone* and has traveled the waters of the Bay of Fundy for 35 years.

8. [anon.] *The Way We Were: Calais-St. Stephen-Woodland-Eastport-Campobello-St. Andrews.* (St. Andrews, NB: Print'N Press Ltd., n.d.)

9. From *Longman's Magazine*, Little's *Living Age*, vol. 157, April May June 1883, 104.

10. Joseph Gough, Jr., grew up on Campobello and his island roots go back to the 1850s, when an ancestor came from Britain. He is the author of *Managing Canada's Fisheries: From Early Days to the Year 2000.*

11. David Owen to William Owen, Sept. 15, 1791, quoted in Craven, 41n5.

12. Samuel Shackford, "Captain John Shackford Family" in Kilby, 444–445.

13. Maxwell Vesey, *Letters from Mrs. Arnold, covering the period from February 26, 1792 to June 30, 1802.* Hitherto Unpublished, 6. University of New Brunswick Archives.

14. He was a captain in the Queens Rangers, on parole when Major André came from meeting with Arnold, after Underhill was for two years and nine months imprisoned by the Continental Army. Underhill told André to go to Captain Kipp's Company in the woods, and they would get him within the lines.

Chapter 15

1. Everyone is so poor Chipman to E. White, May 26, 1786. New Brunswick Museum.

2. Willard Wallace about renting out house in St. John Willard M. Wallace, *Traitorous Hero: The Life and Fortunes of Benedict Arnold* (New York: Harper and Brothers, 1954), 300.

3. Quoted in Wilson, 204.

4. Quoted in Sereisky, "Benedict Arnold in New Brunswick," *Atlantic*

Advocate, March 1962, 32. These witnesses may have been aware that two black men were burned alive for supposed arson in New York.

5. Quoted in Quigley, 51.

6. Sereisky, 38.

7. Wilson, 206.

8. Quigley, 52.

9. McNutt, 86.

10. Isaac Newton Arnold, 372.

11. The descendant of Loyalist refugees who settled in Saint John, New Brunswick, Stephen Davidson had shared his passion for history in numerous magazine articles, the *DCB*, and a loyalist history book.

12. September 26, 1792, Benedict Arnold to J. Bliss. New Brunswick Museum.

13. BA to W. Chipman, undated letter in reply to Chipman's of Aug. 30, 1792, in Wilson, 218.

14. Ruth B. Phillips, *Trading Identities* (Seattle: University of Washington Press, 1999), 124.

15. Phillips, 222.

Chapter 16

1. Philbrick, 35.

2. Sir George Trevelyan, *George the Third and Charles Fox: The Concluding Part of the American Revolution* (London: Longmans, Green, and Co., 1916), vol.1, 308.

3. Jared Sparks, *The Life and Treason of Benedict Arnold* (Boston: Hilliard, Gray and Co., 1835), chapter 17. https:www.gutenburg.org/files/49500/495-h/495=\-h.htm.

4. *The Parliamentary History of England from the Earliest Period to the Year 1803*, vol.29, 1519.

5. Isaac Newton Arnold, 376. This was the only duel Benedict fought in England.

Chapter 17

1. McCusker and Menard, 145.

2. Susan Dwyer Amussen, *Caribbean Exchanges: Slavery and the Transformation of English Society, 1640–1700* (Chapel Hill, NC: University of North Carolina Press, 2007), 40.

3. Amussen, 228.

4. Elizabeth Abbott, *Sugar: A Bittersweet History* (NY: Overlook Press, 2011), 168.

5. Abbott, 16

6. Charles-Maurice de Talleyrand-Perigorde, *Memoires*, vol. 1, 3rd part, 1791–1808, 227. http://www.gutenberg.org/files/25756/25756-h/25756-h.htm.

7. Sherwin, 363.

8. Wallace, 300.

9. See a major work for its treatment of slave revolts—Robin Blackburn, *The American Crucible: Slavery, Emancipation and Human Rights* (New York: Verso, 2011), 174.

10. Jared Sparks, *The Life and Treason of Benedict Arnold* (Boston: Hilliard, Gray, & Co.), 335.

11. James Walvin, *The Slave Trade* (Gloucestershire, UK: Sutton, 1999), 49–50.

12. Oscar Sherwin, 354. The supposition was that Arnold had been granted a favorable contract to furnish supplies for British troops at New Brunswick, and that this explained the bustle at the "sort of Ynirian [probably Welsh for temporary] headquarters." A.H. Wetmore, "Saint John's Old and Historic Buildings: a paper read before the Fortnightly Club, Oct. 15, 1934," Saint John Free Library. 14.

13. BA to JB, Jan. 3, 1795, New Brunswick Museum.

14. BA to W. Chipman, Jan 14, 1795, in Joseph Wilson Lawrence, *Foot-Prints, Or, Incidents in Early History of New Brunswick* (NY: McMillan, 1883), 76.

15. Edward H. Hall, ed. *Reminiscences of Dr. John Park, Proceedings of the American Antiquarian Society*, vol. 7, Oct. 1892, 72–73.

16. BA to JB, Jan. 26, 1793, New Brunswick Museum.

17. BA to JB, August 15, 1795. New Brunswick Museum.

18. MSA to Edward Arnold, July 1, 1801, New York Public Library Archives.

19. Quoted in Wilson, 228.

20. Duncan Campbell Scott, *John Graves Simcoe* (Toronto: Morang & Co. 1906), vol.7, 104.

21. BA to Earl Spencer of the British cabinet, manuscript letter of Dec. 29, 1796. Isaac Newton Arnold, 389.

22. MSA to ES, May 20, 1797, in PMHB, vol. 25, 467.

23. Peggy to ES, May 20, 1797, in PMHG, vol. 25, 467.

Chapter 18

1. BA to JB, December 20, 1799. New Brunswick Museum.

2. "To have one's close friend suppose all is well...Loss is unbearable" BA to JB, 1795. New Brunswick Museum.

3. MSA to W. Chipman, June 4, 1795. New Brunswick Museum.

4. MSA to Elizabeth Chipman, June 12, 1792. New Brunswick Museum.

5. Alessandro Barbero, *Charlemagne: Father of a Continent*, translated by Allen Cameron (Berkeley: University of California Press, 2004), 116–117.

6. Martina Scholtens MD MPH CCFP is a family physician practicing in Vancouver, British Columbia, and a Clinical Instructor with the Faculty of Medicine at the University of British Columbia. Her article appeared in *CMAJ* October 7, 2008, 804–805.

7. W. Eamon, "The tale of Monsieur Gout," *Bulletin of the History of Medicine* 1981, vol.55, 564–567.

8. G.P. Rodnan, "Early Theories Concerning Etiology and Pathogenesis of the Gout," *Arthrutus Rheum* 1965, vol. 8, 599–610.

9. Horace Walpole to Sir Horace Mann, July 25, 1788, *Letters of Horace Walpole, Earl of Oxford*, vol. 8, 574–575.

10. W.S.C. Copeman, *A Short History of the Gout and the Rheumatic diseases*. Berkeley, University of California Press, 1964.

11. Mather Byles to E. Winslow, Jan. 25, 1785 in *Winslow Papers*, 265.

12. J. Bliss to B. Arnold, February 16, 1793, New Brunswick Museum.

13. J. Bliss to B. Arnold, July 2, 1793, New Brunswick Museum.

14. *Ibid.*

15. B. Arnold to W. Chipman, Oct. 15, 1792, New Brunswick Museum.

16. J. Bliss to B. Arnold, January 22, 1794, New Brunswick Museum.

17. B. Arnold to J. Bliss, July 2, 1793. New Brunswick Museum.

18. MSA to J. Bliss, June or July 1794. New Brunswick Museum.

19. B. Arnold to J. Bliss, September 5, 1795. New Brunswick Museum.

20. J. Bliss to B. Arnold, November 17, 1795. New Brunswick Museum.

21. B. Arnold to J. Bliss, March 26, 1796. New Brunswick Museum.

22. B. Arnold to J. Bliss, May 17, 1799 New Brunswick Museum.

23. B. Arnold to J. Bliss, December 20, 1799. New Brunswick Museum.

24. B. Arnold to J. Bliss, September 19, 1800. New Brunswick Museum.

Chapter 19

1. MSA to Mrs. W. Chipman, June 4, 1795, quoted in J.W. Lawrence, *Footprints, Or, Incidents in Early History of New Brunswick* (Saint John, NB: J& A. McMillan, 1883), 77.

2. *PMHB*, vol. 2, 473.

3. MSA to Edward Shippen [ES], May 20, 1797, *Live of Margaret Shippen, wife of Benedict Arnold*, 166.

4. Isaac Newton Arnold, 221.

5. MSA to Edward Arnold, July 1, 1801 in J.G. Taylor, *Some New Light* (London: G. White, 1931), 59–60.

6. Milton Lomask, "The Aftermath of Treason," 1967, vol.18, issue 6.http://www.americanheritage.com/content/benedict_arnold_aftermath_treason.

7. Peggy to Edward Burd, in Lomask.

8. Ann Fitch to Edward Shippen, June 1801, in Isaac N. Arnold, 393.

9. "Life of Margaret Shippen, Wife of Benedict Arnold," *Pennsylvania Magazine of History and Biography*, The Historical Society of Pennsylvania, University of Pennsylvania Press, Vol. 26, no. 4 (1902), 467.

10. MSA to ES. *PMHB*, vol. 25, 2, 166.

11. MSA to Edward Arnold, January 1804 in Taylor, 21.

12. Taylor, 38.

13. Taylor, 40.

14. Taylor, 41.

15. Taylor, 42.

16. Taylor, 38.

17. Carrie Rebora and Paul Staiti, *John Singleton Copley in America* (NY: Metropolitan Museum of Art), 1995), 282.

18. MSA to Edward Arnold, in Taylor, 31.

19. MSA to Edward Arnold, in Taylor, 60.

20. Ann Fitch to ES, June 29, 1801 PMHB, 472.

21. MSA to ES, March 1786. PMHB, 167. Peggy knew she had suffered in the dislocations of her life with General Arnold, as well as the aftershocks of his

treason. Yet, ruminating in letters, she qualified remarks about her uneasiness, with those about his unbounded love and how she did not repent of her life choices. MSA to Edward Shippen (son), July -?- 1802.

22. Rogan, 208–209.

23. MSA to JB, in Taylor, 3.

24. Peggy to JB, December 23, 1801. NBM

25. MSA to Richard and Henry, Nov. 5, 1802, in PMHB vol. 25, 482.

26. MSA to Richard and Henry, November 5, 1802. PMBH vol.25, 173.

27. MSA to ES June 1804, in Taylor, 33.

28. MSA to Richard Arnold and Henry Arnold in in Arnold, M., and Joyce D. Goodfriend. "Notes and Documents: The Widowhood of Margaret Shippen Arnold: Letters from England, 1801–1803." *The Pennsylvania Magazine of History and Biography*, vol. 115, no. 2, April 1991, 250: (1991): http://www.jstor.org.proxy.library.stonybrook.edu/stable/20092605.

29. MSA to Richard and Henry, July 27, 1801 in "The Widowhood of Margaret Shippen Arnold, 194–195. January 5, 1803, PMHB, 484.

30. MSA to ES, Jan. 17, 1804, in Taylor, 65.

31. The Arnold Family Papers in the Archives and Special Collections section of Penrose Library, University of Denver has some of Peggy Arnold's letters to Richard and Henry Arnold as well as letters of the sons. Daniel Coxe to Edward Arnold, July 5, 1804. University of Denver Special Collections and Archives [UDSCA].

32. https://archive.org/stream/some newlightonla00tayl/somenewlightonla00 tayl_djvu.txt.

33. MSA to Sarah Shippen, PMHB vol. 25, 2, 176.

Appendix

1. BA to Margaret Arnold. Newbrunswick.net/Saint_John/benedict/benedict 2.

2. MSA to JB, December 5, 1795. New Brunswick Museum.

3. The May 29, 1776 letter of Arnold to Reverend Booth when hastening the two sons off to boarding school give an apercu not only into Arnold's ideals of education

but his degree of humility about his role of father. He apologized that his "situation has prevented my paying that attention to them I otherwise should have."

4. James to Brother(s), April 2, 1832. The Arnold Family Papers 1781–1991, University of Denver Special Collections and Archives [UDSCA].

5. BA to JB, February 20, 1796, New Brunswick Museum.

6. McEwan's Commemorative... (Toronto: J.H. Beers, 1905) 434.

7. James Arnold to Margaret Arnold (his niece), March 1848. USDCA.

8. Arnold's letter of concern about his son Henry, to J. Blakesly, Sept. 20, 1794 in Wallace, 303.

9. James Arnold to Richard Arnold, March 15,1819. UDSCA.

10. James Arnold to Richard Arnold March 6, 1827. UDSCA.

11. BA to Edward Arnold, Sept. 7, 1800, NYPL archives William Smith papers. Taylor has Benedict's letter of advice, 56.

12. MSA to Edward Arnold, Jan. 11 and 17, 1804. NYPL.

13. MSA to Edward Arnold, Sept. 7, 1800, in Taylor, 57.

14. James Arnold to brothers, August 16, 1814. UDSCA.

15. James Arnold to brothers, August 7, 1815. UDSCA.

16. James Arnold to Richard Arnold, Jan. 22, 1837. UDSCA.

17. Quoted in Isaac Newton, 408.

18. Lorenzo Sabine, *Biographical Sketches of the American Loyalists* vol.1, 180.

19. James Arnold to Richard Arnold, March 15, 1819. UDSCA.

20. MSA to Edward Arnold, July 31, 1801, in "The Widowhood of Margaret Shippen Arnold," 239.

21. See Chapter 10, note 1.

22. Thanks to Barry Murray of the St. Andrews Historical Society for this story.

23. The Last Will and Testament of Benedict Arnold is reproduced in the *PMHB*, vol. 26, no. 2 (1902).

24. BA to JB, March 7, 1798. NBM.

25. Taylor, 18.

26. James Arnold to Richard Arnold, April 2, 1832. UDSCA.

27. James to Richard, April 2, 1833. UDSCA.

28. MSA to Sons, November 5, 1803 in Isaac Arnold, 403.

29. James Arnold to Richard Arnold, March 6, 1827. UDSCA.

30. MSA to ES, Jan. 17, 1804, in Taylor, 65.

31. William to Richard, Oct. 22, 1816 NYPL.

32. William to Richard, Oct. 25, 1813 UDSCA.

33. Sophia Arnold to William Arnold, Dec. 1814, in Taylor, 33.

34. William Arnold to Richard Arnold, Oct. 22, 1816. NYPL.

35. Nathaniel Hawthorne *Our Old Home* (Boston: Houghton Mifflin, 1887), vol.1, 490.

36. Isaac Newton Arnold, 304. After the 1780 treason, Hannah was writing an old friend in New Haven. Hannah apologized for unburdening herself of her bad news when the friend had recently lost a child.

37. Hannah Arnold to MSA. PMHB, vol. 25, 1, 43.

38. MSA to Richard Arnold and Henry Arnold DATE? in "The Widowhood of Margaret Shippen Arnold," 240.

39. James Arnold to Richard Arnold, March 15, 1819. UDSCA.

40. James Arnold to Richard Arnold, June 22, 1837. UDSCA.

Bibliography

Abbott, Elizabeth. *Sugar: A Bittersweet History* (New York: Overlook, 2008).

Acheson, T.W. *Saint John: The Making of a Colonial Urban Community* (Toronto: University of Toronto Press, 1985).

African Americans in Exile After the American Revolution (New York: Garland Publishing in Association with The New England Historic Genealogical Society, 1996).

Allen, Jack I. "The Loyalists and Slavery in New Brunswick" in *Transactions of the Royal Society of Canada*, Series 2, Vol. 4, Section II, 1898, 137–185.

Allen, Thomas B. *Tories: Fighting for the King in America's First Civil War* (New York: HarperCollins, 2010).

Allison, Robert J. *The American Revolution: A Concise History* (New York: Oxford University Press, 2011).

Amussen, Susan Dwyer. *Caribbean Exchanges: Slavery and the Transformation of English Society, 1640–1700* (Chapel Hill, NC: University of North Carolina Press, 2007).

Andreas, Peter. *Smuggler Nation: How Illicit Trade Made America* (New York: Oxford University Press, 2013).

Armour, Charles A., and Thomas Lackey. *Sailing Ships of the Maritimes; An Illustrated History of Shipping and Shipbuilding in the Maritime Provinces of Canada, 1750–1925* (New York: McGraw-Hill Byerson, Limited, 1975).

Arnold, Isaac N. *The Life of Benedict Arnold; his Patriotism and his Treason* (Chicago: Jansen, McClurg & Co., 1880).

Bell, D.G. *Early Loyalist Saint John: The Origin of New Brunswick Politics, 1783–1786* (Fredericton, New Brunswick: New Ireland Press, 1983).

Berkin, Carol. *A Sovereign People: The Crises of the 1790s and the Birth of American Nationalism* (New York: Basic Books, 2017).

Blakeley, Phyllis R., ed., and John N. Grant, *Eleven Exiles: Accounts of Loyalists of the American Revolution* (Toronto: Dundurn Press Limited, 1982)

Bobrick, Benson. *Angel in the Whirlwind: The Triumph of the American Revolution* (New York Simon & Schuster, 2011).

Boylan, Brian Richard. *Benedict Arnold, the Dark Eagle* (New York: W.W. Norton, 1973).

Brandt, Clare. *The Man in the Mirror: A Life of Benedict Arnold* (New York: Random House, 1994).

Buckner, Phillip, and John Reid. *The Atlantic Region to Confederation: A History* (Toronto: University of Toronto Press, 1995).

Callahan, North. *Flight from the Republic: The Tories of the American Revolution* (New York: Bobbs-Merrill, 1967).

Canadian Encyclopedia of Biography.

Case, Stephen, and Marc Jacobs. *Treacherous Beauty: Peggy Shippen, the Woman behind Benedict Arnold's Plot to Betray America* (Guilford, CT: Lyons Press, 2012).

Cecere, Michael. *The Invasion of Virginia 1781* (Yardley: Westholme).

Chadwick, Bruce. *The First American Army: The Untold Story of George Washington and the Men behind America's First Flight for Freedom* (Naperville, IL: Sourcebooks, 2007).

Chopra, Ruma. *Unnatural Rebellion: Loyalists in New York City during the Revolution* (Charlottesville, VA: University of Virginia Press, 2013).

Cody, H.A. "The United Empire Loyalists" in *Loyalist Souvenir: One Hundred and Fiftieth Anniversary of the Landing of the Loyalists in the Province of New Brunswick, 1783-1933* (New Brunswick Historical Society, n.d.).

Condon, Ann Gorman. "The family in exile: Loyalist social values after the revolution" in Margaret Conrad, ed., *Intimate Relations: Family and Community in Planter Nova Scotia, 1759-1800* (Fredericton: Acadiensis Press, 1995), 42-53.

Condon, Ann Gorman. "Loyalist Arrival" in Phillip A. Buckner and John G. Reid, *The Atlantic Region to Confederation: A History* (Toronto: University of Toronto Press, 1994).

Craven, Paul. *Petty Justice: Low Law and the Sessions System in Charlotte County, New Brunswick, 1785-1867* (Toronto: Published for The Osgoode Society for Canadian Legal History by the University of Toronto Press, 2014).

Daigler, Kenneth A. *Spies, Patriots and Traitors: American Intelligence in the Revolutionary War* (Washington, D.C.: Georgetown University Press, 2014).

Dallison, Robert L. *Hope Restored: The American Revolution and the Founding of New Brunswick*. The New Brunswick Military Heritage Series, volume 2 (Fredericton, New Brunswick: Goose Lanes Editions and The New Brunswick Military Heritage Project, 2003).

Decker, Malcolm Grove. *Benedict Arnold, Son of the Havens* (New York: Antiquarian Society, 1961).

Dictionary of Canadian Biography. University of Toronto and Université de Laval (Toronto: University of Toronto Press, 1955-).

Duncan, Roger F., and John P. Ware. *A Cruising Guide to the New England Coast including the Hudson River, Long Island Sound, and the Coast of New Brunswick* (New York: Dodd Mead, 1983).

Ferreiro, Larrie D. *Brothers at Arms* (New York: Knopf, 2016).

F.J. My Story: Being the Memoirs of Benedict Arnold: Late Major-General in the Continental Army and Brigadier-General in that of His Britannic Majesty (New York: Charles Scribner's Sons, 1917).

Flexner, James Thomas. *The Traitor and the Spy: Benedict Arnold and John André* (New York: Little, Brown, 1953).

Forman, Samuel A. *Dr. Joseph Warren: The Boston Tea Party, Bunker Hill, and the Birth of American Liberty* (Gretna, Louisiana: Pelican, 2012).

Fortescue, John E. *The War of Independence: The British Army in North America, 1775-1783* (Mechanicsburg, PA: Stackpole Books, 2001).

Gallagher, Mary W. *The Outer Island: A History of Campo Bello Island* (mimeographed, n.d.).

Gipson, Lawrence Henry. *American Loyalist Jared Ingersoll* (New Haven: Yale University Press, 1920).

Griggs, Walter S., Jr. *Historic Disasters of Richmond* (Charleston: The History Press, 2016).

Hill, George Canning. *Benedict Arnold: A Biography* (New York: Worthington, 1888).

Hodges, Graham Russell, ed. *The Black Loyalists Directory*.

Hoffer, Peter Charles. *Stresses of Empire: Selected Articles on the British Empire in the Eighteenth Century* (New York: Garland, 1988).

Hornsby, Stephen J., and John G. Reid. *New England and the Maritime Provinces* (Montreal: McGill/Queen's University Press, 2014).

Jasonoff, Maya. *Liberty's Exiles: American Loyalists in the Revolutionary World* (New York: Vintage, 2012).

Johnson, Ryerson and Lois, and the Lubec Historical Society. *200 Years of Lubec History, 1776-1976* (Lubec, Maine: Lubec Historical Society, 1976).

Kilby, William Henry, ed. *Eastport and Passamaquoddy* (Eastport, Maine: Edward E. Shead & Co., 1888, rep. Forgotten Books, 2017).

Kranish, Michael. *Flight from Monticello: Thomas Jefferson at War* (New York: Oxford University Press, 2011).

Lehman, Eric D. *Homegrown Terror: Benedict Arnold and the Burning of New London* (Middletown, CT: Wesleyan, 2015).

Letters and Papers Relating Chiefly to the Provincial History of Pennsylvania with some notices of the writer by Thomas Balch (Philadelphia: Crissy & Markley, 1855).

Martin, James Kirby, and Mark Edward Lender. *A Respectable Army: The Military Origins of the Republic, 1763–1789* (Wheeling, IL: Harlan Davison, 2006).

Martin, James Kirby. *Benedict Arnold, Revolutionary Hero: An American Warrior Reconsidered* (New York: New York University Press, 1997).

Matson, Cathy. *Merchants and Empire: Trading in Colonial New York* (Baltimore, MD: Johns Hopkins University Press, 1998).

McCuster, John J., and Russell R. Menard. *The Economy of British America, 1607–1789* (Chapel Hill: University of North Carolina Press, rep. 1991).

McNutt, William Stewart. *The Atlantic Provinces: The Emergence of Canadian Society, 1712–1857* (Oxford University Press, 1965).

Middlebrook, Louis F. *Maritime Connecticut during the American Revolution* (Salem, MA: The Essex Institute, 1925).

Milner, Marc, and Glenn Leonard. *New Brunswick and the Navy, 500 Years* (Fredericton, NB: Goose Lane, 2010).

Moore, Christopher. *The Loyalists: Revolution, Exile, Settlement* (Toronto: Macmillan of Canada, 1984).

Mowat, Grace Hellen. *The Diverting History of a Loyalist Town* (St. Andrews, NB: Charlotte County Cottage Craft, 1937).

Murphy, Jim. *The Real Benedict Arnold* (New York: Clarion, 2007).

Nelson, Eric. *The Royalist Revolution: Monarchy and the American Founding* (Cambridge, MA: Belknap Press, 2014).

Norton, Mary Beth. *The British-Americans: The Loyalist Exiles in England, 1774–1789* (Boston: Little, Brown, 1972).

Nowlan, Alden. *Campobello, the Outer Island* (Toronto: Stoddart, 1993; copyright Clarke, Irwin & Co., 1973).

Olasky, Marvin. *Fighting for Liberty and Virtue: Political and Cultural Wars in Eighteenth-Century America* (Washington, D.C.: Regnery, 1995).

Paine, Lauran. *Benedict Arnold, Hero & Traitor* (London: Robert Hale, Ltd., 1965).

The Pennsylvania Magazine of History and Biography

Pesha, Ronald. *Remembering Lubec: Stories from the Easternmost Point* (Charleston, SC: History Press, 2009).

Philbrick, Nathaniel. *Valiant Ambition: George Washington, Benedict Arnold, and the Fate of the American Revolution* (New York: Penguin, 2017).

Puls, Mark. *Henry Knox, Visionary General of the American Revolution* (New York: Palgrave Macmillan, 2008).

Quigley, Louis. *Benedict Arnold: The Canadian Connection* (Riverview, NB: Queue Publishing, 2000).

Randall, Willard Sterne. *Benedict Arnold: Patriot and Traitor* (New York: William Morrow, 1990).

Rees, Ronald. *New Brunswick: An Illustrated History* (Halifax: Nimbus Publishing Limited, 2014).

Rogan, Roger Kemper. *Benedict Arnold, Our First Marine: His Contemporaries and the Story of his Life* (Cincinnati, OH: Jones Brothers Publishing Co., 1931; rep. Kessinger, 2010).

Rogers, N.A.M. *The Wooden World: An Anatomy of the Georgian Navy* (New York: Norton, 1996).

Sherwin, Oscar. *Benedict Arnold* (New York: The Century Co., 1931).

Smith, Joshua. *The Rogues of Quoddy* (Dissertation, Univ. of Maine: Proquest, 2003).

Smith, Joshua M. *Borderland Smuggling* (Gainesville, FL: University Press of Florida, 2006).

Sparks, Jared. *The Life and Treason of Benedict Arnold* (Boston: Hilliard, Gay, & Co., 1835).

Stark, James H. *The Loyalists of Massachusetts and the Other Side of the American Revolution* (Boston: James H. Stark, 1910).

Stauber, Leland. *The American Revolution: A Grand Mistake* (Amherst, NY: Prometheus Books, 2009).

Stevens, John Austin. "The Expeditions of Lafayette against Arnold. A Paper read before the Maryland Historical Society, Jan. 14, 1878" (Baltimore: J. Murphy, 1878).

Stories about Arnold, the Traitor, Andre, the Spy, and Champe, the Patriot: For the Children of the United States (New Haven: A.H. Maltby, 1831).

Taylor, Alan. *American Revolutions: A Continental History, 1750–1804* (New York: Norton, 2016).

Taylor, J.G. *Some New Light on the Later Life and Last Resting Place of Benedict Arnold and of his Wife Margaret Shippen* (London: George White, 1931).

Tillotson, Harry Stanton. *The Exquisite Exile: The Life and Fortunes of Mrs. Benedict Arnold* (Boston: Lee and Shepard, 1932).

Truxes, Thomas M. *Defying Empire: Trading with the Enemy in Colonial New York* (New Haven, CT: Yale University Press, 2008).

Tuchman, Barbara W. *The First Salute* (New York: Random House, 1988).

Van Doren, Carol. *Secret History of the American Revolution* (New York: Viking Press, 1941).

Van Tyne, Claude Halstead. *The War of Independence* vol. 2 (New York: Macmillan, 1902).

Walker, Lewis Burd. "Life of Margaret Shippen, Wife of Benedict Arnold." *The Pennsylvania Magazine of History and Biography*, volumes XXIV-XXVI (1900–1902).

Wallace, Willard M. *Traitorous Hero: The Life and Fortunes of Benedict Arnold* (New York: Harbor & Bros, 1954).

Walvin, James. *The Slave Trade* (Gloucestershire, UK: Sutton, 1999).

Webster, J. Clarence. *Historical Guide to New Brunswick* (New Brunswick: Bureau of Information and Tours and Travel, 1936).

Wells, Kate Gannett. *Campobello: An Historical Sketch c. 1893* (BiblioLife 2011)

Wilson, Barry K. *Benedict Arnold: A Traitor in our Midst* (Montreal: McGill, Queens University Press, 2001).

Wilson, Ellen Gibson. *The Loyal Blacks* (New York: Capricorn Books, 1976).

Winks, Robin W. *The Blacks in Canada: A History* (Montreal: McGill-Queens Press and New Haven: Yale University Press, 1971).

The Winslow Papers. University of New Brunswick. Electronic Edition from 2005.

Wright, Esmond, ed. *The Fire of Liberty* (London: Hamish Hamilton, 1984).

Wright, Esther Clark. *The Loyalists of New Brunswick* (Fredericton, New Brunswick: 1955).

Index